Trance Formation: A Memoir of Trauma, Travel, and Transformation

A Spiritual Quest for Self-Discovery and Healing

TheReal Rayster

About the Author

As a child, I always loved telling stories. Stories and tales have always captivated me, serving as a constant source of inspiration. This lifelong love of storytelling was affirmed when I recently discovered a picture of myself, grinning ear to ear, walking off a stage in 1995, medals clinking against my chest from a school writing contest.

Ever since I started working in the corporate world after graduating with a BS in Computer Science in 2010, I felt a nagging sense of "otherness," a resistance to the traditional path. This feeling sparked a journey of self-discovery that spanned many years, culminating in the upheaval of the pandemic, which forced me to confront inner truths and ultimately led to the writing of this book.

Being a first-time author, it was challenging to maintain the motivation to write daily. However, after everything I've experienced and now having completed my first book, it was undoubtedly worth it. The unconventional nature of my experiences, along with my extensive travels, inspired me to share my story. I hope you will find this book to be a source of inspiration and offer a fresh perspective on life's challenges and triumphs.

If you've enjoyed reading this book and would like to support my journey as an author, I would be deeply grateful if you could leave an honest review on Amazon or any online platform where you purchased the book. Your feedback is invaluable to me as I continue to grow and evolve as a writer.

If you'd like to connect or follow my journey, you can find me on Instagram and most social media spaces as @therealrayster. I'd love to hear your thoughts on the book!

ISBN: 978-621-06-2263-8 (eBook)

ISBN: 978-621-06-2265-2 (Paperback)

ISBN: 978-621-06-2264-5 (Hardcover)

Cover Design by Nin (Sanctum Press)

Published by Raymond P. Janayon (The Real Rayster)

therealrayster.com

Quezon City, Philippines 1226

The information contained in this book is for general informational purposes only.
It is not intended as a substitute for professional medical advice and should not be
relied upon as such. If you have any concerns about your mental health, please
consult with a qualified healthcare provider

Contents

Author's Note

In 2022, I began writing this book, never imagining it would evolve into a 25-chapter memoir chronicling my journey of self-discovery. I vividly remember penning the first and third chapters, eager to share my story with the world.

At the time, I debated between fiction and a novel, but the abundance of self-help books and novels already available inspired me to write a memoir—a story uniquely mine. I believe I have a story to tell, a transformation, a hero's journey of turning life's challenges into gifts.

Trance Formation is a collection of personal stories exploring my path of self-discovery and finding my true calling. I'm a software engineer turned storyteller—just a fellow human sharing my experiences.

A warning: This book contains stories about mental illness, psychedelic use, long meditation retreats, and solo travels that may be triggering for some readers. If you find yourself struggling, please seek support from a healthcare professional.

I encourage you to approach this book with an open mind and a willingness to explore new possibilities.

Thank you for taking the time to read my story. I hope you find it helpful.

With love and authenticity,
TheReal Rayster

Part One

Foundations

"We are not makers of history.
We are made by history."

- Martin Luther King, Jr.

Chapter 1

The Girl Who Introduced Me to Magic

On a clear, sunny day in 2022, just after lunch—that awkward time when you're sleepy, but restless too—I was sprawled on a mat on the balcony, gazing out the open door. The familiar tug-of-war between wanderlust and laziness had me daydreaming of Japan, a country I hadn't visited since before the world changed. The gentle breeze carried the sounds of birds chirping, a soothing contrast to the bustling city below. Little did I know, an unexpected journey was about to begin, not across continents, but deep within the forgotten corners of my own memories.

"Oh, wonderful sky of might," I mumbled dramatically, bored enough to talk to myself, "Where is my next flight?" My recent trips to Japan had awakened a thirst for adventure, but the pandemic had clipped my wings. Now, staring at the endless blue, I longed for the bustling streets of Tokyo, the tranquility of Kyoto's temples, the taste of authentic ramen... yet the thought of packing, planning, and navigating a changed world felt exhausting.

I sighed, watching the clouds drift by, when my eyes landed on a giant, dusty storage box tucked away in the corner. It was a relic from my last move, overflowing with forgotten treasures. A flicker of curiosity ignited within me. Maybe revisiting the past could offer an escape from the present. With a surge of energy, I hauled the box into the center of the room, anticipation tingling through me. I had no idea that hidden within its depths was a spark that would reawaken a part of me I thought I had lost.

As I delved deeper into the box, unearthing old photographs, travel trinkets, and finished journals, I couldn't help but reflect on the people who had shaped my life's journey. Teachers who challenged me, strangers whose kindness surprised me... each encounter, big or small, had left an imprint on my soul.

I've come to believe that every person we meet serves a purpose in our lives. That sometimes, they come along at just the right time, offering a lesson, a nudge towards growth, or even a sprinkle of magic. My journey is shaped by the people who've crossed my path—and maybe even a girl who shared her love of a certain boy wizard...and a certain pop-punk princess who inspired me to pick up a guitar and find my own voice.

These encounters, big and small, molded me into the person I am today—flaws, unexpected strengths, and all. High school was where that "me" began to truly take shape. Think of it as my coming-of-age story, complete with awkward first crushes, epic failures, and the kind of friendships that leave a mark on your soul.

2001-2002: High School: The Middle Ground

High school, for me, was the sweet spot. Elementary school was all about wide-eyed wonder, exploring the world for the first time. College felt like a focused sprint towards a future career, where I thankfully had way nicer bathrooms. But high school? That was the messy, glorious in-between. A time for self-discovery, first crushes... and honing my ability to hold my breath longer than diving in the ocean, all to survive a trip to the guys' bathroom.

Freshmen year. Hormones raging, voice cracking, and the daily trauma of just trying to survive the bathroom gauntlet. Every morning, the same internal debate: "Okay, which door of doom do I choose today? The cavernous main bathroom with its unidentified objects littering the floor (and the lingering fear of bringing a souvenir back to class), or the solitary one, mysteriously locked half the time?" Seriously, you haven't experienced true terror until you've dodged suspicious stains, tried to decipher the cryptic graffiti on the walls ("Dave + Lisa 4eva???"), and held a staredown with the overflowing trash can in the corner, all while navigating the labyrinthine stalls that offered little privacy and even less sanitation. My breath-holding practice was clearly preparing me for future swimming lessons. Welcome to the unique charm of public schools in Iloilo, where the janitors were heroes, and the bathrooms were...character-building. Let's just say it made me appreciate clean restrooms for the rest of my life.

The First Magic

First day of class, I was running late, sweat dripping down my face, frantically searching for our classroom. It was tucked away at the far end of campus, a gauntlet I'd face every morning. Finally, I burst through the door, relieved the teacher wasn't there yet. Shuffling to an empty desk, I took it all in... the chipped paint, the dusty chalkboard... this was my new world.

"High school won't be so bad," I muttered, trying to convince myself. It was a fresh start, a chance to be anyone I wanted. That idea was both exciting and terrifying. I'd always felt a little...offbeat. Not a genius like my mom claimed, but aware of things other kids didn't seem to notice.

Slowly, friendships started to form. Life settled into a rhythm: Wake up, struggle through classes, study, play. It was comfortable in its own way.

Then, November 2001. *Harry Potter and the Sorcerer's Stone* hit the theaters. My heart pounded with excitement – just like my father's used to when he'd pop in a Superman tape, transforming our living room into Metropolis. Theaters were strictly off-limits for me, but the allure was impossible to resist. So, I did what any desperate Potter-wannabe would do – scored a bootleg VCD from the nearest SuperMart.

One afternoon, finding the house empty, I raced home from class. That flimsy plastic felt like a victorious heist in my hands, a bit of rebellion fuelled by years of my father's superhero obsession. The living room became Hogwarts. Even though I was alone, it felt strangely real – every flicker of the screen transporting me to that world of magic and hidden depths.

The next day, I desperately wanted to share that feeling. Showing the blurry VCD to my friends, my voice probably cracked with enthusiasm. But while they liked flying broomsticks, it wasn't their thing. Still, something had shifted in me. Maybe I was imagining it, but I started noticing...little things. Glimmers at the edge of my vision. Thoughts that felt like whispers from some-where else.

Until one day, <u>the magic found me</u>. It wasn't fireworks or a talking hat, not at first. Just a quiet sense of certainty in the most unexpected of places – our math classroom. But the feeling that washed over me was undeniable, a simple thought that defied logic, a whisper that told me the abandoned *Harry Potter* book I'd spotted on a vacant desk earlier that week belonged to someone I didn't know yet.

Days later, our advisor's "Be back soon!" note scrawled on the blackboard was barely visible amidst the usual pre-class commo-tion. A familiar roar of voices filled the room, each one louder than the last, making me think I'd stumbled into a Pokémon battle. Shuffling to my new desk, barely surviving a backpack collision, I heard it – the magic words whispered behind me: *"Harry Potter..."*

My heart did a little leap. Finally, someone else who got it! I whipped around. Two girls, both beaming, were glued to the pages of a book. One of them was Angeli. "Wait," I blurted out, "the movie? *Harry Potter and the Sorcerer's Stone?*"

Angeli looked up, a mischievous grin spreading across her face. "Don't tell me you haven't read the book!" And for the record, it's the *Philosopher's Stone*. They changed the title a bit for US viewers."

A flash of recognition. Wait... was that the same book I'd eyed a few weeks ago? Was she the mysterious owner?

That was it – the spark that lit the fire. Instant connection. We became the resident Hogwarts experts of that class, sharing theories, excitedly debating who our favorite characters were. Turns out, Angeli had the book! I begged her to let me borrow it, and by lunch break I was lost in J.K. Rowling's world, fumbling through a language that felt both magical and frustrating. Movies were easier back then, just sit and watch...but this? This was a whole different level of adventure.

The String Connection

In City High (that nickname always cracked me up), students had a choice: join the Music Club, locally known as "The Banda," or sweat it out in PE Class. Easy decision for me. I opted for guitar lessons. Seemed logical – you don't see many string players out there, but a guy with a guitar can always serenade someone at a party, right? ...Or at least that was my teenage logic.

One day, I was making my way to the "Titanic." Yep, that's what everyone called the music classroom – a ramshackle building located in the middle of a pond, reached by a rickety wooden bridge. The squeak of old planks underfoot, the smell of damp wood...every crossing was a minor adventure. But once inside...it was like a different world. Posters of rock legends plastered the peeling walls, musical notes swirled across every surface. This place felt like magic.

From the entrance, I spotted Mr. Delmonte, perched on a stool, surrounded by instruments I couldn't even name. There were only a few other students, so I didn't hesitate. "Sir," I said, thrusting my application form at him, "Guitar slot, please." We chatted briefly, and I left smiling. I'd scored the last spot!

Classes were a mix of fun and frustration. My fingers protested against the strings, but slowly, chords started to make sense. The handful of us bonded quickly, a motley crew of music nerds, a world away from the noise of the regular school day.

Then, one afternoon, there she was. Angeli. I'd always admired her ungirly nature, like a real-life Hermione, but this...this was unexpected. There she sat, cross-legged on the floor, carefully adjusting the tuning pegs of a bandurria.

"What are you doing here?" I asked, unable to hide my surprise.

"Hi Raymond!" she grinned, as if it was the most normal thing in the world. "I just applied for the bandurria slot," Angeli added. "Good thing Sir Delmonte is kind enough to let me in, I just have to catch up with the lessons."

"That's great!" I replied.

"What about you?" she asked.

"Oh, I'm the guitar guy," I said, trying for casual but probably just sounding shy.

"So it was you! Sir mentioned we only got one guitarist this year. With so many students in this school, I wonder if they even know the 'Banda' exists," she mused.

"Beats me." At least I have someone to hang out with during music class, I thought.

"Yeah, for sure," I said out loud.

As the days went by, Mr. Delmonte noticed Angeli and me always together. One afternoon, he had to ask, "Are you two...going together?"

"Uhh sir, we're from the same section," I replied. He leaned in, whispering, "Oh, I thought... but have you made any moves on her?"

"Uh, no. I'm here for the guitar, sir." Please stick to music, I grumbled inwardly. Angeli caught a glimpse of our exchange and went back to her music. I grabbed my guitar, tuning it frantically. If he just knew what we were discussing, he'd probably be even more confused... magic.

Even with his constant reminders, I began to question my own feelings. My mother's words echoed in my mind, a shield against romance. "We're still kids," she'd say, "focus on school."

Besides, I was a mess. Not just the usual teenage awkwardness, though that was bad enough, but something deeper. A nagging feeling that I was...incomplete, pieces of me still undiscovered. So, while Mr. Delmonte might dream of teenage band romances, the reality was a lot less dramatic.

Angeli and I fell into a comfortable rhythm, me fumbling with guitar chords, her picking out melodies on the bandurria. We talked about Hogwarts, about classes, about which pop songs might actually be decent if played with our instruments. Friendship, not romance, fueled our musical adventures. And with the constant reminder of my own unresolved issues, maybe that was for the best.

But as the months passed, those reminders turned into questions. Was my reluctance to consider dating all about Mom's rules and insecurity? Or was something else holding me back? A thought, unformed and terrifying, began to take shape in the back of my mind...

Discovering Friendship

During this time, I was obsessed with online games. They were a whole new world, and I couldn't wait to share my enthusiasm with my classmates, including Angeli. When I mentioned *Ragnarok Online*, she surprisingly agreed to try it out. So, we headed to a local gaming café. She peeked through the glass door and immediately balked.

"I don't want to go inside! It's full of boys!"

"Says the tomboy," I retorted. "I thought you wanted to play *Ragnarok?*"

"Okay, fine. But don't leave me behind!"

I opened the door, and in her haste to avoid the crowd, she nearly tumbled inside! Scrambling to her feet, face flushed, she shot me a glare.

To divert attention, I quickly asked the person at the desk, "Do we have space for an hour of playtime?"

"Yes, in 15 minutes," he nodded.

While waiting, she whispered, "Why is that most of them are playing that gun game? Is it that fun?"

"That's called *Counter-Strike*. I've played it before, but it's not my thing. *Ragnarok* is superior," I said.

We settled in, and as I guided her through the Ragnarok tutorial, the gaming cafe faded away. Guiding her hands on the mouse felt strangely intimate. The whole experience – the shared excitement, the awkward moments – was one of those indelible memories that define our early friendships.

We became close friends. Over the next few years, that shared connection only deepened. When we moved to sophomore year, we landed in the so-called 'Star Section', a class for top-performing students. With each passing year, a handful of 'new wizards and witches' joined the Harry Potter fan ranks within our little wizard club.

Angeli was practically the president of the club. Her enthusiasm was infectious. In fact, one teacher scolded her, hands on hips, saying, "I don't like your attitude!" Apparently, Angeli's habit of eagerly interjecting Harry Potter references during class was a bit much. The whole scene was hilarious.

She might be one of the most mischievous people I know, but she's also fiercely true and loyal. If I have to label it, she was my best friend. The kind who'd call, "Hey Ray, I got the new Harry Potter book! Let's talk about it!" Of course, the rumors swirling around the classroom insisted otherwise, but we just ignored them, immersing ourselves in our Hogwarts discussions. Little did I know, this friendship, forged over a shared love of magic and stories, would soon be tested in ways I couldn't imagine.

Chapter 2

Love and Lies

2 **003: Junior Year**

Honestly, a love letter? The last thing I ever expected. I'm the shy kid, the one who blends into the background, guitar in hand and nose in a book. Letters like that are for people who actually have lives.

One day, an empty English classroom meant "Library work" scrawled on the board. I rushed over, hoping for a lifeline, but found something unexpected instead: "Read a book. Reaction paper." My eyes scanned the shelves, landing on *Of Mice and Men*. As I settled into a worn armchair in the corner, the musty scent of old books and dust motes danced in the sunlight streaming through the windows. Steinbeck's words resonated with a quiet ache: "Guys like us, that work on ranches, are the loneliest guys in the world." I wondered if that loneliness was an inevitable part of life, a shadow that followed even the most well-intentioned.

Someone tapped me on the shoulder.

"Someone is looking for you outside," a girl I didn't even recognize mumbled, her eyes glued to her open book.

Confusion mingled with curiosity. Who could be looking for

me in the middle of library time? I clumsily pushed back my chair, bumping into the table leg and earning a few irritated glances from my nearby seatmates. Heart pounding, I made my way towards the door, a sense of anticipation growing with each step.

In the hallway stood a familiar face – a former classmate, her expression nonchalant, arms crossed. She was short, with straight, long hair and a mischievous glint in her eye.

"This is for you!" she blurted, shoving a thin, light-pink envelope into my hand before turning on her heel and disappearing back into the sea of students, their uniforms a blur of green and white as they rushed between classes, laughing and chatting.

The envelope was made of textured paper, the handwriting on the front elegant and unfamiliar. The faint scent of strawberries wafted from it as my pulse quickened. Not another homework assignment, then. A love letter? No one had ever...

I retreated to the sanctuary of my armchair, clutching the letter to my chest like a lifeline. My heart pounded, a frantic drum solo against my ribs. A furtive glance around the library confirmed that nobody seemed to be paying attention. With trembling fingers, I carefully opened the envelope, the strawberry scent intensifying as the delicate paper unfolded.

"You're so cool when you play the guitar," the letter read in elegant handwriting, signed simply "From your Secret Admirer." A wave of warmth engulfed me, overwhelming my usual shyness. Did someone actually see me, the real me, beyond the quiet exterior? Did she hear the music in my heart as I fumbled through chords in the old music room? Or was this some cruel joke?

Days turned into a blur of stolen glances at the letter, each rereading a confirmation of my worth, a secret talisman against the gnawing loneliness. The mysterious admirer remained elusive, her identity a tantalizing enigma that both thrilled and tormented me.

Angeli just laughed when I showed her. "Who even writes letters anymore?" she teased. Still, she swore she had no idea who sent it. Some classmates found out, a few playful jeers of "Raymond's got an admirer!" echoed through the hallways. I stopped asking, let the mystery linger, a secret source of warmth in my lonely heart.

2004: Senior Year

Graduation year – that pivotal point between childhood and the vast unknown, full of possibility and pressure. For me, it was one of the most memorable, and not for the reasons I'd expected.

As the end of high school approached, the intense text exchanges with Angeli filled my days. We talked about everything – our dreams, our fears, our plans for the future. I even got swept up in the cheesy "I miss you" messages, cringing even as I typed them. But a nagging doubt, a whisper in the back of my mind, said, *"Maybe this isn't what you think it is." I always tried to be kind...it's just how I was raised. But how could I know if someone was genuine? I didn't realize then that some people see kindness as weakness, an opening to exploit. Too nice, that's what I was.*

The weeks leading up to graduation were a whirlwind of emotions. Balancing the excitement of finishing school with the uncertainty of what lay ahead left me on edge. Amidst the chaos, Angeli's messages became a comforting constant. We made plans to hang out after graduation, to explore colleges together, to keep our friendship alive even as our paths diverged. The thought of losing her, the one person who seemed to truly understand me, filled me with a quiet dread.

But that dread turned into a cold reality a few days before graduation. I was at Sunday mass with my classmates, the air thick with incense and the murmur of prayers, when my phone buzzed. It was a text from Angeli: "All those heartfelt messages we'd been sending? Just a joke."

Each hymn, each prayer, felt like a hollow echo in the cavern of my despair. The incense, usually comforting, now choked me, its sweetness a mockery of the bitterness twisting in my gut. I stole glances at my classmates, their faces serene in the flickering candlelight. Did they know? Were they in on it too?

"It's just a joke!" Angeli's words, a poison-tipped arrow, pierced through the haze of disbelief.

And that love letter in Junior Year? Another joke, another cruel trick orchestrated by my classmates, their laughter a chorus of mockery echoing in my ears.

"We're very sorry, we just want to see how you react." Their apology felt hollow, a flimsy bandage over a gaping wound.

I became their entertainment, a puppet dancing to their whims, my heartstrings their twisted playthings. Each beat of my pulse was a drum of humiliation, a rhythm of rejection. I thought all this time, she was my soulmate. I thought she was my crush. All this time, I was just a pawn, a plaything to my own lack of self-esteem. I just wanted to be seen and heard at times, but why does life do this to me again and again?

The world tilted, the familiar pews and stained-glass windows warping into a grotesque carnival. I was the main attraction, the clown with the painted-on smile, his heart a shattered mirror reflecting their amusement.

I stumbled out of the church, the celebratory atmosphere a cruel joke. The sun beat down on my back, but I felt cold, hollowed out. The taste of salt mingled with the metallic tang of blood as my lip quivered, each sob a jagged shard piercing my chest. The world blurred, each jeepney a smear of color against the gray backdrop of my despair.

My room became a refuge of desolation. Each tear was a shard of my shattered trust. The prank wasn't just a harmless joke; it was a deliberate attack on my vulnerability. This betrayal confirmed my deepest fears: I was unlovable, unworthy of genuine affection.

"I don't want to trust anyone ever again."

The pain was so deep, the betrayal so complete, that I felt a part of myself shutting down. The words echoed in my empty room, a mantra of self-protection, a prison I'd built for myself. This was the moment I began to close off my heart, a shield against future pain. Looking back, I see how that decision, born out of hurt and betrayal, would shape my relationships for years to come. I became guarded, suspicious, hesitant to let anyone in. The echoes of those text messages, the memory of that love letter turned prank, haunted me long after graduation.

Even with the girl in Junior Year who'd confessed her feelings, I'd pushed her away, convinced I wasn't worthy of her affection. The pattern was painfully clear: hurt begetting hurt instead of love.

Angeli didn't give up easily. She would call my name in the hallway, try to catch me after school as I walked to the jeepney stop, even enlist our mutual friends to pass along her apologies. Each time, her eyes would plead for forgiveness, her voice a soft whisper against the backdrop of the bustling school day. But I remained steadfast in my silence, a fortress of hurt and resentment.

As the days passed, however, the fortress around my heart began to crumble. I realized that holding onto anger and resentment was only hurting me. One day, as Angeli approached me with tears in her eyes, I finally found the strength to forgive her.

"I'm sorry, Ray," she sobbed. "I never meant to hurt you. I truly value our friendship, and I don't want to lose it over a stupid prank."

I looked at her, seeing the genuine remorse in her eyes, but the hurt was still too raw. "Angeli," I began, my voice shaking, "I need to understand something."

She looked up at me, her eyes filled with a mix of regret and sadness. "What is it?"

"About the text messages," I continued, my voice barely a whisper. "I... I never thought you were joking. The way you talked about your feelings, your dreams..."

Her eyes widened in surprise. "But... but I thought you were playing along," she stammered. "You know, joking around like we always did."

A wave of confusion washed over me. "But the messages felt so real," I said, my voice cracking. "How could you not see that?"

"I guess I didn't realize how much they meant to you," she admitted, her voice barely audible. "I just thought... I don't know, I thought you were being your usual kind self, humoring me."

"Kind?" I scoffed, the bitterness rising in my throat. "You thought my kindness was a joke?"

"No, no, that's not what I meant," she said, reaching out to touch my arm. "It's just... I've always seen you as so strong, so sure of yourself. I guess I underestimated how much my words could affect you."

"And I," I countered, "underestimated how easily you could dismiss my feelings."

A heavy silence settled between us. The realization that we had both been operating under false assumptions, fueled by our own insecurities and misinterpretations, was a bitter pill to swallow. But in that shared moment of vulnerability, a glimmer of understanding emerged. Perhaps it wasn't just her betrayal, but also my own self-doubt and inability to fully trust, that had led to the misunderstanding. The confusion and hurt remained, but now, there was also a hint of hope for healing.

"I forgive you, Angeli," I said softly, my voice still thick with emotion. "But I won't forget."

We embraced, the weight of the past few weeks lifting slightly from our shoulders. It wasn't a complete reconciliation, but it was a start. We both knew that trust, once broken, takes time to rebuild. But as we stood there, on the cusp of graduation, I felt a glimmer of hope that our friendship could be salvaged.

After graduation, things were different with Angeli. The easy intimacy we once shared was replaced by a cautious politeness. We saw each other occasionally, when I was back in Iloilo, but that was it. The pain of the betrayal lingered, a dull ache that never fully faded. Our paths eventually diverged as she moved abroad, and I embarked on my own journey to Metro Manila, carrying the weight of that experience with me.

The betrayal, while devastating, wasn't entirely unexpected. It was a painful echo of an earlier hurt, a wound that had festered for years, shaping my beliefs about myself and my place in the world. The roots of my insecurity, my deep-seated belief that I wasn't worthy of love or trust, ran deeper than any teenage prank.

Is this the pain of my first love? Or does this stem much deeper from something of my past?

To truly understand why I reacted so strongly to Angeli's betrayal, I need to take you back to a simpler time, a time before love letters and text messages, before the complexities of high school friendships. I need to take you back to my childhood, to the house that built me, and to the man who unwittingly laid the foundation for my lifelong struggle with self-worth.

Chapter 3

The House That Built Me

His ragged pants rustled against his skin as fingers finally found the coins. A hoarse cough. "Here," he rasped, his voice roughened by years of cigarettes. "Get yourself some candy at Torres's. Bring back a Coke and a pack of Hope."

I grinned, teeth bared. Those errands were the best. Bazooka bubblegum, sweet and pink, was my prize – and the feeling I'd done something important, just like him. Coins clutched in my fist, I dashed through the double doors, the final one's spring slamming a triumphant BAM behind me.

Back home, I handed him the soda and smokes. He went to his corner, the crinkle of the cellophane loud in the quiet room. Watching him open the pack, pour the dark fizz into a glass...this was happiness, I thought. He looked at me, and for a second, there was something in his eyes. Almost like he was sorry, but I didn't understand for what.

That was how it should be, right? Dads with their drinks and smokes, kids with their candy. That's all it took. At least, that's what I thought.

Family Story: Early Childhood (Ages 4-9) [Year 1994-1999]

Two years before my sister was born, I was the 'prince' of the family. We lived in a breezy bungalow in a subdivision, and I had brand new toys & cars, you name it – especially my favorite, the 'Polar Bear', a sleek white truck my father brought back from Singapore. I even had my own 'Yaya' or 'Nanny' when he was sailing the seven seas. I cherished those two years, living like royalty.

Two years later, my sister was born. Papa was happy because she looked like him, but the center of attention inevitably shifted to my younger sibling. Papa decided we should move back near my grandfather. We built a two-story house nearby, with one of the rooms upstairs usually empty.

My relationship with my sister was a constant push and pull, a dance between love and rivalry. She, the vivacious social butterfly, always ready with a quick joke or a playful jab. Me, the quiet observer, more comfortable with books and my own thoughts than with crowds and chatter. Mama, ever the peacemaker, would shake her head and mutter, "Cats and dogs," whenever our bickering escalated.

As for Mama, she's the best mother in the world (like most mothers!). The perfect example of unconditional love, caring for all of us no matter what happens. With Papa, she was gentle and patient, always trying to soothe his anxieties. But with me, she was firm yet loving, encouraging me to be strong and independent. Perhaps she sensed that I would need that strength to navigate the unpredictable storms brewing within our home.

My relationship with my father was more complicated. The 'drama' you see in television, everyone has a story to tell.

His fall from 'King of the Seven Seas' had a devastating impact on his mental health. In his prime, my father was a man of sharp wit and quiet intensity. His brown skin, weathered by the sun, contrasted with his clean-shaven head, giving him an air of authority and discipline. My mother, with her warm smile and gentle touch, was the perfect complement to his intensity. Her porcelain skin, a trait I inherited, glowed with a radiance that seemed to defy the troubles that surrounded us.

Mama always said I inherited my smarts from him, and we shared a love for intellectual pursuits. We bonded over the family computer (NES), TV shows like Ripley's Believe It or Not, and his vast collection of VHS and Betamax movies, especially Superman. This shared passion was our common ground...until the tides of fortune turned against him.

He couldn't take the emotional burden of losing a high-paying job. He couldn't accept that those people he helped eventually fled with his money. He couldn't accept the low wage of being a seaman instructor. His family didn't know how to support him emotionally. Because he was a man, he felt the need to put on a strong exterior, negating his inner turmoil.

It became a depression. A never-ending spiral of suppression. Drugs and nicotine were his saviors on the seas, and turned to sugar and cigarettes later – still addictions.

That was the kind of environment I was exposed to as a child. I was innocent, observing from a standpoint: "Why is my father like that?" I didn't have the answers back then, but I tried my best to be a good son.

As a kid, I could always tell if someone was lying or hiding something. My father wasn't immune to that. No matter how he pretended or drowned himself in soft or hard drinks, I could see his misery behind the mask. The smell of those sweet drinks mingled with stale cigarette smoke, clinging to the walls the way sadness clung to him. He'd sit in his corner for hours, pretending to watch the TV, but his eyes were distant. Sometimes, I'd catch him looking at me — not the proud gaze of before, but something almost...apologetic. Like the prince he used to see had been replaced by a pauper, and he wasn't sure what to do with me anymore. When we did interact, it was always with an undercurrent of tension. He expected me to be tough, to hide my emotions, to never show weakness. It was as if he wanted me to be a miniature version of himself, the man he could no longer be.

Eventually, it all became a façade, the illusion of a normal, happy family we put on for the world. Because that's how families were supposed to behave, right? We had to show our neighbors that we were fine.

A Shattered Screen and a Broken Heart: Around 2000-2001

The crash of glass ripped through my sleep, shattering the world of Pokémon I'd been dreaming about. My heart hammered as I scrambled to the window, peering down at the chaotic scene on the balcony. A mess of wires snaked across the concrete, glinting chrome appliances scattered like fallen soldiers. My breath caught – was that a video cassette in the sunlight? Had Papa thrown out my Pokémon tapes?

From my perch at the top of the stairs, I could see just enough of the living room and kitchen to make my heart sink. Mama stood amidst the laundry, her usually bright face etched with sadness. She scrubbed at our underwear, her movements jerky and uncoordinated. As I watched, a single tear escaped, tracing a glistening path down her cheek. I wanted to run to her, ask what was wrong...but a sudden certainty held me back. I knew, without knowing how I knew, that asking questions would be useless.

My hands trembled as I returned to my room, confusion swirling inside me. *Why was everything always so unpredictable?* Desperate for something to cling to, I prayed to the Almighty God, hoping that at the very least the VHS would survive – without a player, my recorded Pokémon movies meant nothing.

My words tumbled out in a rush. As I finished, I heard my Mom storm at my father in the balcony, asking what he was doing. Her tolerance had reached its limit. I watched from above, sobbing and glaring at my father. Once he seemed calmer, they went to my grandfather's house next door to discuss his latest episode.

Despite the damage, I immediately went downstairs, gathered the remaining working appliances back to our living room. The TV's crystal screen was fully shattered and the Betamax was full of indentations. That TV – the one we watched *Titanic* on – was now submerged in crystal fragments, a void staring back at me. My movies and recordings – what if they were gone? The thought felt like a reflection of the growing void in my heart. That fear, that emptiness...it was almost unbearable.

The shattered glass on the balcony mirrored the shattered feeling inside me. Desperately, I just wanted to watch my favorite movies, to escape into a world where things made sense. Miraculously, the VHS survived, the outer ring damaged, but the play button still visible. It must have been the last thing he struck before Mama intervened.

I opened my VHS recordings, fumbling hands searching for my Pokémon tapes. When I found them, untouched, a wave of relief flooded my senses. I played one of my Pokémon episodes. The familiar music, the bright colors...it was a beacon of normalcy in the chaos. "It was not that bad after all," I said to myself.

When my parents came back, I told him to not ever touch the VHS ever again. He looked at me with a hollow, voided eye. Something in me shifted that day. The man I called Father was becoming a stranger, his actions fueled by a force I couldn't understand.

The House of Echoes

The sizzle of frying oil turned into a scream as he plunged his hands into the pan, the smell of burning flesh mingling with the stench of despair. Another morning, the sickening sweetness of toilet bowl cleaner filled the air, followed by his choked cries for help, a symphony of agony and regret. The metallic click of the main switch echoed his silent plea for release, a desperate attempt to silence the demons that tormented him. And then, the refrigerator - the dull thud of his fist against cold steel, a percussion of rage that reverberated through the house, leaving a chilling silence in its wake. The dent, a grotesque scar on its once-pristine surface, became a haunting reminder of his inner turmoil, a constant echo of the helplessness that gripped our family. Each morning, I braced myself for the unpredictable symphony of his despair, my own hands trembling in silent fear, the weight of his pain pressing down on my young shoulders.

All of these happened when I was at the dining table, a witness to his private circus. I'd learned where the floorboards creaked least, which cupboard door provided the best view of the kitchen. It became a kind of survival, my childhood measured in shattered glass and swallowed poisons.

The days bled into a blur, every thud, every splash of liquid a potential prelude to disaster. A few years after these incidents, his condition worsened. My mother decided to take him to the Mental Hospital. I tagged along, but when she decided to stay with him overnight, I went home alone. She said I had to, someone needed to be with my sister, there was food already prepared...the excuses of a mother stretched too thin.

The next day, I remember going back to the hospital for my mother's errand. She told me that the night she was with my father, he grappled with one of the other patients, his hands around the man's neck as if he wanted to choke him. After that, the staff decided to restrain him, a white-wrapped mummy on the bed, fighting against unseen enemies in his sleep.

His therapy continued for many weeks. I remember talking to him one day. We both sat on chairs near the window, overlooking the grassy field and stairs going down – a rare moment of connection in those dark times. He began, "To, I noticed something..." Then, "Why aren't you playing anymore? You used to love running around out there..."

I bowed my head, unable to look him in the eye, tears threatening to betray the composure I'd so carefully built. I wanted to scream, to tell him this was his fault, but all I could do was cry. His hug was brief, then he left me there, descending the stairs to prepare for dinner. There were no words spoken, not then. But the message echoed in the silence that followed: I was denied, hurt, and betrayed.

He tried his best to understand the kind of world where I could thrive – a world unexplored in his own time. Yet, even in his fractured state, he clung to the ideals he'd known: boys should be strong, weakness a thing to be hidden at all costs.

As his depression worsened, my role elevated to a temporary adult. In most cases, I was alone at the house. My mother, her hands often clasped in worry, was always at my father's side, her eyes filled with a mixture of love and concern, my sister away with her school activities. It wasn't until years later that I understood: **I'd been left behind not out of cruelty, but necessity.**

After the Silence: January 2002

After returning from school, an eerie atmosphere enveloped both our house and my grandmother's. Gazing at the sky, it felt as if a dark cloud had paused for the day, unwelcome and lingering. Approaching the gate of our home, a moment of unexplainable silence greeted me. From a distance, I observed our small *sari-sari* store, closed.

I proceeded through the balcony then opened the main door. I discovered one of my aunts arranging figurines near the television, each one meticulously placed. Several relatives sat on the couch. Despite my entrance, no one seemed to notice, as if everyone was consumed by the mysterious cloud.

"Ta? What's happening?" I asked.

Immediately my aunt looked around and hugged me tightly.

"You Father is..." she said while trying to contain her tears

"Huh? Where is Mama?" asking the confused me

"She's with your grandmother in the other house" she replied while wiping her eyes.

I immediately dashed through the door like Sonic for the first time, leaving my bags on the floor.

As I ascended the stairway to my grandmother's house, I saw

my father's older brother, Tito R. He noticed my approach and instantly blocked my way like a guard, halting any unruly visitor.

"Calm down, don't shout or anything, just calm down" he said in a not-so-composed way.

He was trying to distract me, but I could already see Mama from afar. What is she doing on the floor?!

"No, I'm okay" I replied, leaving him near the door.

I continued my gaze. Mama lay half on the floor of the living room, sobbing in tears. My grandmother sat beside her, their mingled cries a sound that would haunt me.

Her arms flew open as she realized I had arrived.

I won't ever forget what Mama said, her voice breaking with each word: "To, wala na si Papa mo" – "Your father is now gone."

The words hit me like a physical blow, knocking the air from my lungs. Gone? *Gone?* A hollow emptiness opened up inside me, threatening to swallow me whole. Time seemed to distort, the world around me blurring as I struggled to grasp the finality of her words.

I collapsed onto the floor beside Mama, my grandmother's arm already around her. The three of us clung to each other, a tangled mess of limbs and sobs. The sound of our combined tears filled the room, a symphony of pain and disbelief. Minutes stretched into an eternity of grief.

Finally, through the fog of my sorrow, a single question emerged, a desperate plea for understanding:

"What happened?" I asked, my voice barely a whisper.

"He was seen at Molo Plaza, sitting on a bench, then went inside Molo Church...it's under repair, so parts are unlocked..." He went upstairs," she whispered, her voice barely audible. The unfinished sentence hung between us, as heavy as the silence of the church he'd chosen for his final act. Outside the window, a bird sang, its melody a cruel parody of peace.

"Some witnesses thought he was with the carpenters because of the clothes he wore..."

There's a long pause in between while we remove our tears. "What about my sister?" I ask.

"She's coming home early as well," Mama replied, her voice still thick with emotion. "We'll wait for her to arrive."

"Okay," I murmured, a dull ache settling in my chest.

I went back downstairs and picked up my bag on the floor. With heavy steps, I headed to my room upstairs, but before I entered, I saw our family portrait. It was a collection of mugshot photos, one for each of us, laid out like a compass.

The north was me, smiling during my recognition day in 1997. The south, my sister, as an innocent 2-year-old. The west, Mama, smiling during her teenage days. And finally him, the east, face all serious in his mid-20s.

My footsteps slowed. Below, my sister shrieked – home from school, and now initiated into this world of loss. But my anger wasn't for her.

I looked back at his portrait, to the east. My voice cracked, the words jagged, "So this is your plan all along?" The disappointment felt like a fist around my heart, tighter than any of the tears I'd shed.

I entered my room, slamming the door with such fury it felt like the entire structure could break if I didn't restrain that ethereal force.

Chapter 4

Weight of Inheritance

February 2002

The weight of his absence pressed down on me like a leaden blanket. I hated him. He couldn't just bail out like that. It wasn't fair. *What am I supposed to do now? What's going to happen to our family?* Big questions for a kid like me, but they kept swirling around in my head, a whirlpool I couldn't escape. The funeral, held in the same church where we'd once attended Mass together, was a blur of incense and murmured prayers.

My mom and sister were crying their eyes out, and I should be too, right? But I didn't. I just stood there, in the middle of the funeral ceremony, watching them, feeling numb. People kept looking at me, their eyes full of pity, probably wondering why I wasn't crying... Inside, though, my thoughts were racing.

I remember his words, how he always said, "Real men don't cry." So maybe by not crying, I'm doing him a favor? It's like a weird way of showing respect, even though it doesn't make much sense.

And then there's his stupid morning routine. I got used to hating it, all the chaos before school. There was that one time my father punched the refrigerator, leaving a dent. Now, whenever I sit in the morning for breakfast, it's like a reminder of that episode. But now, knowing I won't have to deal with it anymore, it's like a weight off my shoulders. Still, it doesn't make things right. The dent remains, a silent reminder of his anger and the pain he inflicted.

He thought he had to do this, that it was inevitable. But was it really? Couldn't he have stayed for us? It feels like he's left us behind, like he chose to go on his own.

After the burial, my sister's friend sends her a message. "I didn't see your brother crying," she writes. But I didn't say anything when my sister mentioned it later during dinner. What was the point? I was already a pariah in my own mind, misunderstood and adrift. So I just kept eating, trying to swallow down all the emotions that threatened to overwhelm me.

The Early Days of Triumphs: Early Childhood (Age 4-8)

Amidst the somber atmosphere of the funeral, my mind drifted to happier times. I recalled the countless hours spent with Papa, engaged in playful battles of wit and skill. "Checkmate!" I declared triumphantly, the final move snapping into place on the chessboard. The room echoed with the clatter of pieces, the tension of the duel finally broken. My heart thumped in my chest – victory!

Papa, a hint of pride etched on his face, leaned back in his chair. "Nice game," he rumbled, his voice warm with admiration. "You're quite the strategist. Ever considered entering a school tournament?"

The suggestion sent a jolt through me. Competition, the chance to prove myself on a bigger stage – it was thrilling. Yet, a familiar fear snaked its way in – the fear of failure. "I don't know..." I mumbled, the excitement dimming. He always inspired me to push my boundaries, to try new things. But stepping out of my comfort zone, facing the unknown – that was a challenge I wasn't sure I was ready for.

My hunger for triumph, however, wasn't confined to the chessboard. In the fantastical realm of *Super Mario Brothers*, I found another arena to conquer. Level after level, I pressed on, sweat beading on my brow as I timed jumps with heart-pounding precision to clear chasms of molten lava. With each discovery – a secret warp pipe, the elusive final dungeon (something Papa had never managed) – came a surge of satisfaction.

My victories extended beyond the screen. I remember an exciting visit to old SM Delgado, our usual family hangout when I was small. Now that I was a big kid, the arcade was my target, its flashing lights and beeping sounds a siren song. We moved next to the console and cartridge area, where a lineup of games waited to be hauled. My heart raced as I spotted the *Pokémon Blue* cartridge, the one I'd been saving for. Papa saw my wide-eyed desire, and I soon held it in my hands, his smile a silent seal of approval. Inserting it into my Game Boy felt like putting on a backpack for the first time – a whole new world to explore! Engrossed in choosing my first Pokémon, I felt a surge of happy ownership I hadn't experienced in a long time. Papa chuckled at my intense focus, squinting at the screen as if trying to decipher an alien language.

"Having fun?" he asked, his eyes twinkling with amusement.

"Yes!" I replied, grinning back, the thrill of the unexpected adventure coursing through me. It felt good to escape the confines of our home, to explore the world beyond our familiar routines.

In those pre-internet days, victory tasted sweeter, each accomplishment a small, hard-earned beacon of hope amidst the chaos swirling in our living room.

Bonding that Ties

Other cherished memories transport me back to our house and backyard, where we often played tag. Laughter filled the air as I chased after Papa, my determination unwavering. He was far stronger, but sometimes, in fleeting moments of victory brought by a well-timed dodge, the joy of a son would wash over me. And each game of tag inevitably led to an arm-wrestling match, a testament to our competitive spirits.

Amidst moments of connection, there were also academic challenges. Seeking my parents' approval, I'd borrow test booklets filled with intricate mathematical equations and puzzles. And when the rigors of school became overwhelming, childhood games like "Wizard of Oz" and "Snakes and Ladders" provided a nostalgic escape.

My father's ingenuity shone through as he skillfully crafted a kite for me. The sight of it soaring across the grassy fields near our home, carried by the wind, ignited a sense of freedom and boundless possibility. Though we didn't always see eye to eye, one thing that united us was our shared enthusiasm for "Ripley's Believe It or Not." We would eagerly watch the TV show together, competing to guess the outcomes of its mind-boggling feats and stories. A playful rivalry emerged, followed by good-natured teasing from the winner.

The One Mission that I Fail

"Raymond," my father said, his voice unusually solemn. "I have a mission for you today." A weighty silence followed, thick with unspoken expectations. "Catch a chicken," he finally added, "and then we'll talk."

Mixed emotions surged within me as I processed his words. Determination to please him battled with a rising tide of fear. Over the years, I'd conquered him in chess, outsmarted him in tag, even aced equations that left him scratching his head. But this? This was a challenge of a different breed – one that required taking a life.

I stood there, frozen in a sea of conflicting thoughts. On one hand, I craved his approval, the silent acknowledgment that I could handle anything he threw my way. But on the other hand, the thought of harming a living creature sent shivers down my spine. Chickens weren't just feathered providers of dinner; they were feathered companions, a constant presence in my childhood memories.

The memory of that day is etched in my mind: My father's patient, yet firm, instructions on how to slaughter a chicken for dinner. The glint of the blade as he demonstrated the technique, each precise movement a chilling reminder of the task at hand. And then, the weight of that same blade, cold and unforgiving, pressed into my trembling hand.

But I couldn't do it. The act of ending another life, no matter how commonplace, was an insurmountable hurdle. In that moment, I saw the chasm widening between us – the stark difference between his upbringing and mine, between his values and the ones I was starting to forge for myself. In the end, I turned away, retreating into the safety of the house, leaving behind the unfulfilled mission and a father whose face, etched with disappointment, held a flicker of something else – perhaps a nascent understanding of the burgeoning man I was becoming.

The experience left me shaken, questioning the very core of my being. It was a brutal lesson in compassion and empathy, a stark reminder that sometimes, true courage lies in defying expectations, in standing firm for what you believe in, even when faced with the weight of a father's disappointment. And although I may have failed the mission he set before me, I emerged from it with a newfound clarity – a newfound understanding of myself and the world around me.

The Last Cry: Year 2000

Growing up without a father was like living in a house where the foundation kept shifting – cracks appearing overnight, a constant reminder of instability. While other kids had parents attending school activities, it was just Mama showing up for me. My world was held together by her strength alone. No one saw the struggle behind the facade.

Being forced into a parental role at a young age was overwhelming. I had to be the strong big brother for my sister and support my tired mom as she struggled to keep our fragile world afloat. Isolated and betrayed, I had no one to talk to about chess or intellectual TV shows, forced to carry on with a false smile hiding the turmoil inside. Was this the society I was supposed to follow? Was this the humanity they envisioned for the future?

Something felt off that day – the familiar tension in the house had intensified, as if a storm was brewing. It's a helpless feeling, watching someone you love slowly unravel, unable to do anything about it. My heart sank, knowing I couldn't stop it, the guilt mixing with fear.

One evening at 5 pm, I was in my room, engrossed in television. He marched upstairs, directly to my door just as I was about to go downstairs, carrying a screwdriver. "Take this to your Tito T," he commanded, his face stern and eyes clouded with that familiar darkness.

"Huh? I don't want to, I'm busy watching," I protested.

In an instant, he grabbed my shoulder tightly, his grip burning through my shirt, and tried to force the screwdriver into my hand. I clenched my fist, refusing. His voice rose, strained with anger. Fear started to creep in as I trembled.

"NO, I DON'T WANT TO!" I shouted, pushing back.

But he kept pushing, down the stairs, still refusing to let go. The relentless pressure continued until I found myself at his brother's door. I still couldn't understand why I had to do his bidding. Couldn't he return the screwdriver himself?

At that moment, I felt like I had lost him for good. In his eyes, I saw a vacancy, a void where connection had once resided. Repeating the same demand over and over. "Return this screwdriver to your Tito T."

"Why can't you do it yourself?" I pleaded, my voice cracking.

"Basta," was his only, echoing reply.

In that moment of helplessness, I realized I had no other choice but to obey, if only to save myself. It wasn't just the words, it was the emptiness in his eyes, the hollowness that mirrored the growing void within me. This was the final straw, the moment I understood that his silence, his refusal to confront his pain, had become a destructive force that threatened to consume us all. It was a stark realization: men, burdened by societal expectations, often suffer in silence, their unspoken struggles festering until it's too late.

"OK, I'll do it," I said, wiping away my tears and sweat.

As I reached Tito T's house, he welcomed me warmly and directed me to return the screwdriver to the boxes near the dining table. I could sense something was up, but he tried to not make a deal out of it. It was a small task, and when it was done, I left his house, the weight of the screwdriver still lingering in my hand long after it had been returned... and the echoes of my own unanswered questions stuck with me, heavier than any tool.

Back home, the silence was deafening. The familiar tension had reached a fever pitch, leaving a palpable emptiness in its wake. I sought solace in the virtual world, losing myself in online games where I could create a new identity, a world where I wasn't defined by my father's actions. It was an escape, a temporary reprieve from the pain. But even as I delved into these digital realms, the weight of my father's choices, the burden of his inheritance, never truly left me.

Chapter 5

Stuck Between Two Worlds

The First World: Year 2006

The familiar chime of the game's login screen was a welcome invitation to leave behind the stresses of college life and embrace the thrill of adventure. Today, however, was no ordinary login; today, I was leading my guild on a HERO Expedition, a crucial step towards achieving the coveted HERO status in the game, a feat that mirrored my own real-life quest for recognition and belonging.

The guild chat buzzed with excitement as we prepared for the expedition. ValerieMae, always the life of the party, was her usual exuberant self, teasing and joking with the others. Cuddles, Anna, and Frostburn responded with laughter and playful retorts, their messages a flurry of anticipation.

I took a deep breath, the weight of leadership settling on my shoulders. A quick check confirmed Cedie and Blu were present, though lagging behind.

"Where are you guys? We're already in Darkon!" I typed, hoping they wouldn't hold us up too long.

"Big brother Ray, I'm right beside you!" Blu's message popped up, followed by Cedie's confirmation.

The chat continued its frantic pace, questions and jokes flying back and forth. I handed out "phanbubbles" as fast as I could, trying to maintain order amidst the chaos.

"Where are you guys going?" DevaPain asked, his curiosity piqued.

Reboy, ever the joker, replied, "We're going on a trip, on our favorite rocket ship – blast off!"

As Reboy's words faded, I took off on my Sky Board. Soaring above the spectacular volcanic landscape of Darkon in our game world, Flyff, I felt awe at the scale and dangers ahead. "Wow," I thought, "this is one of those moments you can hardly believe is happening."

The reverie shattered with my real name: "ValerieMae: Raymond Janayon, Raymond Janayon." The chat exploded with impatient messages– "Paken: they're taking forever!" and "Frost-burn: Ray, where are you?".

I pushed my flying skills to the limit, but game restrictions held me back. Finally, I reached the volcano zone's edge, dismounted my board, and landed amidst my boisterous guildmates, all clamoring for "phanbubbles." ValerieMae stepped forward first, followed by Cuddles and the others.

Once everyone was ready, we approached the "Mysterious Girl" and initiated the group teleport into the dungeon. "OFF WE GO!" The screen flickered to black, and we plunged into the heart of the volcano. The ruby-red floor glowed beneath us, teeming with swarms of flying, dragon-like "Meteos." As the expedition leader, I unleashed my magic, drawing the creatures away from my less-experienced teammates. They were low-level compared to my Elementor – master of elements, though frail in close combat, but I could easily handle them.

Deeper into the volcano we ventured, the guild chat a constant buzz of banter and strategy. I tried to focus, guiding us through the fiery labyrinth towards the final dungeon.

Finally, the teleport spot appeared. "Finally, Ray, you've arrived." Valerie declared, landing beside me with a playful swat to my character's head. Players were buzzing with restless energy, waiting for instructions.

"Nightwatcher: I came~" proclaimed a latecomer, prompting laughter. Valerie continued her playful assault. "What's our formation?" I asked, desperate to get this show started.

"A circle, duh!" Valerie quipped back. "Hurry up! But," she added with a mischievous grin, "maybe a straight line would be better? Hmm..." A flicker of playful confusion rippled through the crowd. "But with all these people..."

My voice rose above the din, "Okay, a circle! Gather around the Mysterious Robed Girl!"

It took some coaxing and good-natured squabbles, but eventually, our crowd shifted into a lopsided heart. Close enough! I signaled to ValerieMae that we were ready, then strode to the center of our ragtag troop.

As I looked out at the assembled avatars, awe struck me. Every Flyff character class was represented. Around twenty-eight dedicated players were here for my hero ceremony. The weight of their time and faith settled on my shoulders. And then, with a force that left me breathless, it hit me:

This is it. This is the kind of community, the kind of support, I've always craved.

"Rayster, Speech! Speech!" Brawnzon shouted, the others joining in the chaotic chorus.

Panic hit me like a cold splash. Okay, okay, what to say...?

"Aheem, everyone – thank you for coming! A special thanks to the Bubble people, those who borrowed characters from another server, and, of course, my friends from other guilds for joining in. And finally, to my own chaotic guildmates, who waited while I gathered everyone..." My voice trailed off, a lump forming in my throat. "Smile guys, you're in a video!"

The chat exploded with a mix of excitement and self-consciousness.

I scanned the crowd, trying to locate the Mysterious Robed Girl, but she was buried within a pile of overlapping characters. With a bit of maneuvering, I finally spotted her and initiated the dialogue.

"Goddess of Rhisis bless you. You have proven your mastery in both thought and deed. If I tell you who I am, will you be surprised? Hmmm." The Goddess paused, her voice both playful and cryptic. "I am the Goddess of Rhisis."

I clicked her again, a tingle of anticipation running through me.

"Do no question me and do not look at me for too long. Go and bring me 10 Dragon Hearts, 10 Dragoon Teeth, and 10 Mysterious Eyes. Then I will make you a HERO with new power. Prove your ability to me. You can get what you need from the monsters nearby."

A familiar thrill coursed through me. I had prepared the quest items in advance. Confident, I approached the Goddess again.

"Go and show the world your new power. I, the Goddess Rhisis, name you a Hero of this world! A protector of Madrigal!"

I held my breath. After the last click, BOOOM! The screen erupted in digital fireworks as my status shifted – from "Master" to the coveted "HERO." The chat exploded alongside the light show, a whirlwind of messages flooding my screen. Everyone was going wild!

"Congrats Ray!" The greetings poured in as I stood there, stunned. Whoa, this was it – the highest of highs. As the digital fireworks faded and the congratulations poured in, I felt a surge of emotion I hadn't experienced in a long time. This was more than just a game; it was a validation of my skills, my leadership, my worth. In this virtual world, I had found a place where I could shine, where my voice mattered, and where I belonged. It was a stark contrast to the isolation and uncertainty of my real life, where the pain of my father's absence still lingered.

Suddenly, players started disconnecting – I guess the digital fireworks caused some lag. As more people said goodnight (it was almost 10 pm anyway), a wave of amazement and accomplishment surged through me. To reach level 120 as an Elementor – a class so few dared to choose for its difficulty – already felt like a miracle. But now, here I was, one of the server's top ten Elementors. Honestly, I never imagined I could pull this off, or that so many would join to celebrate it.

"This," I realized, "is the power of the internet. It can connect us across continents, transcend boundaries, and create communities where we can truly be ourselves."

The Second World: Year 2008

The scratchy plastic chair dug into my back as the faint scent of whiteboard marker hung in the air. Sunlight streamed through the dusty windows of the computer lab, casting long shadows on the rows of humming machines. A daydream about my next Flyff adventure was shattered by a familiar voice calling my name.

"Mooond...? Do you mind if we talk..?" Lyn sounded eager, with a hint of nervousness in her voice. We slipped to a corner of the lab, away from the clattering keyboards and the blinding fluorescent lights.

"I hope you won't mind me asking, uhmm..." she started, then stopped. "I rented a pink costume last weekend, so... uhmmm... I would like to play the role of Sita."

Oh no, I thought, a knot forming in my stomach. *This is going to be complicated.* Lyn, with her porcelain skin and flowing dark hair, possessed a classic Filipina beauty that turned heads wherever she went. She had her heart set on the spotlight.

"Oh, that," I replied, trying to hide my surprise. Wait, the *Sita* role? My mind raced. Arlyn, with her sun-kissed skin and striking features, had always radiated an exotic allure that captivated everyone in our class. "Uhmm, I'm not sure yet. I heard Arlyn has her costume ready too. I'll talk to you both, okay?"

"Okay, Mond..." she replied, a touch of disappointment clouding her delicate features. She barely nodded, and I could see a hint of hurt in her eyes.

As we returned to our seats, I couldn't shake the feeling of Arlyn's gaze from across the room. We were supposed to be working on a computer assignment, but the previously relaxed lab now felt stifling, a silent war playing out between glances.

Okay, now this is interesting, I thought, feeling a headache coming on. Two girls vying for the same role. Honestly, Arlyn seemed perfect for the part, but how could I let Lyn down without causing drama? *Just what have I gotten myself into?*

Just what's going on here? Let me back up a bit...

It all started in my third year of college, in an English literature class shared with HRM students.

"No final exams for this class!" Sir Jun proclaimed.

A ripple of excitement ran through the room. It quickly died down as he continued, "But you will present a play based on one of the stories I give you."

We stared at him, a mix of confusion and apprehension clouding our faces.

"So for this class, let's divide into three groups. Two HRM groups and one Computer Science. Any leftover HRM students will join the Computer Science team. With that said, I have 3 papers here to pick from, so choose your representative and draw."

The HRM students quickly chose their representatives. I could feel the weight of expectation as my classmates turned to me. I stood, walked to the front, and picked the last crumpled paper.

"'Ramayana'... What the heck is this?"

"The stories you receive will inspire what you're about to do," Sir Jun explained. "You can adapt them directly, or reinterpret them – just tell your version of the tale. Choose a leader, discuss, and get to work. Any questions? If not, class dismissed."

The bell rang, and the HRM students bolted out the door, leaving my Computer Science classmates staring at me expectantly.

"Mond? You'll be the leader, right?" Jess asked, her voice a mix of hope and trepidation.

I didn't answer. My mind was still reeling from the announcement. *Plays? Group work? On top of all my programming classes? My scholarship depends on my grades. This feels like a disaster waiting to happen.* A knot of anxiety tightened in my stomach. I could feel my heart pounding in my chest, a familiar rhythm that always accompanied the fear of failure. I had always excelled in my academics, but this was different. This wasn't about memorizing formulas or writing code; it was about creativity, collaboration, and stepping outside my comfort zone.

One glance around the room was enough. They knew this silence meant a bad mood. With endless homework and the pressures of third year, who had time for this?

The next English class arrived, and Sir Jun requested a list of group members with the leader's name at the top. More murmuring and hesitation filled the air.

"Si Mond na lang!" (Mond, we choose you, come on), Mary pleaded, echoing the silent sentiments of the room.

A flicker of defiance sparked within me, but then fizzled. It wasn't like I had a choice anyway, was it?

"Okay, I'll write down our names on this paper," I said, my hand shaking slightly, then reluctantly submitted it to Sir Jun.

"Now that's settled, remember: you have creative freedom with the stories. Extra credit goes to those who take it to the next level," he announced.

"Before I forget, you'll find different versions of your assigned story in the library – short, long, even poems. It's up to you to adapt the material into a short trailer-style play, so don't feel obligated to act out every scene." After these final instructions, Sir Jun moved on to the regular lesson.

This was another challenge I'd have to overcome. It wasn't just my work on the line anymore; my classmates' grades depended on me too. I had to give it my all. As we parted ways, the task of casting loomed over us. The pressure was on. If we chose poorly, the whole thing would be a disaster.

Initial roles were tentatively agreed upon, until Lyn approached me with her plea to swap parts with Arlyn.

Sita is the story's heroine, and Lyn saw herself in the spotlight thanks to her rented pink dress. Perhaps, there was something else playing at her heart, a desire for more than just a pretty costume. So, during our first dress rehearsal – with Arlyn and Lyn already sporting their costumes – the confrontation finally unfolded.

"If you noticed, Arlyn is much better suited to be Sita," I told the group bluntly. "Look at her – the costume, her exotic beauty... It's obvious. Lyn, I know you wanted the part, but the majority agree that Arlyn would be a better fit. You'd shine as Queen Kaikeyi, the King's wife."

Lyn's face fell, the pink dress suddenly seeming to lose its luster. Though disappointed, she understood. The majority had spoken, and Arlyn did look the part. Maybe Queen Kaikeyi wasn't so bad after all. A wave of whispers and approving nods rippled through the group as Arlyn basked in the validation, her heart swelling with gratitude.

Meanwhile, a problem of a different sort had emerged: no one seemed willing to play Rama. "Mary, I need you as Hanuman." I declared. "Instead of Rama, you'll lead the war against Ravana."

"Ehh, is that the Monkey God?" Mary replied with a grimace.

"Yes," I confirmed. A headache was brewing. This was going to be harder than any programming assignment. But my scholarship, my future, depended on pulling this off. And not just for me - my classmates were counting on me too. I couldn't let them down. I had to find a way to make this work.

So I explained who would play which role, that the team would be divided into two: the dark team with Ravana and the good Monkey team with Hanuman. Everyone seemed as attentive as ever.

After finalizing the cast list, a wave of relief briefly lifted the weight of responsibility I felt as the director, scriptwriter, and audio person. But days later, panic set in: I'd completely over-looked costumes for everyone except Arlyn and Lyn! With only three to four weeks until the performance, I gathered my class-mates during a break.

"Guys, we have a problem. I totally forgot about costumes for the rest of you!" I blurted out, my voice tinged with anxiety. "Can anyone help? I'm swamped with audio and don't think I can handle making them too..." My voice trailed off, hoping someone would step up.

Thankfully, Jess stepped forward. "Don't worry, Mond. I'll volunteer, and I'll ask Mary and Lyn to help as well." Relief replaced the worry knotting my stomach. I quickly gave them a sketch for inspiration – Indian garments for our play. While I had zero experience in costume design, I trusted them to make it work, even with our shoestring student budget.

Two weeks before the performance, we held a chaotic rehearsal in an empty room. The audio was ready... At first, it went smoothly...until the forest scene. Arlyn, as Sita, wandered as planned, only to be 'abducted' by Ravana, played by Jeniel. What was initially a funny scene soured with repetition. Instead of the menacing presence the scene demanded, Jeniel pranced around Arlyn with exaggerated movements, drawing laughter from some of our classmates. She bit back a frustrated sigh.

We were wasting precious time – time our schedules barely allowed – and couldn't move on to the next scene. Despite telling them to stop, the giggling continued, echoing in my pounding head. The pressure, the lack of sleep, the looming deadlines of my other classes...it all coalesced into a boiling rage. I felt like I was carrying the weight of the entire production on my shoulders, and they were making a mockery of it.

Each failed attempt pushed me closer to the edge. My knuckles whitened on the chair. Finally, I snapped. "Enough!" I shouted, the force of it surprising even me. I stormed out of the room, fury battling anxiety. I was so done – stressed, overworked, and now this! Heading to the bathroom to cool off, I stared at myself in the mirror. "Raymond, get a grip," I muttered. "This isn't just about you – it's about them too. It's a chance to learn how to work with different people, even when they're being impossible."

After about 15 minutes of pacing and self-lecturing, I marched back to the classroom. Just outside the door, I overheard Arlyn say, "Okay, I'll take it from here." A jolt went through me – they were taking charge, maybe doing it without me was suddenly possible. But as I lingered, their voices drifted into the hallway. Gone was the playfulness, replaced by serious focus. A small smile tugged at my lips. Maybe my outburst had made a difference. I waited until they hit a snag, a confused pause in their dialogue, before casually strolling back in. Relief surged through their faces, mixed with a hint of apology. I was sorry too. It was unspoken, but understood.

That day, we pulled it together, capturing multiple takes. I left feeling confident that, amidst the chaos, we'd all earn good grades.

The Play

Our class advisor, Sir Arlie, surprised us with a gesture of support after witnessing our chaotic dress rehearsal. "Mond, I'll lend you my laptop for audio playback. It'll give your play a bit more polish." His offer was a lifeline compared to scrambling with my Nintendo DS Lite.

The day of the performance arrived. We'd been relegated to a small classroom for our stage, the school's auditorium already occupied by the dance troupe's rehearsals. The air crackled with nervous energy as we flicked off the lights, leaving the room in near darkness. The faint glow of Sir Arlie's laptop was all that illumi-nated the faces of Sir Jun and the three judges, their expressions a mix of surprise and curiosity.

One teacher, the other two...one rumored to be Sir Jun's girl-friend. Her eyebrows shot up in surprise as the play began.

Three figures stood in a circle, each representing a key figure from the Ramayana. The laptop's faint glow was all that broke the darkness. Just as Sir Jun stirred, ready to break the silence, the play began.

"It all started in darkness – then Brahma, the creator." A flicker of soft light hinted at a face, paired with the sound of birdsong and rustling leaves.

"Then, Vishnu, the maintainer and preserver." Another flicker of light, this time with the sounds of a bustling village.

"And Shiva," a pause, then a single beam illuminated a face, "the DESTROYER!" The narrator's booming voice echoed against a backdrop of thunder and screams. The lights snapped back on, momentarily blinding the audience.

But soon, Lyn swept onto the stage as Queen Kaikeyi, her posture regal, meeting Mary as Hanuman, who bowed before her, hand outstretched to receive the boon.

Then came Arlyn, radiant as Sita, wandering lost in the forest... until Ravana swooped in for the 'kidnapping'. As "Can You Feel the Love Tonight?" swelled in the background, Ravana's attempts at seduction were met with Sita's unwavering defiance. To my relief, their scene flowed as practiced, building tension that had Sir Jun shifting forward in his seat. His girlfriend's knuckles whitened on his arm. A hint of jasmine perfume filled the air as Sita clutched the flower Ravana had offered, a symbol of both beauty and his sinister desire.

Next, Mary, in a hastily constructed monkey mask, rallied the monkey troops! A clash of dark and light forces loomed – under-scored by a rousing track from *Final Fantasy IV DS - Prologue*.

The music swelled as the battle tableau formed, Sita and

Queen Kaikeyi stood amidst the chaos, faces carved in determination. Silence hung heavy. Then the clash of Ravana and Hanuman's sword echoed through the room, freezing the fight in the center. At that precise moment, the narrator's voice rang out, each syllable clear and powerful: " AD -- LO -- WIS!"

A flash of light pierced the darkness - Sir Jun snapping a photo of the frozen tableau.

"The journey of Adventure, Love, and Wisdom! Now showing in theaters nearby."

Thunderous applause filled the room. A standing ovation – it surged through me, and tears of joy streamed down my face.

The applause slowly faded, leaving a ringing silence in its wake. I stood there, heart still pounding, the taste of triumph mingling with the bittersweet knowledge that this chapter was ending.

As the lights came back on, I caught a glimpse of Sir Jun's girlfriend wiping away a tear, her smile a radiant beacon in the dimly lit room. It was a moment of validation, a confirmation that our hard work had touched hearts and minds beyond our own. In that instant, I understood the power of storytelling, the ability to transport an audience to another world, if only for a fleeting moment.

But the real world awaited, with its own challenges and uncertainties. As I packed up the props and costumes, my thoughts drifted back to the digital realms I knew so well. The virtual victories, the sense of belonging and purpose I found online, served as a stark contrast to the messy complexities of real life.

In Between

College hadn't changed that. I was still the same kid, haunted by the past, but now with the added burden of responsibility. I kept to myself, wary of forming close bonds after the betrayal I experienced in high school. The online world of Flyff offered a refuge, a place where I could shed my insecurities and be someone else entirely. But even as I soared through virtual landscapes and led my guild to victory, the desire for a fresh start, to escape the memories and limitations of my hometown, burned ever brighter. I knew I needed to finish college quickly, leave Iloilo behind, and create a new life where the weight of the past wouldn't hold me down.

In the stuffy silence of my bedroom, the sharp clicks of my Gameboy's buttons echoed through the room, a comforting rhythm amidst the chaos of my thoughts. The scent of old plastic and worn-out batteries filled the air, a familiar smell that transported me back to simpler times.

Around 2001, a worn cartridge of *Zelda: Link's Awakening* found its way into my hands, a loan from a classmate. Unlike the digital camaraderie of Flyff, this adventure was solitary. Yet, it wasn't devoid of connection. In those pre-internet days, gaming was a social activity in its own right. Sharing tips, swapping cartridges, huddled conversations over pixelated puzzles – these were the building blocks of a different kind of community, one forged in shared experiences and face-to-face interactions.

I vividly remember being utterly stumped in the Angler's Tunnel, a maze-like dungeon filled with traps and monsters. I had the Angler Key, but I couldn't figure out where to use it. I wandered through the same corridors again and again, growing increasingly frustrated with each dead end. I knew there had to be a way in, but it eluded me.

Finally, after days of fruitless searching, I swallowed my pride and approached the cartridge's owner, a boy in a different section, after class.

"Hey, I'm the one who borrowed your *Zelda*," I mumbled, clutching my backpack where my Gameboy was hidden. "Can I ask you about Dungeon 4? I'm totally lost."

He grinned, a mischievous glint in his eyes. "Sure thing," he replied, "but you might have to give the game back afterwards."

"Oh, right..." I hesitated, then offered, "What if I trade you a different cartridge for a while? I have this 8-in-1..."

He perked up, intrigued. "Let's go talk more about this – I need some fresh air."

We ended up on an open-air second floor, a warm breeze ruffling our hair as we discussed the trade. He patiently listened as I described my struggles in the Angler's Tunnel, his face a mask of concentration as he tried to recall the solution. Then, a lightbulb seemed to go off in his head.

"Do you have the Angler's Key?" he asked.

"Yes, but..." I trailed off, suddenly realizing my mistake. "Wait! You mean that skull thing by the waterfall? I thought it was just decoration!"

He laughed, handing me back my Gameboy. "Give it a try."

As Link placed the key in the skull-shaped slot, a hidden door creaked open. I stared at the screen, then back at him, a mix of embarrassment and gratitude flooding over me.

"Thanks!" I exclaimed. "I feel like such an idiot for not seeing that."

"Don't worry," he said, patting me on the back. "We all get stuck sometimes."

In that moment, I realized that even in the solitary world of gaming, connections could be forged and challenges could be overcome through collaboration. While the vastness of the internet allowed for anonymous friendships in Flyff, there was something undeniably special about the tangible connection forged over a shared love for *Zelda*. Both experiences, in their own way, offered a sense of belonging and purpose, a welcome escape from the lingering pain of my past. They taught me the importance of community, the power of resilience, and the enduring appeal of adventure.

But life wasn't just about virtual victories and shared quests. The real world, with its complexities and demands, was always there, waiting. And as I neared the end of my college journey, a new adventure beckoned – one that would test my resilience and force me to confront the shadows of my past in ways I never could have imagined. The corporate world, with its promise of stability and financial security, seemed like a world away from the pixelated battles and fantastical landscapes of my childhood. Yet, as I prepared to step into this unfamiliar territory, I couldn't help but wonder if the skills and lessons I'd learned in those virtual realms would translate to the harsh realities of the workplace.

Chapter 6

Navigating the Corporate System

Year **2010-2012**

A wave goodbye to Mama and my sister marked my journey to the urban jungle of Metro Manila – the promised land of job opportunities. It wasn't my first time venturing into this chaotic world. Years back, Tito N had whisked me and my cousin away for a whirlwind city adventure – flashing neon signs, a symphony of car horns, the tantalizing smell of street food we never got to try. That trip sparked a hunger in me to experience this intensity firsthand. Now, he'd groomed me for the corporate world, and fresh out of college, that's exactly where I was headed.

The aroma of garlic and onions sizzling in oil mingled with the scent of freshly brewed coffee. Tito N and I huddled over breakfast, his booming voice a stark contrast to the early morning quiet.

"So, how many companies did you apply to yesterday?"

"Uhmm, around ten," I admitted, feeling a familiar wave of guilt wash over me. Was I doing enough?

"Good." A satisfied nod, the kind only a man of his generation, steeped in a different kind of work ethic, could deliver. Me, their millennial 'prince,' still grappled with those pre-dawn starts. "Are you coming?" His voice echoed from the doorway.

A scalding gulp of coffee, I was out the door, keys jingling a frantic rhythm. Two months under their roof – a crash course in ironing, navigating traffic, and most importantly, self-reliance. Independence was on the horizon, a promise whispering through the rumble of the city traffic.

Chasing the Corporate Ladder

My hunger to climb that corporate ladder burned bright. Days blurred into a frenzy of job applications, the scent of stale coffee lingering on my hands as I hunched over my phone. With each tap, Google Maps revealed another office building, another dot on the vast sprawl of Makati City. The thrill of possibility battled a prickling fear – what if this search led nowhere? Then, like a beacon amidst the endless job postings, a flicker of hope online: an old forum friend, Elio, messaged with news of a tech giant opening.

That first interview alongside Elio... The air crackled with nervous energy as we squeezed into chairs in the waiting room. A woman in a power suit tapped her phone anxiously, while a young man's resume trembled in his hand. I took a deep breath, trying to calm the butterflies in my stomach as we waited for our turns.

My turn came. I entered the interview room, my clammy hands betraying the nerves I tried to hide. "So, hi! Please have a seat," the interviewer said with a smile. A wave of relief washed over me. At least I'd cleared the first hurdle.

"I appreciate your interest in this position. Your exams were impressive – that's why you're here today," she began, then surprised me with a shift in conversation. "Upon reviewing your resume, I can't help but notice that you're from Iloilo City. That's quite a journey! That's brave of you, starting fresh in a city like this." Her words held a warmth I hadn't expected, a flicker of recognition of the challenges beyond my skills and qualifications.

"Well, I'm just trying my best, ma'am," I replied, my voice a bit steadier.

"I like you already," she said, her smile widening. "We'll be in touch soon with an update."

I left the room feeling strangely buoyant. The interview was barely about my experience, yet that focus on my journey, on the boldness of my move, gave me a sliver of hope. Spotting Elio on my way out, I couldn't hide my grin.

"So, how was it?" His voice held a familiar mix of nerves and anticipation.

"It was...different," I said, unable to fully explain the strange optimism bubbling up inside me.

We promised to keep each other updated, and then waited. Each day felt like an eternity, my phone glued to my hand as I waited for any sign of news. I clung to that sliver of hope, visualizing it as a rung on the corporate ladder I was desperate to reach.

A Lifeline Appears

The tech giant's silence gnawed at me. Days blurred until another Yahoo Messenger ping broke the monotony – Jacob. He messaged with exciting news: the company where he worked was hiring! A lifeline to cling to in the midst of my limbo. This time, the interview was set for Boni Avenue. At least I knew where that was, even if the commute from Las Piñas was still a beast.

By the time I found Jacob outside Mang Inasal, the smell of roasted chicken in the air made my stomach growl, a sharp contrast to the nerves jangling beneath my crumpled suit.

"Rayster!" His familiar grin cut through the rush hour crowd.

"Long time no see, Jacob!"

"Yeah, the last time we met was still in Iloilo when we had our vacation in Guimaras," he replied.

"Speaking of vacations, I could use one," I admitted. The exhaustion settled heavy in my shoulders as I searched for any sign of the office building.

"So for the interview, you have to proceed to the third floor of

Robinsons Forum, that's the hub for their recruitment process. It's pretty straightforward. I will have to go back to the office, but good luck!" he said.

"Okay," I said, standing up and rushing my way to the mall. I proceeded to the third floor, marveling at the rows of office cubicles within a bustling mall. Back in Iloilo, offices were always in their own buildings. This was different, and the sheer novelty of it added to my nerves. Finally, I reached the applicant check-in desk, Jacob's description echoing in my head.

The clock ticked relentlessly as I stared at the screen during the interview, my mind racing to recall the obscure technical terms we had just learned during training. Each question on the exam felt like a barbed wire fence I had to crawl under, each answer a gamble. I did my best, but as always, the doubts crept in. Another routine in this seemingly endless job hunt.

After a week that dragged like a year, the call came: thanks to Jacob's referral, I'd gotten the job! A rush of disbelief, then elation. "I got in? No way! Wait, yes – YES!!! " I practically shouted over Yahoo Messenger at Jacob, barely able to process the good news.

Paperwork, forms, a blur of requirements. Then, the training. Those 8 am starts, the brutal commute from Las Piñas, the endless hours...it felt like a test of endurance. Some days I barely made it, fueled by a mix of desperation and stubborn determination.

The Training Grind

The MRT doors slid open, and I was swept into a sea of bodies, the stench of sweat and desperation filling my nostrils. Two hours later, I stumbled into the training room, my shoulders aching from the weight of my backpack. The taste of stale coffee lingered on my tongue as I scanned the room, twenty pairs of eyes sizing each other up with a mix of nerves and excitement. Flashback to my first day of school, but this time with way more on the line.

I found a chair and tried to act cool, but the newbie *provinciano* vibes were strong. Luckily, my accent broke the ice – the second I spoke, everyone was curious about this sweet-sounding Ilonggo in their midst. We laughed and chatted, and some of that tension started to melt away. Mark, Josie, and Gemma were among those that I eventually befriended.

Then the instructors arrived – two seasoned pros in their 50s who promised to alternate and train us in the tech we'd need. They laid out the rules – grades, group projects, all of it – but also made it clear they wanted us to enjoy the process too. They got how crazy those first weeks could be.

And yeah, it was a brutal journey. The training itself was a whole different level from school, but the real beast was the commute. Those blurry early morning and late night battles against the crowds... I was drowning in coffee, three cups a day just to survive. We had those dreaded test cases after each lesson hanging over our heads, and there were times I was ready to lose it. My mind was a runaway train, and finishing them felt impossible. I even had to beg my teammates for help once, which was humiliating. Honestly, I thought I wouldn't make it.

But as those grueling weeks neared their end, a weird thing happened. The day we were supposed to get our grades... it felt like a mini-graduation, with some food and jitters all around. Deep down, I was terrified I'd flunked, especially after those killer test cases. But I guess that's where my group project saved me. We even snagged second place in a contest! It was that never-give-up spirit, wanting to help the team and make up for my own weaknesses. When I opened those grades and saw an 83, I was stunned. I'd thought I'd barely scrape by with a passing score. This was different, the stakes were so much higher than back in the province, and everyone here was so competitive.

Through those two months, I made some amazing friends, people I'd work alongside for years to come. Training, as crazy as it is, ends up something you cherish. It's that shared struggle, that camaraderie...you build bonds that last way beyond those first few weeks. Two months flew by, and suddenly, it was official: I was an employee! Even now, it feels surreal. Me and Elio both hoped for that other company, the one that never called. But life takes funny turns. Now here I am, right in the heart of the Manila madness, just where I've always longed to be.

My Rollercoaster First Project

After two grueling months of training, the moment finally arrived – I was an official member of a project team. Turns out, I hadn't just landed any project. From nervous whispers among my former classmates, now coworkers, I learned this one had a reputation for being...well, let's just say "intense." But hey, fresh out of training, fueled by a mix of ambition and naiveté, I saw a challenge, not a reason to run.

That third month marked a turning point. It was time to move on from Tito N's house in Las Piñas and its soul-crushing commute to Boni station. No way was I going to survive actual project work if I was already half-dead from travel. Luckily, I found a place within walking distance of the office – a cramped bedsit maybe, but with one jeepney ride, I was at work. Crisis averted!

Those first few weeks on the project felt welcoming. Friendly faces, the usual new-hire training sessions... it was starting off smoothly. As a programmer, I was eager to dig into the code, to understand the system from the inside out. I was fortunate to land on a testing team, where my task was to meticulously check every function across the whole project. It sounded tedious, but I saw the bigger picture. This was a strategic move. Mastering this would set me apart from the other newbies.

My team leader was a quirky guy, a total pro who somehow managed to simultaneously teach and poke fun at my overly serious nature. Okay, maybe I was a bit too intense. But between his guidance and those endless cups of coffee, I started to find my rhythm. A few months in, a new batch of fresh graduates arrived – wide-eyed and eager, just like I'd been. And suddenly, I was the one doing the explaining, the teaching. It was a strange but satisfying shift.

My first company promoted me quickly. After a few months mastering my initial tasks, I was given the opportunity to teach new hires – a big deal for someone so early in their career! It meant more responsibilities, but I was ready to take them on.

Then came a twist I hadn't anticipated: a smaller, focused project with just me and an associate manager. This was it – the real deal. I was no longer just a trainee. I soaked up everything I could about client calls, those dreaded admin tasks...it was like a crash course in how projects actually functioned beyond the code. Looking back, I realize just how lucky I was. At 21, while my peers were still learning the ropes, I was getting a front-row seat to project management. Plus, this manager was great to work with – laid-back, focused...a total change from my often-frantic first team leader. I thrived under his guidance.

My time with that associate manager felt like a turning point. Looking back, it was a huge privilege. None of the other new grads had the same opportunity, the same level of hands-on experience. That small project ended up a success story, and I genuinely liked working with him. His laid-back style, the way he taught without making me feel stupid...it was a welcome change from my first, frantic team leader who often left me floundering. While I'd learned a lot from him too, this new style fueled my desire to become a leader who could empower, not just manage. I was just getting started.

The Project Swap Request

Although working with the new associate manager gave me valuable experience, my work was becoming monotonous. I yearned for the spark of inspiration that came with learning new programming languages like JAVA or .NET. One day, during a chair shuffle, I was moved to the edge of our project area, right next to a different team. The buzz of their conversations was infectious – snatches of tech jargon I didn't fully understand, but recognized as the language of innovation. My curiosity was piqued by their use of modern languages, and by one employee, Alfonso. Even from a distance, I could tell he tackled problems with focus, a stubborn determination mirroring my own. Could a transfer reignite my motivation?

It had been almost a year trapped in legacy systems. I wanted new challenges! A few weeks later, I decided to approach my manager. Armed with my recent promotion, I explained my desire to transfer to the other team and learn new technologies. Despite understanding corporate processes weren't that simple, my manager explained the difficulty in my request. Still, he promised to send an email on my behalf, offering a sliver of hope. While I waited, I was given a new project to focus on. I took this as a temporary setback. But years of academic success had made me an entitled millennial, used to getting things my way. My motivation plummeted alongside my mental health. Staying in the same project, facing the same routines, felt suffocating.

No Way Out

But that change wouldn't last. My next assignment was a whole different beast: a new project led by a woman, Miss J. And let's just say our personalities were like oil and water. One day I'd swear she was yelling at me, the next, she'd be giving me the silent treatment. And, of course, the inevitable happened: I messed up. It wasn't even a huge mistake, but with my disinterest in the legacy systems growing, sloppy work had become a bad habit. Having to shuffle into her cube and explain my blunder felt like going to the principal's office. Was I in trouble, or just incompetent? It was hard to tell, which made it even worse.

The chaos seemed to escalate, day by day just trying to survive under her leadership. Until one fateful night... actually, it was closer to a fateful midnight. Just as I was settling in with my pre-bed milk, my phone blew up. It was her – Miss J. Disaster had struck. There was a critical mistake I'd made during a production migration. As the developer with exclusive access to the dev environment, it was on me, and we were hours away from launch.

"Get back to the office ASAP," she barked, then hung up. I groaned, knowing I might as well kiss my sleep goodbye. Changing back into my work uniform, all I could think was, "How did I screw this up? I'm usually so careful!"

The office was eerily quiet at that hour. To my shock, another team leader was there, someone I hadn't worked with directly before. This was serious. Miss J spotted me, her face tight.

"Raymond. What happened? You need to double-check, triple-check, everything! We're launching soon; there's no time for this." I slunk back to my computer, dread weighing me down. It took almost two hours of tense work until I was finally ready to ask Miss J for a final check.

The installation day itself was a blur. All I remember is Miss J messaging me, "It's okay now. You can go home. Come in late tomorrow, 10 AM is fine." Relief washed over me, along with a lingering sense of shock. I'd never experienced this kind of pressure before. It made me question myself – even with my cautious nature, was I cut out for this? Had I just been lucky until now?

The next day was awkward, to say the least. But Miss J surprised me – she was smiling. Turns out the installation went perfectly. When I finally arrived, exhausted at 10 AM, she was already at her desk, looking like she'd never even left. We even had a mini-celebration (she brought corn on the cob, oddly enough), but that wasn't the end of it.

For a brief moment, it felt like things might be turning around. The installation went well, my confidence was starting to return, and I'd even built some rapport with my difficult boss. But that optimism was soon shattered. In an attempt to boost my morale, I believe, management transferred me to a different project. Unfortunately, this move backfired. The new team dynamic was a stark contrast to the camaraderie I'd built with Miss J. While I tried my best to be a good team member, one team member's negativity was too much to handle as the days passed.

During a knowledge transfer session, I was explaining a complex feature to the team. As I walked them through the code on the screen, this team member kept interrupting, interjecting with irrelevant comments or trying to finish my sentences. Their tone was condescending, as if they were trying to prove they already knew everything I was saying. Their constant interruptions broke my concentration and made it difficult for me to convey the information clearly. It felt less like a collaborative learning session and more like a competition.

This negativity, a final blow after the disappointment of my transfer being denied, shattered any remaining joy in my work. The office, once a place of possibility, now felt suffocating, a petty battleground where my skills were overshadowed by envy and my dreams put on hold. It made the office feel suffocating, like a place where my skills weren't valued, and where I had to navigate negativity instead of focusing on interesting projects. I realized then that it wasn't just about having good skills or being a contributing team member. It was also about knowing how to navigate difficult personalities and office politics. But ultimately, I was done wasting my energy on people who didn't respect me or my skills – their problems weren't my responsibility. This realization, while important, couldn't erase the toll it had taken. Quite simply, the office just didn't feel inspiring anymore. It felt like a place where my dreams were put on hold, and I just didn't want to go back.

Chapter 7

Denial, Debts, Determination

Silence. My apartment felt emptier than ever now that the pressure of the job was gone. The relentless hum of the old refrigerator mirrored the emptiness in my chest. February 14, 2013. Valentine's Day had brought not love, but the bitter-sweet taste of freedom — and a whole lot of unanswered prayers. No more imposter syndrome, no more suffocating deadlines... but no more salary either. I'd broken up with my first workplace, a leap from stability into a future clouded with uncertainty.

The phone's shrill ring pierced the silence, jolting me back to reality. My stomach tightened as I hit the answer button.

"Ma?"

"Raymond, what is this? Why did you resign without warning? You know I worry!" Her voice was sharp, a tremor of panic beneath the anger.

"Hold on, Ma. Didn't we talk about this last night?" Confusion laced my words.

"I still can't believe you did this! You're alone there! How will you survive?" The question hung heavy in the air, her usual concern replaced by a desperate fear.

"Ma, I know this is sudden, and yes, things look messy right now. But please, you have to trust me." I tried to soothe her, to project a calm I didn't truly feel.

"The fact remains: I'm safe here, and I have some savings. I'll figure it out," I insisted, the promise more for myself than her.

Her frantic voice echoed in my head with every sip of bland coffee. "How will you survive?" the question circled back around, a vulture picking at my newfound freedom.

The phone clicked off, leaving a sterile silence in its wake. My hands trembled as I set it down on the worn, wooden table beside my bed. The scent of stale coffee clung to the air, a bitter reminder of the conversation I'd just had with Mama.

How will you survive? Her words echoed in my mind, each syllable a sharp jab to my gut. Doubts gnawed at me. *Was I being reckless? Foolish? Was this newfound freedom just a mirage, a cruel trick of fate?*

The cramped room, with its peeling paint and flickering fluorescent light, suddenly felt claustrophobic. The hum of the old refrigerator, a constant companion in my solitary existence, seemed to mock me with its steady rhythm. *How am I going to pay for this? For food? For... life?*

I closed my eyes, willing the panic to subside. *Breathe, Ray,* I told myself. *You've got this. You always find a way.*

But the truth was, I was terrified. The familiar weight of responsibility, once a comforting anchor, now felt like a crushing burden. The future stretched before me, a vast, uncharted territory filled with uncertainty.

Weeks turned into a blur of restless nights and aimless days. The initial thrill of freedom gave way to a gnawing anxiety. I spent hours staring at the blank walls of my apartment, the only sound the rhythmic ticking of the clock, a relentless reminder of time slipping away.

The once-comforting scent of home-cooked meals was replaced by the cheap, greasy aroma of fast food, a constant reminder of my dwindling finances. The weight of unpaid bills pressed down on me, a tangible manifestation of my growing despair.

But amidst the darkness, a flicker of hope remained. A stubborn refusal to give in, a determination to claw my way out of this pit of self-pity. I started scouring the internet for freelance gigs, anything to bring in a few extra pesos. I sold my old phone, pawned a few belongings, and even resorted to using my credit card to cover basic necessities. It was a desperate scramble, a high-wire act with no safety net. But it was also a lifeline, a way to keep my head above water while I searched for a more sustainable solution.

One day, as I rummaged through a box of old belongings, my fingers brushed against a familiar texture. I pulled out a faded poster board, a relic from a seminar I'd attended a year ago. It was a dream board, filled with images of faraway lands, exotic cuisine, and smiling faces. A forgotten dream resurfaced, a reminder of a time when I dared to believe in a brighter future.

A spark ignited within me, a tiny flame of hope amidst the darkness. *Why not?* I thought. *Why not re-create the life I truly want?*

I unearthed boxes full of treasures – remnants of seminars I'd attended a year ago. A forgotten dream board surfaced, a reminder that most people forget to dream. Trapped by society's expectations, they lose sight of what's possible. Hadn't that been my experience working a job? Always following orders, never daring to think for myself.

The seminar's message echoed clearly: for the dream board to work, you have to picture – truly visualize – what you want to manifest. Cars, mansions, whatever your heart desires. It had been such a fun exercise before, scouring magazines for images that resonated, then transforming a blank wall into a collage of possibilities.

Another concept came back to me: 'Preparing the field'. A

metaphor for planting seeds, it meant making practical steps towards your goal.

My strongest desire? To travel to Japan. Practical steps meant... checking flight prices, of course!

Google Chrome became my portal, revealing the reality of my dream: a round-trip ticket during sakura season would cost 20-30k PHP. A hefty sum, but at least now I had a target. A prayer to the universe, a flicker of hope...and my daydreaming commenced. To an outsider, I might have seemed crazy, but to me, it was reclaiming the playful spirit I cherished as a child.

One day, while doing groceries near my old workplace, the disinfectant smell of the supermarket making my stomach churn, my heart sank as I spotted two familiar faces entering the mall.

"Oh, Raymond! Fancy meeting you here." Officemate 1 eyed the grocery bags dangling from my hands – a single wilting onion, a bag of bargain chips, the evidence of my meager existence.

"Just doing some errands..." I mumbled, my cheeks burning. I wished I'd changed out of the faded gym shorts I practically lived in now.

Officemate 2 merely nodded, a hint of pity in her eyes.

"Alright, gotta go..." I managed, escaping the awkwardness as quickly as possible.

Their laughter, sharp and carefree, bounced off the storefront windows as the two of them disappeared inside the mall, their carefree energy a stark contrast to the weight in my chest.

Months flew by. No job, no steady income, debts mounting. The travel photos on my dream board seemed to mock me. Was this all the progress I'd made toward my dream?

My trusty 3DS and Fire Emblem: Awakening became reliable companions. Games had always been my haven, a way to escape and unwind. But that double-edged sword could also turn into an addictive crutch. I still found joy in writing about my favorite games, but in the tangible world... I was adrift. Each hour spent immersed in that virtual world felt like one more step away from the life I yearned to create.

My approach was one of experimentation, of playful exploration. Integrity mattered, a compass guiding my actions even when I lacked a clear path. I moved forward with blind faith that things would work out, relying on a force larger than myself to fill in the blanks.

How long could I sustain this balancing act between bold dreams and the crumbling foundation of my finances?

First Attempt

My next adventure leads me to SM MegaMall. From that "Manifest Your Dreams" seminar I attended a year ago (taught by the super enthusiastic Ms. Meg), I learned the secret art of vending machine mind control. At 23, I was a self-help warrior, ready to prove the skeptics wrong!

As I fumbled with the joystick, my fingers trembling, I closed my eyes and whispered a silent wish: "Please, Magic Vending Machine, I just want one cute plushie!" With the clink of a coin, our battle of wills began. Left, right, up, WHOA too fast! The claw dangled precariously over the prizes. My original target was a fluffy white sheep I found incredibly adorable. As the claw swooped down, it brought something else up with it... a flash of red! A voucher? Was that...?

Hope ignited in my chest. It looked like a Jollibee voucher – could it be?

"Don't drop it, don't drop it!" I willed the claw, my heart pounding a frantic rhythm against my ribs. With agonizing slowness, the prize neared the drop zone... and held!

I'd won! A 500-peso Jollibee voucher! Amazement overwhelmed me – people had been trying for ages, and I'd succeeded! Suddenly, winning a plushie seemed insignificant. It was time to celebrate at Jollibee itself!

The aroma of sizzling chicken and sweet spaghetti sauce greeted me as I dashed to the nearest branch, barely taking in the mall's bustle. The line snaked out the door, but my grin was even wider than Jollibee's. What should I order? The crispy chicken? A burger dripping with pineapple goodness? My stomach rumbled in anticipation. In that moment, worries about debts and joblessness melted away. I scanned the menu, the possibilities endless.

Second Attempt

My second slot machine adventure unfolded in a Pasay casino on a Saturday afternoon. The guard eyed me suspiciously, a routine I'd grown accustomed to, the forever-young face on my passport my only defense against being turned away.

Inside, the casino was a sensory assault – a cacophony of electronic cheers, bells, and that distinct jingle of coins hitting metal. Rows of blinking machines lined a dimly-lit room, each promising a different kind of escape from the world outside.

One of Ms. Meg's techniques echoed in my head: find "your" machine. Feel the energy. It sounded absurd, but hey, the vending machine had worked, right? I surveyed the room, a strange sense of anticipation tingling in my fingers. One machine, tucked away in a corner, had an almost magnetic pull. No one was playing it, and the flashing jackpot numbers seemed to pulse with my own racing heartbeat.

Each pull of the lever, each coin swallowed, brought a mix of adrenaline and the nauseating fear of loss. Small wins fueled my delusion – a few rounds more, and I'd double this! No... triple it! Rent money, grocery money... maybe even a ticket to Japan? It WAS possible! Then, blinding lights exploded and victorious music blared! The jackpot was mine – 4,000 pesos! Not THE jackpot, but still... enough for a splurge. And deep down, a nagging whisper – could the next pull wipe it all out?

My heart raced as I cashed out, the clerk's indifference a stark contrast to the euphoria bubbling within me. I couldn't wait to share my unexpected triumph with my cousin. With trembling fingers, I texted her: *Change of plans! Meet me at Mall of Asia(MOA).* Her surprised reply brought a wave of conflicting emotions. She was thrilled for an unexpected outing, while I... I felt a flicker of guilt, quickly overshadowed by the intoxicating thrill of my secret win. For a moment, I saw the face of a street vendor outside the mall, his worn clothes and tired eyes a stark counterpoint to my sudden fortune.

When I met my cousin at the mall, her excited chatter washed over me. "What happened? Why meet here? Did you win the lottery?"

"Something like that," I grinned, the lie catching in my throat. "I just won four thousand pesos at the casino! Let's ride the Ferris wheel!" It felt good to say it out loud, to share a small victory after months of solitude and shame.

The Ferris wheel groaned as it carried us higher, the wind whipping at my hair. Below, the MOA complex burst with color – the blur of arcade lights, the shouts of kids on thrill rides, families strolling down to the bay. For just a few precious moments, my worries faded. Yet, even as we laughed and pointed out distant ships in the harbor, a shadow began creeping over my joy. Tonight's extravaganza felt less like a deserved treat and more like a desperate attempt to drown out the gnawing fear in the back of my mind.

We spent the rest of the night enjoying each other's company, riding the Ferris wheel, playing arcade games, and indulging in a feast at Jollibee. As we finally arrived back at my apartment, the weight of reality settled back upon my shoulders. The fleeting joy of the evening couldn't erase the fact that debts were piling high, untouched by side-hustles and seminar promises. One year... and I was no closer to the life I'd envisioned. Despair seeped into my bones, a bitter taste in the back of my throat. I was a failure, and soon, everyone would know it.

A week went by, the thrill of the casino win a distant memory. Each day was a struggle, a balancing act between hope and despair. *Would I ever escape this cycle of disappointment and unfulfilled dreams?*

Then, one afternoon, during lunch, my phone rang. It was a foreign number. My heart skipped a beat. *A debt collector?* I hesitated, a familiar dread creeping over me. The call ended, then flickered back to life five minutes later.

Answer it, a voice inside me urged. *What if it's an opportunity?*

With trembling fingers, I pressed the answer button.

"Am I talking to Mr. Raymond Janayon? Might you be interested in a career opportunity with our client?"

A flicker of hope ignited within me. This was it. A chance to prove myself, to rebuild my confidence, to create a life beyond the shadow of debt and disappointment.

The future, once a hazy blur, now shimmered with possibility. I accepted the offer, eager to embrace this new chapter. Little did I know that this job would lead me to a far greater opportunity, one that would transform my life in unimaginable ways.

Chapter 8

The Unexpected Mentor

I never expected my mentor to be a woman I'd only heard about in secondhand stories. It all started one Sunday afternoon in 2011, my world a messy blur of yesterday's t-shirt and game controllers. Tita N and Cousin Jil burst into my apartment, their breathless excitement a stark contrast to my lazy sprawl.

"You have to go to this seminar!" they exclaimed in unison, thrusting a complimentary ticket into my hands.

A quick online search revealed a self-help seminar here in Metro Manila, boasting a lineup of speakers I'd only heard whispered about in reverent tones: Kiyosaki, Canfield... and **Anthony Robbins**, his face flashing on the screen, his book *"Awaken the Giant Within"* a beacon of hope in my otherwise aimless existence.

The seminar itself was a whirlwind of positive affirmations and promises of transformation. Robbins's words crackled with energy, igniting a spark of recognition within me. The idea that I could manifest my dreams by simply visualizing them felt both exhilarating and terrifying.

As the seminar ended, excitement gave way to a different kind of buzz – the upsell. Whispers of "another seminar," one held at the shiny new SM Arena, filled the air. It wasn't free, but it was the next step on a path I was suddenly eager – and just a little afraid – to follow. This was the engine that was needed to kickstart my own journey.

My mom's stories about a preschool teacher who'd supposedly found success through this seminar swirled in my head. Could this be my path too? Or would I just end up another sucker, broke and disillusioned? Filled with both hope and skepticism, I signed up for the final, three-day seminar in a cool, breezy city. It promised techniques to relinquish fears and manifest the life I envisioned.

The first day, I scanned the room, a mix of established network marketers and lost souls like myself. Among them, a familiar face emerged – the teacher from my mom's stories! Eager to connect, I made a mental note to approach her after the introductions.

Later that day, during an exercise that involved a bonfire, I spotted her from a distance, intently focused on the flames. Her expression was pensive, almost melancholic. It mirrored the knot of uncertainty in my own chest. After the exercise concluded, I gathered my courage and introduced myself, eager to learn from her experiences. Little did I know, this was the beginning of a mentorship that would change my life.

Soon enough, she became my guide in this world of networking and sales.

Year 2013

"Do you meditate?" Ms. Kris asked, a hint of curiosity in her voice.

"Not really," I replied, my tone dismissive. "But I get the idea... sit cross-legged, eyes closed, right?" "There's more to it than that," she chuckled softly. "Try these videos I'm sending you. Aim for ten minutes a day at first, and gradually increase the time as you're able. Make it a part of your daily routine, along with your calls and prospecting. I'll check in with you tomorrow to see how it's going."

The line went dead, the silence punctuated by the hum of the refrigerator and the echo of her challenge.

I struggled with meditation at first. Thoughts ricocheted around my skull like angry wasps – bills, work tasks, past failures. But day by day, something shifted. The buzzing in my head quieted, if only for a few minutes. The days of endless gaming slowly lost their appeal, replaced by a budding desire to create something of my own.

Yet, social anxiety still plagued me. My heart pounded with each presentation, and even with an old college classmate one day at the mall, it was no different. The scent of cinnamon buns from a nearby stand twisted a knot in my stomach as I met her kind but hesitant smile, a flicker of pity in her eyes that fanned the flames of my old insecurities.

"Meditation won't fix everything," my mentor had said. "But it gives you space. Space to see your patterns, space to choose a better way."

I could use some space right now.

Sweat prickled the back of my neck, and my hands trembled as I reached for my coffee cup. The muffled announcements from the mall's PA system competed with the honking jeepneys outside, creating a jarring symphony that echoed the chaos in my head. My old college classmate, Sarah, sat across from me, a flicker of pity in her eyes igniting a familiar burn of shame.

"Is there something you want to say, Raymond?" she asked, noticing my distraction.

"Sorry, just...excited to share!" I fumbled with the presentation book, pages rustling in the tense silence. "As I was saying, once you buy the package deal, you not only get the product, but also services and health benefits..." I rushed through the spiel, desperate to regain control.

Her hesitant "I need to think about it" felt like a death sentence. I knew I'd come on too strong, pushing her for a decision before she was ready.

"Think about what package you want," I stammered, any semblance of professionalism gone. "We have different variants..."

"No, but I'll let you know soon," she said, her voice trailing off. "I have to leave..."

"Alright, we'll keep in touch," I muttered, the lie ringing hollow even to my own ears.

As I watched her walk away, a wave of defeat washed over me. The old familiar voices of self-doubt filled my head: *You messed it up again. You'll never be good at this.* The mall's bright lights seemed to dim, and the cheerful music turned into a mocking soundtrack to my failure.

The walk back to my apartment felt longer than usual, each step a reminder of the sting of rejection. Back in my cramped apartment, I replayed the conversation over and over in my head. Maybe sales wasn't for me. But then again, wasn't the seminar all about not giving up?

Jobless in Manila, borrowing money from relatives was proving fruitless. Even those I'd helped in the past couldn't spare a dime. It felt like the universe was conspiring against me...yet, something inside me still clung to those seminar promises.

With my job prospects dwindling and my savings running low, I found solace in an unexpected place - my video game blog. It was a fun hobby, a creative outlet that offered a welcome distraction from my worries. As I typed away, my mind drifted to Japan, a strange obsession that had reappeared on my Vision Board. The photos of cherry blossoms and serene temples offered a stark contrast to my current reality. I checked flight prices, a foolish daydream given my lack of finances, but a persistent voice whispered, *"Someday."*

Just as I was starting to find some inner peace, my phone's shrill ringtone shattered the tranquility. It was Ms. Kris.

"Good morning, Eaglet," Ms. Kris's voice, a mix of warmth and that familiar no-nonsense tone, filled my cramped apartment.

"How was your day? Did you start with meditation? And what are you up to today?"

Her energy was a jolt to my system, a reminder that even in this state of limbo, there were still things to be done, routines to be followed.

"I had a presentation yesterday — it went well, I think! My potential client seemed interested, said she'd get back to me," I replied, trying to inject a note of optimism into my voice.

"Did you utilize the sales script I gave you?" Her tone sharpened. "Remember, in sales, you have to be persistent and assertive to seize opportunities."

"I did ask her about it," I mumbled, already feeling the familiar knot of self-doubt tightening in my stomach. "But I didn't want to come across as impolite to my former classmate."

"I understand that you have a connection with her," Ms. Kris said, her voice firm but not unkind. "But in sales, you need to be resolute and unyielding in pursuing leads. If you take people lightly, you won't generate any sales."

Her words struck a chord, but the thought of being that pushy salesman made my skin crawl. "I see your point," I sighed, "but I don't think sales is my calling." The confession felt like a weight lifting off my chest, but it also brought a wave of uncertainty. What was I supposed to do now?

A pause hung in the air before Ms. Kris's voice softened. "Did you have your morning meditation session today? It's a good practice to cultivate inner peace and clarity."

"Yes, I did meditate this morning," I replied, grateful for the change in topic. The rhythmic sound of my breath during meditation had been the only thing keeping the chaos at bay recently.

"And what are you doing with your free time now that you're not working?" Curiosity tinged her voice.

"I'm writing on a blog about video games," I said, a spark of enthusiasm flickering to life. "It's a fun hobby to keep me occupied. Would you like to check it out?"

"Oh really?" Her voice brightened. "Send me the link." I quickly found the link and sent it to her. A few minutes later, she exclaimed, "You're really into this, huh? Lots of detailed reviews here! I can barely write one paragraph!"

"Thank you, Ms. Kris," I said, a tentative smile spreading across my face. Her unexpected praise felt like a warm ray of sunshine piercing through the clouds of my self-doubt. It had been so long since I felt genuinely proud of something I'd created.

"Well, keep it up," she encouraged. "I'll touch base with you again in a few days. Don't forget to complete your assignments."

"I won't forget. Thank you, Ms. Kris," I said before the call ended.

I put down the phone, a strange mix of emotions swirling within me. Relief, gratitude, a renewed sense of purpose, and a lingering fear of the unknown. What did the future hold for me?

Despite the uncertainty, Ms. Kris's call had reminded me that even in the midst of failure, there was still room for growth and new beginnings. I grabbed a pen and paper, determined to chart a new course for my life. Money, a bigger house... the usual aspirations filled the page. But at the top, in bold letters, I wrote: Japan. A dream that seemed laughable given my current circumstances, but as the ink dried, it felt like a promise. A promise to myself that I wouldn't give up on my dreams, no matter how far-fetched they seemed.

A few days later, Ms. Kris texted, "Eaglet, let's meet in BGC. Wear something nice. I'll text you the place."

Intrigue mingled with a hint of nervousness. What was she up to this time? I decided to go for a casual yet stylish look, opting for my favorite polo shirt and a pair of dark jeans.

We met at a children's park in Taguig, an unexpected choice given the sophisticated setting of BGC. But that was Ms. Kris for you – always surprising, always finding joy in the simple things. We spent the afternoon swinging, laughing, and indulging in a bit of childlike fun. It was both liberating and a little embarrassing to be playing on the swings at my age, but Ms. Kris's infectious enthusiasm made it impossible not to join in.

As the sun began to set, we walked towards the heart of BGC. The iconic tree in the center, adorned with twinkling lights, was a beacon against the darkening sky. Before heading into a nearby restaurant, Ms. Kris stopped and gave the tree a playful hug, her face lit up with a childlike wonder that was both endearing and contagious.

"I'll text you when it ends," she said, disappearing into the restaurant.

As I watched her disappear into the warm glow of the restaurant, a wave of curiosity washed over me. What surprise did Ms. Kris have in store for me this time?

"Have fun!" I replied, a wave of warmth washing over me. Did I have feelings for her? The thought surprised me. Sure, I was drawn to her energy and zest for life, but it felt more like the affection one would have for a sister or a close friend. Besides, equality was one of my core principles.

My mind wandered back to the seminars. Were they working? Was *anything* working? The posh malls I passed seemed to mock my thin wallet.

Suddenly, my phone buzzed. "Ray, where are you? Come back to the restaurant," Ms. Kris texted, a hint of urgency in her tone.

A knot of excitement and fear twisted in my stomach. What had happened? I raced back through the darkening streets, my heart pounding.

I found her seated alone at a table, a half-finished glass of wine in front of her. Her usual composure was replaced by a hint of flustered energy.

"What happened? Where's your date?" I asked, breathlessly.

"Let's order first," she said with a mischievous smile. "It's my treat. Then, I'll tell you the whole story."

The waiter approached, and we ordered. I splurged on a green spaghetti and a shake I'd never dared to try before, a small rebellion against my usual frugal habits. As we waited for our food, Ms. Kris's smile widened.

"I didn't actually meet him," she confessed. "He left before I got here."

"Wait... did you *ghost* him?" I asked, disbelief giving way to a burst of laughter.

She nodded, a giggle escaping her lips, and soon we were both laughing uncontrollably. It was the kind of laughter that makes the world blur, leaving you and your companion in a bubble of pure joy. I felt a pang of sympathy for the ghosted guy, but hey, weren't the seminars all about manifesting what you want? Standards were standards.

As the waiter set down our food, we composed ourselves. "Let's make the most of this fancy place anyway," Ms. Kris suggested, her eyes sparkling with amusement.

And in that moment, with free food, a beautiful setting, and the company of someone who could make me laugh like no one else, my problems seemed to fade away.

As we ate, the conversation flowed easily, a comfortable rhythm of laughter and shared stories. Ms. Kris regaled me with tales of her own mishaps and triumphs in the business world, her honesty and vulnerability a refreshing change from the usual bravado of motivational speakers.

"You know, Raymond," she said, leaning in conspiratorially, "Sometimes, the most important lessons aren't the ones taught in seminars. They're the ones we learn through experience, through stumbling and picking ourselves up again."

Her words resonated with me, echoing my own recent struggles and doubts. "I'm starting to see that," I admitted. "Maybe sales isn't my path, but I'm not sure what is yet."

"That's okay," she said, her eyes twinkling with understanding. "Sometimes, the path reveals itself when we least expect it. Just keep exploring, keep learning, and most importantly, keep believing in yourself."

Her words were a balm to my wounded spirit. It was as if she could see right through my insecurities and fears, offering a reassurance that I hadn't found anywhere else.

After dinner, we strolled through the illuminated streets of BGC, the city lights reflecting in Ms. Kris's eyes. We talked about our dreams, our fears, our hopes for the future. It was a connection I hadn't anticipated, a friendship that blossomed from the unlikeliest of circumstances.

"You know, Eaglet," she said, as we reached the edge of the park, "I've always admired your spirit, your willingness to try new things, even when you're scared. Don't ever lose that."

"Thank you, Ms. Kris," I said, my heart swelling with gratitude. "Your support means the world to me."

As we parted ways that night, I couldn't shake the feeling that this unexpected encounter had been more than just a mentor-mentee outing. It was a turning point, a reminder that even in the midst of uncertainty and self-doubt, there was always the possibility of connection, growth, and new beginnings.

The memory of that evening stayed with me, a source of comfort and inspiration as I continued to navigate the twists and turns of my journey. It was a reminder that sometimes, the most profound connections are the ones we least expect, and that even in the face of adversity, hope can bloom in the most unexpected places.

Chapter 9

The Priestess's Prophecy

Year 2014

"Do you meditate?" Pat's question caught me off guard, mid-bite of my crispy chicken.

"Yes, but why the sudden interest?" I asked, wiping my mouth with a napkin.

"I've been meaning to ask," she said, already digging into her own lunch. "What do you use?"

"No app for me," I said. "Just an old MP3 I downloaded years back. It's my morning ritual."

"Interesting," she said, fingering a worn mala bead bracelet on her wrist. A serene expression engulfed her face. "I've been exploring different meditation techniques lately. Maybe we could compare notes sometime."

We were both Software Engineers at the same start-up, our paths crossing by chance. Somehow, our schedules synced, our breaks aligned. We'd message, grab coffee, venting about code bugs and life outside the office. Like that day by the pond, the setting sun casting long shadows across the water as the air filled with the gentle quacking of ducks and the rustling of leaves in the breeze.

The earthy scent of damp soil and the soothing murmur of the flowing river added to the tranquil atmosphere.

"Ray, would you believe I was almost a nun?" Her laughter rang out, a stark contrast to the unexpected confession.

"Well...I could picture it," I admitted. A playful nudge to my shoulder earned me a half-hearted punch in return. Nothing serious, we weren't *that* kind of friends. Still, (and not to brag) I've always been comfortable around women...

"It was an experience," she said, the smile fading. "One that made me realize I didn't buy what the Bible was selling anymore."

Her candidness was refreshing, and it sparked a deeper conversation about our individual journeys.

I raised an eyebrow. "Like, missing chapters? Because that seriously messes with a person's worldview."

Her eyes met mine, a heavy undertone in her voice. 'Control,' Pat said.

I nodded in understanding. "I know, right? That's how I ended up reading all sorts of esoteric stuff. What about you? What do you believe?"

Her eyes held a genuine curiosity. "We are like fragments of the one, searching for connection, for meaning. God, the divine...it used to feel simpler." Her words hung in the air. Then, cautiously, "But Law of Attraction, yeah, I believe in that. Manifesting what you focus on... I first learned about it years back, some metaphysical seminar or other."

Her smile was a flash of understanding. "So, you're not completely new to this. That makes it easier for me to understand why you're interested in this."

Easier? What did she have in mind?

"A few months ago, I had a 'Soul Reading' done by this psychic. Basically, she reveals what you need to know. Go in with questions."

A psychic? That was a leap I hadn't considered. "Intriguing..."

My mind raced, a mix of excitement and the familiar twinge of skepticism.

"Long story, Ray, but she told me I'm a Priestess...from Atlantis."

My mind reeled. *A priestess? From Atlantis? Was she serious?* "The Atlantis? Like, the mythical lost city?"

"That very one," she confirmed.

"Tell me more," I urged. This wasn't just idle curiosity anymore; it was something deeper.

"Well, if you must know, I was a Priestess who sang for the dead," she said, her voice hushed.

"You sang... why?" It sounded both strange and oddly beautiful.

"Like a ceremony, helping souls transition smoothly to the spirit realm."

"I see...or maybe I'll see, someday," I replied. "So, a past life connection?"

"Exactly," she said.

"You know, I've always felt a mysterious affinity for Egypt," I admitted, a sheepish grin spreading across my face. "I've had count-less dreams of wandering through ancient temples and gazing up at the pyramids. Even as a kid, something about that civilization captivated me. I mean, I was obsessed with Yu-Gi-Oh! for a while."

Pat's eyes widened with interest. "Dreams, huh? That's defi-nitely a sign. What kind of dreams? And what was it about Yu-Gi-Oh! that resonated with you?"

"Mostly fragments," I said, "but there's always a sense of famil-iarity, like I've been there before. I can almost feel the desert heat on my skin and hear the ghostly whispers of the wind through the ancient symbols. As for Yu-Gi-Oh!, it wasn't just the Egyptian mythology aspect, although that definitely played a part. It was the whole idea of hidden knowledge, ancient rituals, and the power of believing in something beyond yourself. It just...resonated with me."

I paused, remembering the hours I'd spent as a kid, poring over my Yu-Gi-Oh! cards, memorizing their intricate designs and fantastical stories. It was more than just a game; it was a portal to a world of mystery and magic that sparked my imagination and fueled my curiosity about ancient cultures.

"Maybe it's not so weird after all," Pat said, a thoughtful look on her face. "Maybe it's all connected somehow. Have you ever considered visiting Egypt?"

A tingling sensation prickled my skin. Could she be right? Was there a deeper meaning behind my lifelong fascination with Egypt?

"Not yet," I admitted, "but it's definitely on my bucket list."

By the time we were back at our desks, she had messaged me the contact info of the psychic, and I found myself surprisingly eager to explore this uncharted territory.

As we walked back to the office, the serene beauty of the surrounding forest, with its tranquil lake shimmering in the afternoon light, felt like a world away from the sterile hum of our computer screens. Ducks quacked lazily in the distance, a stray cat wound its way through the undergrowth, and the air was thick with the scent of damp earth and blooming flowers. The contrast between the animated conversation we'd just had and the peaceful natural setting only heightened my anticipation for the psychic reading Pat had described.

A shaft of sunlight pierced through the blinds as we settled back into our cubicles, illuminating a tiny cactus perched on my desk. Its spiky resilience seemed to mirror my own determination to thrive in the face of uncertainty.

Our esoteric talks became a daily ritual. Some coworkers side-eyed us, probably wondering if we were dating. Didn't matter. I was used to being the odd one out, and Pat's company made me feel less alone in my eccentricities.

The day I finally contacted the psychic also happened to be my 24th birthday. Figured, why not do something completely different? As I messaged her to schedule an appointment, a familiar knot of anxiety twisted in my stomach.

"You're bouncing off the walls, Ray," Pat remarked, catching me mid-stride as I paced by the water cooler. "Caffeine jitters, or something else?"

It wasn't just the extra espresso shot. "More like... what if this is all just a bunch of new-age nonsense? What if she just tells me what I want to hear?" The confession felt surprisingly good, a release of the pent-up tension.

Pat grinned. "Don't worry. Worst case, it's at least going to be a funny story for birthday drinks." She nudged me playfully. "Now go on, time to face your destiny."

Destiny... the word echoed in my head as I approached the Cubao coffee shop where the psychic, Vel, had agreed to meet me. She was easy to spot, seated alone at a tiny table, a pen and scrap of paper before her. A wave of hello, then introductions.

"Raymond," I replied, trying to hide my surprise. She sported jeans and a purple t-shirt, her hair in a simple style—not exactly the flowing robes and crystal ball I'd imagined when Pat mentioned a psychic. Maybe I'd been watching too many fantasy movies. Despite her casual appearance, there was a vibrant intensity about her that made her stand out from the café crowd. Her voice, soft yet clear, held a soothing quality that put me unexpectedly at ease. And though I couldn't place it, there was something strangely familiar about her...a sense of trust I couldn't quite explain.

A mix of skepticism, intrigue, and nervous anticipation churned within me. Part of me wanted to dismiss this whole experience as a silly birthday indulgence, but another part, the part that had been yearning for something more, clung to the hope that maybe, just maybe, there was more to this than met the eye.

"Would you mind writing your full name on this?" She gestured towards the paper.

"Here you go," I said, handing it over, fighting the irrational urge to snatch it back. There was something almost ritualistic in the way she accepted it, a slight bow of her head. *Now, that was definitely my imagination running wild...*

My skepticism wrestled with a growing sense of wonder. Could this woman really tap into the hidden depths of my being? Was there truly a cosmic library holding the secrets of my soul?

Closing her eyes, she placed her fingertips on the paper. "First," she explained, "I connect with your Guardian Angels to access a part of your Akashic Records. Think of it as the cosmic library of your soul."

Permission granted, I thought, feeling a subtle energy shift in the air. Maybe that was just my nerves on edge.

Then, the floodgates opened. "Great leader...teacher...writer, blogger... galaxy far from the Milky Way..." Her words became a blur as my mind struggled to keep up. My heart pounded. *Was she making this up?*

Wait, what? My galaxy? Like, outer space? Panic threatened to drown out the rest of her words. I fumbled for my notebook, scribbling fragments, desperate to capture the important bits. I kept asking for repeats, trying to make sense of it all.

"As for your soul function," she continued, seemingly unfazed by my reaction, "you have a combination of an Alchemist and a Scribe. An alchemist can transform something into another..." Her explanation, filled with concepts I had mostly heard of in video games, like turning common items into potions or exotic materials.

"...a scribe may refer to someone who writes history," she went on. "These individuals act as chroniclers of events, preserving knowledge and stories for future generations. They bridge the gap between the past and the present, ensuring that the lessons of the past are not forgotten."

I fumbled with my notebook, the words a jumble in my head.

"You should trust yourself more, Ray," she reminded me, her voice gentle. "Be your own mentor. Create anything you like – that is how an Alchemist works. Strengthen your willpower and every-thing will come to you."

"Be open to all kinds of experiences. Volunteer & Freelance," she added. "Being alone is temporary, a time to cultivate that inner strength. Then, you can help others as you've helped yourself."

"Thank you so much," I managed to say as our session ended. We both smiled, and I stood up, my legs unsteady. A strange mix of determination and bewilderment washed over me. Was this all real? Or had I just paid for an hour of elaborate storytelling?

The reading ended too soon, leaving me clutching my notes as I stumbled out of the coffee shop. The bright afternoon sun was a harsh contrast to the dim lighting where I'd just spent the past hour. As I hailed a jeepney, my heart pounded with a mix of adrenaline and confusion. Every bump in the road seemed to echo the phrase: "A galaxy far from the Milky Way." *Was I going crazy?*

I reread my scribbled notes, the driver throwing me curious glances. The familiar scent of exhaust mingled with the sharp tang of street food and something acrid – burning plastic, maybe? The jeepney lurched forward, and I clutched my notes tighter, my mind still racing with the possibilities and implications of what I had just heard.

Suddenly, Pat's voice popped into my head, an unexpected burst of enthusiasm. "Dude, that's so cool! Maybe you're, like, an intergalactic ambassador in disguise."

The driver's sidelong glance snapped me back to reality. I almost blurted out, "But do ambassadors write gaming blogs?" Okay, maybe not the best time to share my internal dialogue. Still, the idea brought a flicker of a smile as I stuffed my scribbled notes back into my bag.

A new thought: what if I *did* have some grand purpose here? The idea was both thrilling and terrifying. Okay, maybe not an intergalactic ambassador, but still... this wasn't your average birthday revelation. But it was *mine*, a bizarre chapter to tuck away in my memory. Whatever the truth of my past, the future remained unwritten. Time to start figuring it out.

Crash Landing

My mind still whirled with visions of galaxies and past lives as I sat at my desk, a ping from my computer jolting me back to reality. It was a message from Pat, and a jolt of anxiety joined my post-lunch caffeine buzz. With the psychic's words still echoing in my head, this wasn't going to be a casual chat.

"Okay, Ray, time to spill," Pat messaged, her virtual presence somehow managing to convey a mix of amusement and curiosity.

"But what if she thinks I'm totally crazy?" I muttered under my breath. "She's always been so down-to-earth, and now I'm about to tell her I'm some kind of space emperor..."

I typed a slightly subdued version of my earlier excitement: "It was...interesting. Definitely made me think. I'll fill you in later." Vague, but not a total lie. Pat would understand the need to process before I shared the full alien reveal.

The rest of the day passed in a blur of code and the lingering strangeness of my weekend. Finally, we were by the duck pond, a bit of nature amidst our corporate oasis. The setting sun cast long shadows, and the air was filled with the gentle quacking of ducks and the rustling of leaves.

"Okay, time to spill," Pat said, amusement and curiosity battling in her eyes.

"Well..." I hesitated. "She said I'm an alien."

The silence that followed was broken by a burst of laughter so loud, I worried it might frighten the ducks.

Once she regained control, her eyes held a different glint. "Okay, alien part aside...anything else?"

"That's the thing! The leader stuff, the writing, the blogging...it's like she read my resume, only with things I haven't even done yet. How'd she know?"

"Maybe that's the whole point of being a psychic?" She shrugged, but there was a thoughtful gleam in her eyes now.

"So, how did you find her?" I asked, steering the conversation back to familiar ground.

"An online forum," she replied. "Word of mouth among those who dabble in the esoteric, I suppose."

We both grinned at the thought of finding our tribe among those who embrace the esoteric. "Turns out, there are more of us than I thought."

"So, what's next, Ray? Master of the Universe action plan?" Pat's question hung in the air, a playful challenge in her eyes.

"No grand scheme yet," I admitted. "Maybe it's less about a plan and more about..." I hesitated, trying to find the words, "...being open to possibilities? What about you?"

"New start," she said, her voice filled with a mix of sadness and determination. "Singapore job offer, and well..." Her voice trailed off for the briefest of moments. "Let's just say the boyfriend situation reached its inevitable conclusion. Fresh chapter all around." A small, defiant smile played on her lips. "Seems like change is our theme this year."

"Oh yeah, I heard from others about the breakup. I'm sorry to hear that," I said, my words sincere. "But hey, I bet you'll meet your perfect match soon. You do believe in the universe and all that, right?" I added with a playful grin, hoping to lighten the mood.

She chuckled, a hint of her usual spirit returning. "Maybe you're right, Ray. Maybe the universe has something better in store."

"I'm sure it does," I said, giving her a reassuring pat on the back. "And besides, with your new job in Singapore, you'll have a whole new world to explore."

"Speaking of new worlds," she said, her eyes twinkling with mischief, "What about that whole 'alien from another galaxy' thing? Think you'll be returning home anytime soon?"

I laughed, shaking my head. "Not that I'm aware of. But who knows? Maybe I'll discover a hidden spaceship in my closet one day."

We shared a smile, a silent acknowledgment of the absurdity and wonder of life.

"Good luck with it all, Pat," I said, my voice filled with genuine affection. "Seriously. And thanks for...opening the door to all of this."

"You too, Ray," she replied, returning my smile. "And remember, be open to the possibilities. You never know what the universe might throw your way."

We waved goodbye to the ducks, their serene presence a stark contrast to the turmoil of our lives. As we headed back to the office, the setting sun painted the sky in hues of orange and pink, casting long shadows that danced along the path. It was a beautiful sight, a reminder that even in the midst of change and uncertainty, there was still beauty to be found in the world.

The psychic, Atlantis, even the whole alien thing... it felt less outlandish now. I remembered the spark of magic within me, a flicker that had been buried under layers of self-doubt and societal expectations. This reading, however outlandish it seemed, had reignited that spark. Was it trying to tell me something?

Meeting Pat – all the rabbit holes we've been down together – it's been intense, chaotic, and wonderful all at once. Maybe life was going to be a bit more phenomenal than I'd ever imagined. And maybe, just maybe, there was more to my story than I had ever dared to dream.

As the weeks turned into months, the memory of that reading lingered, a quiet hum in the background of my life. I found myself seeking out new experiences, exploring ideas that once seemed far-fetched. And when my sister suggested a trip to Singapore, I couldn't shake the feeling that it was more than just a vacation – it was a calling, a chance to explore the world with fresh eyes and an open heart.

Part Two

Quests

"The real voyage of discovery consists not in seeking new landscapes, but in having new eyes."

- Marcel Proust

Chapter 10

Singapore: Unveiled

March 2015

The heavy, sweet scent of orchids filled the humid air as I stepped off the plane at Changi Airport. The unfamiliar sights and sounds of Singapore swirled around me, a sensory symphony far removed from the dusty streets of Manila. Excitement warred with a knot of nervousness in my chest. This was my first time leaving the Philippines, my first taste of the unknown, armed with only my younger sister, a backpack, and a misplaced sense of confidence in Google Maps.

My sister, ever the meticulous planner, clutched a meticulously crafted itinerary, her eyes scanning the airport with a mix of anticipation and apprehension. A mischievous glint sparkled in her eyes as she held up her phone, a notification buzzing. "Where are you both going?" Tita G had messaged, curiosity laced with disbelief.

With a playful smirk, my sister typed, "Singapore," unleashing a barrage of exclamation marks in the chat.

"We're not kids anymore, are we?" I teased, a thrill of independence coursing through me. Convincing my mother to let me embark on this adventure with only my younger sibling as my companion had been a challenge, but here we were, about to step into the "Little Red Dot," a city that held secrets and revelations I couldn't even begin to fathom.

Stepping out of the airport, I knew this moment would be forever etched in my memory. The sky blazed with the remnants of a vibrant sunset, a stark contrast to the familiar dusky evenings settling over Manila. We navigated the bustling yet efficient world of the MRT system, our eyes wide with wonder as we weaved through the labyrinthine network of trains. The constant movement and mechanical hums created a symphony of urban energy that both thrilled and overwhelmed me.

Lost in the maze of tunnels and platforms, we finally emerged at the iconic Marina Bay Sands. The sight took our breath away — a majestic structure seemingly defying gravity, its three towers connected by a sweeping skypark. We quickened our pace, eager to reach the haven it promised.

As we approached the entrance, an Indian-looking man in a crisp suit extended a hand towards our bags. My years navigating the bustling streets of Metro Manila had instilled a sense of caution in me. I politely declined, opting to drag the luggage to the side as my sister waited with a flicker of confusion in her eyes.

I approached the reception, my heart pounding with a mix of anticipation and suspicion. "Sir, welcome to Marina Bay Sands. May I please see your passport and reservation number?" the receptionist's voice was a soothing melody.

I handed over the documents, stealing glances back at my sister, who mirrored my own apprehension. The man who offered to help with our bags waited patiently nearby.

"Sir," the receptionist's voice interrupted my thoughts, "we've taken the liberty of making a change to your reservation to enhance your special stay. Happy Birthday!"

A wave of gratitude replaced my initial suspicion. With a subtle nod towards the man who had offered to help, the receptionist transformed him into our designated bellhop. He promptly retrieved our luggage from my sister. A silent apology formed in my mind as I realized my misplaced distrust.

The grand entrance of Marina Bay Sands unfolded before us, its sheer scale and opulent design leaving us breathless. Soaring ceilings, polished marble floors, and glittering chandeliers bathed us in a warm, luxurious glow. The gentle murmur of conversations swirled around us, adding to the vibrant yet sophisticated atmosphere.

Lost in the moment, we barely noticed the elevator doors silently slide shut. A flicker of surprise crossed our faces as we realized the bellhop and our luggage were already inside, leaving us to catch the next one up. A chuckle escaped my lips – just minutes after doubting his intentions, we were surprised by his efficiency.

In the elevator, my impatience mounted when the buttons seemed unresponsive. Then it dawned on me – the magic key in my hand was also the elevator access card. *Technology is amazing,* I thought, impressed.

A melodious "ding" welcomed us to our floor. We followed the bellhop across the hall, the see-through glass floor dizzying us with its view of the floors below. As we reached our room, exhaustion and hunger threatened to overwhelm us. We mumbled a thank you to the bellhop before he departed.

Entering the room, we were immediately captivated. Instead of a plain hotel room, a panoramic view of "Gardens by the Bay" greeted us. The curtains had opened automatically, revealing the sprawling greenery, the towering, colorful Supertrees, their lights twinkling like stars against the darkening sky. This unexpected gesture from the receptionist filled me with gratitude.

My sister excitedly explained the room's amenities while I collapsed on the luxurious sofa, overwhelmed by the sheer opulence. Glancing at the hotel menu, we winced at the astronomical prices. Abandoning the fancy dining idea, we ventured out to explore the nearby streets in search of local, affordable food.

Following Google Maps, we crossed the futuristic Helix Bridge, its double helix structure glowing in the twilight. My sister, ever the dessert lover, suggested finding a birthday cake. We entered a nearby mall, but were quickly disheartened by the extravagant prices. We continued our quest, eventually stumbling upon a bustling row of food stalls recommended by one of my coworkers.

The air was alive with the intoxicating aromas of sizzling meats and fragrant spices, a symphony of scents that made my stomach rumble. "Hainanese Chicken Rice!" I exclaimed, instantly recognizing the dish my colleague had raved about. We ordered two plates and raced back to the hotel, the anticipation of devouring our feast overriding our exhaustion. Our eagerness amused the vendor, his hearty laughter echoing through the bustling food court.

Back in our room, we savored the flavorful chicken and fragrant rice, the day's adventures making it taste even better. The initial jitters of being in a foreign land had given way to a sense of excitement and possibility.

A Surprise Celebration

The following morning, fueled by anticipation for another day of exploration, I awoke before my sister. The sight of the Gardens bathed in the golden hues of sunrise filled me with a sense of peace and gratitude. As I offered a silent prayer of thanks, my phone buzzed. "Let's go swimming!" my sister announced, still half-asleep.

We donned our swimsuits and headed for the rooftop pool. The elevator doors opened to reveal a breathtaking panorama of the Singaporean cityscape, bathed in the warm glow of the morning sun. We couldn't resist snapping countless pictures, capturing the moment before diving into the refreshing water.

The morning tranquility was blissful, broken only by the gentle splashing of water and our excited chatter. As the sun rose higher, the pool buzzed with activity. We decided it was time for breakfast and were thrilled to discover a complimentary buffet offered by the hotel. We luxuriated in the spread fit for royalty, any sibling rivalry forgotten as we piled our plates high with a delicious assortment that mirrored the culinary diversity of Singapore.

Halfway through breakfast, a waiter in attire that contrasted sharply with our casual clothes approached us. "Hello sir and madam," he said in a warm voice, "Would you like some coffee?"

"Sure," I responded, surprised by the attention.

Just then, he followed up with a question. "Sir, mam, from where are you from?" he asked.

Recognizing the accent, I blurted out, "Philippines!"

"Oh, fellow Filipinos!" he exclaimed with a warm smile. "I came from Ilocos Norte. What brings you here to Singapore, specifically to Marina Bay Sands?"

"Oh it's my birthday," I replied, still a bit bewildered. "We just wanted to do something different for a change."

My sister, still engrossed in her food, simply nodded in acknowledgment.

The Filipino waiter smiled, then departed for a moment. We resumed our exploration of the breakfast buffet, the vast array of dishes a testament to the hotel's opulence. My sister, ever the social butterfly, excitedly answered a video call from her boyfriend, sharing all the details of our whirlwind Singapore adventure.

The familiar chatter of the restaurant faded into the background as a group of waiters in black and white attire surrounded us. My mind struggled to process how our quiet breakfast had transformed so suddenly. A melody filled the air as the waiters began singing "Happy Birthday" in perfect harmony.

Overwhelmed, I felt a surge of emotions – surprise, gratitude, and a touch of shyness from suddenly being the center of attention. The urge to hide under the table was strong, but I remained frozen in my seat. My sister, phone still held high, turned her camera toward me with a wide grin. A wave of shyness washed over me as I realized her boyfriend, on the other

end of the call, was witnessing the entire unexpected celebration.

Just then, the Filipino waiter reappeared, holding a beautifully
decorated chocolate cake with a sparkling birthday candle. "Happy
Birthday, sir!" he said, placing it on our table. "Enjoy this, it's a bit
expensive, but the staff wanted to do something special for you."

This unexpected kindness left us speechless. Our fruitless
cake search the previous night was forgotten, replaced by the
heartwarming reminder of the kindness of strangers and how positive energy radiates out into the world.

As the singing faded, my shyness subsided. The waiters
returned to their duties, leaving us with a final farewell from our
new Filipino friend. Glancing at my watch, I realized it was almost
10 am, checkout time, and we didn't want to be late. After hastily
finishing our breakfast, we gathered our gear, and my sister headed
towards the elevator.

As I exited the restaurant, an elderly Chinese lady, who I
recognized from the group who had sung "Happy Birthday,"
approached me. With a warm smile, she simply said, "Happy
Birthday."

This simple greeting, from a stranger of a different culture, left
me speechless for a moment. In all my years, I had never received
such a spontaneous gesture. It was so heartfelt, so unexpected, that
it touched me deeply. Perhaps this was the universe's way of
reminding me that even in the midst of personal struggles, there is
always kindness to be found.

With a renewed sense of warmth in my heart, I continued
towards the elevators where my sister awaited. We checked out
smoothly, the only distraction being the mesmerizing Marina Bay
Sands chandelier that captivated my gaze during the short wait.

Leaving the opulent comfort of Marina Bay Sands, we
embarked on the next chapter of our Singaporean adventure – a
budget-friendly hostel nestled in the heart of Little India.

Back outside, the change in atmosphere was immediate. The

bustling streets hummed with a different energy as we navigated towards the MRT station. The efficient train system whisked us away, and soon we were deposited into a neighborhood thrumming with a new rhythm. The air was alive with the intoxicating aromas of spices and incense, and the faces around us reflected the vibrant tapestry of Little India.

My sister, less accustomed to such a swift cultural shift, commented with a touch of uncertainty, "There are a lot of Indian people here... it smells different."

A chuckle escaped me. "Well, we're in their neighborhood now," I reminded her gently. "We're the visitors here, so let's be respectful of their culture and keep our comments to ourselves."

A bit chastised, she nodded in agreement. We arrived at the hostel far too early for check-in, around 10:30 am. Thankfully, the staff was understanding and happily stored our luggage in a secure room. Relieved, we hopped back onto the train, ready to continue our day of exploration with Universal Studios as our next destination.

Universal Studios: Where Dreams Come True

Our first full day in Singapore was dedicated to reliving childhood dreams at Universal Studios. The train ride was a marvel of efficiency, whisking us to the theme park entrance in a blink. Stepping through the iconic gates, we were greeted by a world of familiar characters and thrilling rides, a kaleidoscope of colors and sounds that ignited our inner child.

The captivating world of the Mummy grabbed us first, its heart-pounding twists and turns sending our pulses racing. We navigated through elaborate sets, feeling the adrenaline rush of a close encounter with the ancient curse. Next, we braved the world of Transformers, battling alongside the Autobots in a mind-blowing 3D adventure that blurred the lines between fantasy and reality.

As the day progressed, we found ourselves laughing, screaming, and surrendering to the pure joy of the theme park. Each ride, each show, each character encounter, transported us to a world where anything was possible. It was a day of unadulterated fun, a temporary escape from the complexities of adulthood.

Beyond the Walls of Exploration

Back at the hostel that evening, the shared bathroom echoed with the soft murmurs of fellow travelers preparing for bed. As I waited my turn, a window framed the cityscape, now bathed in the golden hues of sunrise. The scene triggered a wave of nostalgia, and the memory of "The Polar Bear" filled my mind. This treasured toy truck, a gift from my father when I was young, held special significance as he'd bought it during his time in Singapore.

I recalled the excitement I felt as a child when my father returned from his travels, his suitcase overflowing with exotic treasures. The bustling streets below, a stark contrast to the quiet serenity of my hometown, sparked a desire to continue his legacy of exploration. This realization filled me with a newfound sense of purpose and a yearning to venture into the unknown, just as he had.

For the first time in my life, I felt a sense of freedom that I had only dreamed of as a child. Not the carefree freedom of youth, but the autonomy of an adult charting his own course. But I also knew that to truly test my independence, I needed to go beyond this shared experience with my sister.

Chinatown Charms and Clarke Quay Nights

Our explorations continued with a visit to a magnificent Buddhist temple in vibrant Chinatown. The intricate carvings and vibrant colors of the exterior left me awestruck. Although my sister, dressed in a short skirt, was unable to enter due to the temple's dress code, she was a good sport and waited patiently outside while I explored inside.

The air inside was thick with the scent of incense, and the gentle murmur of prayers filled the hallowed space. Witnessing the faithful in their rituals and observing the various statues and paintings sparked a deep sense of respect and curiosity about this unfamiliar religion. As I wandered through the temple's tranquil courtyards, I spotted a lone traveler dressed in black, meticulously capturing the essence of the temple through his camera lens. His quiet dedication piqued my curiosity, planting a seed in my mind about the possibility of embarking on a solo adventure in the future.

Exiting the temple, we met up with our friend Cleo, a Filipino banker living in Singapore. He took us to a renowned restaurant in Chinatown, where we indulged in a unique crab feast. The crab soup, a symphony of rich flavors and aromatic spices, stole the show, and we observed the cultural nuances around us, from the communal dining style to the meticulous cracking of crab shells.

While initially fascinated by the meal, my thoughts drifted back to my father and the connection I felt to this place where he'd also walked. The bustling streets, the vibrant colors, the intoxicating aromas – they all seemed to whisper his name, reminding me of the shared experiences that had shaped me.

As the sun dipped below the cityscape, we said our goodbyes to Cleo and ventured towards the beckoning lights of Clarke Quay. The contrast between Chinatown's traditional charm and the district's neon energy was exhilarating. The riverside thrummed with activity, its reflections shimmering on the Singapore River. Bars and restaurants overflowed with lively chatter, making the perfect backdrop for our evening photos. We strolled along the water, snapping shots of the colorful facades and illuminated skyline, my determination to uncover even more of Singapore's hidden gems burning brighter than ever.

A Clash of Styles

Our Singapore adventure spanned almost five days, a whirlwind of breathtaking sights, cultural immersion, and the occasional sibling disagreement. Our contrasting personalities – my sister's meticulous planning versus my adventurous spontaneity – added a layer of complexity to our journey. This fundamental difference came to a head during our designated "free day" in Singapore.

The morning began with breakfast at our hostel. The common area buzzed with the energy of fellow travelers, each embarking on their own Singaporean adventure. The air carried the familiar scent of a canteen, and the chatter of voices rose and fell like the clatter of dishes. We settled into our usual spot, a corner table that had become our breakfast base for the past four days.

I was eager to hit the streets and explore new neighborhoods, while my sister, ever the planner, insisted we finalize our itinerary with a map and a list of "must-see" attractions.

"Just wing it?" my sister questioned, her voice laced with concern, as I suggested exploring without a fixed itinerary.

"Don't worry," I reassured her with a playful grin, "we'll stumble upon hidden gems that way."

She rolled her eyes, but a smile tugged at the corner of her lips. "Fine, but don't blame me if we get lost in the middle of nowhere."

Truth be told, my confidence in navigating solely with Google Maps was slightly misplaced. We ventured beyond familiar tourist spots, into a vibrant local market overflowing with unfamiliar sights and smells. As we delved deeper, my initial confidence started to wane.

"Hey," my sister nudged me subtly, her phone screen displaying a map with a red dot blinking suspiciously far from our current location. "Are we... lost?"

A sheepish chuckle escaped my lips. "Maybe a little," I admitted, feeling the familiar heat of sibling rivalry flare. "But getting lost is part of the adventure, right?" Deep down, I knew I was pushing things a bit, but the thrill of discovery was intoxicating.

Our wandering eventually led us to the waterfront near the Merlion, the iconic symbol of Singapore. My sister's eyes lit up, and she whipped out her phone, eager to get the perfect photo with the famous landmark.

Inspired by a surge of adventurous spirit, I suggested we take a detour around the harbor before snapping our souvenir photo. My sister, ever cautious, hesitated, scanning the map with a skeptical eye. After some gentle persuasion, she reluctantly agreed, and off we ventured.

Our walk, filled with lively banter and playful teasing, was enjoyable...until it wasn't. As the sun began to dip below the horizon, we realized we'd lost track of our route back to the Merlion. My sister, her dark hair like a midnight waterfall tumbling down her back, groaned, a playful pout forming on her lips. Her morena skin, reflecting the fading sunlight, glowed with a hint of frustration. "I knew this would happen," she groaned, a playful pout forming on her lips.

As the tension mounted, a wave of maturity overwhelmed me. I was the elder brother, after all, and it was my responsibility to set a good example. Taking a deep breath, I softened my tone.

"Okay, look," I conceded. "Maybe we can find a compromise. How about we pick a general direction and explore for another few minutes? If we haven't found a familiar landmark by then, we can pull out the map and regroup."

My sister, still slightly flustered but appreciating the olive branch, nodded in agreement. A few minutes later, we stumbled upon a familiar path, and the gleaming Merlion came into view, its illuminated splendor a welcome sight.

In the end, we got our photo with the Merlion, even if it involved a few extra detours and a minor sibling squabble. Our day of spontaneous exploration solidified a newfound appreciation for each other's travel styles. It was a reminder that sometimes, the most rewarding experiences lie outside the neatly planned itinerary. Our differences, once a source of friction, had become the foundation of a stronger bond. We learned to embrace each other's strengths, finding a balance between structure and spontaneity.

A Bittersweet Farewell and a Taste of Home

The last day of our Singapore adventure arrived, bringing with it a mix of emotions. The grandeur of Changi Airport, a destination in itself, soothed our travel fatigue. However, my sister's aversion to missing flights had us arriving ridiculously early, with hours to spare before our departure.

To pass the time, we indulged in a hearty breakfast of nasi lemak, the fragrant rice and spicy sambal a comforting reminder of home amidst the unfamiliar surroundings. The airport's mesmerizing gardens filled the pre-flight hours, their manicured beauty a stark contrast to the bustling city we'd just explored.

The insatiable explorer within me couldn't resist one last adventure. Leaving my sister, comfortably settled near a floral statue, engrossed in her phone, I embarked on a solo exploration of the sprawling airport. Every corner I turned revealed a new wonder: a cascading waterfall, a butterfly garden teeming with vibrant colors, even a movie theater. It was a city within a city, a testament to Singapore's dedication to innovation and beauty.

As I wandered through Changi Airport's enchanting gardens, a sense of liberation bloomed within me. Each step without a plan felt like a small rebellion against our meticulously crafted itinerary. The world beckoned, a vast map waiting for my solo exploration. This newfound freedom, a stark contrast to traveling with my sister, ignited a yearning for independent adventures. While I cherished our bond, I craved to test my own wings, to discover hidden corners that resonated with my own rhythm.

With a newfound appreciation for my sister's patience and a heart full of gratitude for the experiences we'd shared, I made my way back to her.

She looked up from her phone, a knowing smile on her face. "Find anything interesting?" she asked, her tone a mix of amusement and relief.

I nodded, recounting my discoveries with enthusiasm. In that moment, our differences faded away, replaced by a shared sense of wonder and the unspoken understanding that this adventure had brought us closer than ever before.

Homeward Bound: Reflections on a Journey

Boarding the plane back to the Philippines, I couldn't help but reflect on the transformative power of travel. Singapore had been more than just a destination; it was a catalyst for personal growth, a mirror reflecting both my strengths and my weaknesses. It had shown me the importance of embracing new experiences, of stepping outside my comfort zone, and of appreciating the unique perspectives of others.

But most importantly, it had ignited a spark within me, a yearning for a deeper sense of independence and self-discovery. The Philippines, with its diverse landscapes and hidden treasures, beckoned me to explore its uncharted corners. The idea of a solo journey, once a distant dream, now felt like a tangible possibility.

As the plane touched down on familiar soil, I knew that this adventure was just the beginning. The lessons learned in Singapore, the newfound confidence and resilience, would pave the way for countless more explorations, both external and internal. The Polar Bear, a symbol of my father's adventurous spirit, now rested on my shelf, a reminder of the legacy I was determined to carry on. Singapore had not only been an escapade but also a turning point, a chapter that would forever shape the narrative of my life.

Chapter 11

Finding Freedom in Solitude

October 2015
Act 1: The Spark of Wanderlust
The stale air conditioner breeze did nothing to cool the restless heat that simmered beneath my skin. My reflection stared back at me from the laptop screen – tired eyes, a face etched with a restless dissatisfaction. The familiar clutter of my work-from-home corner felt suffocating. Every click, every travel blog, was a futile attempt to break through the oppressive stillness. It wasn't sadness I felt, but a suffocating sense of stagnation.

The self-planned trip to Singapore months earlier still flickered in my mind. It had been like a desperate gasp for fresh air, a revelation – a glimpse at the thrill of facing the unknown, of relying on my own instincts.

Could I capture that feeling again, push it even further? Would I have the courage to explore somewhere completely alone, proving to myself – and to the world – that I could break free from my own self-doubt and forge my own path? Japan seemed like the ultimate test, but its sheer unfamiliarity was daunting. I needed a stepping stone, a trial by fire. A place where

I could perhaps find the answers I was seeking, a place to test my mettle.

And then, I found it – Ilocos Norte, a northern province in the Philippines, rich in history and natural beauty. A place that whispered promises of adventure and self-discovery.

Act 2: Taking the Leap

The glow of my laptop screen reflected a face etched with doubt. Likes and a few enthusiastic comments trickled in for my Facebook post. "What do you think of solo traveling?" Simple words that held a lifetime of potential – and a whole lot of fear.

Just then, a notification popped up: Kuya Porky, a friend known for his adventurous spirit, had chimed in with a thumbs-up emoji and the words "Life-changing!" His comment was like a jolt of electricity, a spark that ignited a dormant desire within me.

I took a deep breath and clicked "Book Now" on the tour website. It felt surreal, like I was stepping off a cliff into the unknown. But the thrill of the unknown was exactly what I craved.

I spent hours scouring online forums and travel blogs, immersing myself in the virtual world of Ilocos Norte. I learned about the region's history, its natural beauty, and its unique culture. The more I learned, the more excited I became.

The day of departure arrived, and I found myself standing at the designated meeting point in Cubao, a bustling transportation hub in Quezon City. My heart pounded as I scanned the crowd, searching for a familiar face from the online group. There were none. Instead, I saw fourteen pairs of eyes staring back at me, some curious, some indifferent.

A voice broke the silence. "Seems like we're complete," the driver announced. He was a middle-aged man with a friendly face and a mop of salt-and-pepper hair. His tanned skin and calloused hands spoke of a life spent outdoors. His warm smile immediately put me at ease.

"If you wouldn't mind," he started, a smile playing on his lips,

"Could you be our official doorkeeper? Your seat gives you the perfect spot."

Surprise enveloped me, then a flicker of amusement. "Sure, I'd be happy to," I replied, my voice a touch stronger. The van doors slid closed, and with an engine rumble, we were off.

A tap on my shoulder startled me. My seatmate tilted her head, studying the empty space beside me. "Are you by yourself?" Her tone held a mix of curiosity and a hint of something else – was that judgment?

"Yes," I mumbled, a familiar tightness coiling in my chest. Why did people need to highlight the obvious?

"Oh." Her eyes flickered towards the next row. "I'm with my sister," she added, gesturing towards a girl who waved shyly.

A wave of unease washed over me. I forced a quick wave back, a polite mask over my discomfort. It wasn't malicious, but her question pricked at an old insecurity. Did people always see my solitude as something to be dissected? A familiar instinct took over. Instead of engaging further, I simply smiled, a faint tightness in the corners of my lips. "Well, I guess this is where we sleep for the next few hours." My voice was light, but my focus drifted towards the window, seeking refuge in the passing scenery.

We left Metro Manila at a bleary-eyed 4 am, the city's familiar chaos fading as the van rumbled on, revealing a shifting landscape of rural scenes and urban pockets. The minty scent of car freshener mingled with the smell of exhaust. Sleep deprivation gnawed at me, leaving a trail of irritability in its wake. Yet, excitement flickered, battling the restless unease that coiled in my gut.

A jolt of surprise – the van was coming to a stop. The driver announced a breakfast break, and the passengers stirred, my job as the "official doorman" snapping me into focus. The eatery was a flurry of activity, bathed in the bright morning sunlight. The symphony of voices, the clatter of dishes, and a whirlwind of movement crashed over my sleep-deprived senses. I grabbed a quick, nondescript meal and hurried back to the van, longing for a moment of quiet.

Finally, we arrived at our first photo stop: the iconic "Ilocos Norte" sign. The driver, ever kind, helped me capture the perfect shot with a smile. We continued, the majestic Patapat Viaduct winding before us. The wind whipped through my hair, the fresh air a balm to my weariness. The vastness of the scenery was breathtaking, and the relative solitude compared to the bustling eatery was a welcome change. With the driver as my companion, I felt a sense of freedom and adventure as we explored this stunning landmark. It was around midday when we reached Laoag City.

"Alright everyone, we're here now on our first destination, Laoag City. Time is 12nn and it's lunch time. Let's have a lunch break and see you again after an hour."

Act 3: Finding My Way in Laoag City

My job as the official doorkeeper was done. As I slid open the van door, Laoag City greeted me with a blast of warm air carrying the scent of dust and something faintly floral. I took in the old-world charm, the central plaza bustling with tricycles and the chatter of vendors. Though a pang of anxiety lingered, excitement fueled my first solo steps in this new place.

My stomach rumbled a protest. Time for food! A scan of the streets revealed the familiar glow of a Jollibee logo. Relief coursed through me, nearly making me lightheaded... then promptly evaporated as I stepped inside. Every table was packed, the lunchtime chatter deafening, the air thick with the scent of grilled chicken. My eyes darted around, searching. Just as I suspected, it was full. If I didn't adapt to the people's high turnover, I would be left behind.

I made a quick decision and pursued the two girls in school uniforms, as they had another extra chair.

"Excuse me, pwede po bang umupo dito? Walang nakaupo?" (Excuse me, can I sit here? Is no one sitting here?) I asked, pointing at the empty seat with a hopeful smile.

The girls glanced at each other, then nodded and smiled, their faces radiating a warmth that eased my anxiety. I placed my tray on the table, my heart still racing, and began to munch on the rich, savory chicken. Each bite was a victory over my initial apprehension, a testament to my growing confidence in navigating unfamiliar situations.

Around 10 minutes later, the girls left, and just in time, the people in the restaurant started to disperse. I guess we picked the rush hour for it. I went outside and began to walk back to the park where the van was parked.

What an experience. I thought I was going to die just by asking strangers to let me sit for lunch. I hadn't ever done that before. But hunger trumps social anxiety. The food, though, was worth the awkwardness. After I finished, I wandered back to the plaza, my mind buzzing with the sights and sounds of Laoag City. The afternoon heat was starting to get to me, and I realized I needed a change of pace.

Act 4: Solo Explorations

The Ilocos Norte tour finally continued. The first stop was a historical and tourist attraction in Vigan, the UNESCO World Heritage Site called Bantay Bell Tower. It was a 20-minute drive from Laoag City. After our group took some pictures, we head back to the van and proceed to the next destination, which is the Marcos Museum, or as the locals call it, *Malacañang ti Amianan* (Malacañang of the North). I didn't enter the museum because I wasn't really interested at the time, but it was a place I knew I'd come back to someday. I just took a quick rest while everyone is taking pictures.

Next stop: Paoay Church, another UNESCO World Heritage Site. It was the highlight of the trip. I remember staring at the structure from afar; it was like I was on a scene in the movie Zorro, where you could see this church that was a century old. The sun-baked coral stone glowed with a warm, inviting aura, and the intricate carvings around the doorways whispered tales of centuries gone by. Stepping inside, the cool, dim interior enveloped me in a sense of reverence and peace. The scent of incense hung heavy in the air, mingling with the quiet murmur of prayers. In that moment, standing beneath the towering arches, I felt a profound connection to history, a humbling reminder of the enduring power of faith and human ingenuity. I then took a lot of pictures from my camcorder and my phone. The view from afar was breathtaking, especially the blue and clear sky that day. I stayed there for an hour while everyone was busy with their chitchat.

We then proceeded to the Sand Dunes, an endless stretch of rolling hills sculpted by the wind. The rippled patterns etched into the sand seemed like ancient hieroglyphs, telling stories of sun and storms. The heat was intense, the air shimmering with a desert-like haze, yet I couldn't help but feel a sense of wonder. I decided to splurge on the 4x4 adventure – after all, when would I be back in a place like this?

As I climbed into the rugged vehicle, a thrill of anticipation shot through me. The driver, a sun-baked local with a mischievous grin, revved the engine, and we took off. The dunes turned into a blur of sand and sky as we raced up and down the slopes, the vehicle tilting precariously at times. I gripped the handrail, my heart pounding in my chest as we crested each hill, the world dropping away below us.

The wind whipped through my hair, carrying a symphony of screams and laughter from my fellow passengers. We were like kids on a roller coaster, our cares forgotten as we surrendered to the exhilarating ride. When the 4x4 finally rolled to a stop, I was breathless, dizzy, and covered in sand – but I couldn't stop grinning. It was an experience I'd never forget, a reminder that sometimes, the most unexpected adventures are the most rewarding.

I took my time with my camera, capturing the vastness of the dunes and the thrill of the 4x4 ride, as if I was the only one in that massive desert, then we all head back to the van.

We arrived at our accommodation at around 5 pm and had

some time to settle in before dinner. The lodging house was quite far from the town center, which gave me an excuse to just relax in the room for the rest of the night. We had a delicious dinner of bagnet and pinakbet, two of the most popular dishes in Ilocos. Afterwards, I enjoyed a peaceful walk under the starry night, marveling at the quiet serenity of the countryside. I knew this trip was more than just a vacation; it was a chance for me to recharge and reconnect with myself.

Act 5: Facing Fears and Finding Courage

Sleep came fitfully amidst the lingering adrenaline of the sand dunes. Each time I drifted off, visions of cresting hills and tumbling down sandy slopes flashed through my mind. The dawn brought a mix of soreness and eagerness. After a quick breakfast at the lodging, we piled back into the familiar van. While chatter didn't flow as easily as yesterday, tiredness was offset by a quiet energy born from a good night's rest.

Our first stop was the Bojeador Lighthouse. Drawn by its isolated beauty, I hurried ahead of the group to capture photos undisturbed. The driver, ever kind, even let me pose with the travel tour logo, adding a touch of playfulness to the scene. Before starting the climb towards the lighthouse, I treated myself to a mango ice cream from a local vendor, its sweet and tangy flavor a refreshing counterpoint to the rising heat. There's something about lighthouses that fascinates me – their solitary presence, the implied journeys, the tales of storms weathered.

The uphill trek might have deterred others, but it felt symbolic in a way. Each step, each labored breath, mirrored the challenges I'd faced back home. But with every step, the fear that had gripped me for so long lessened. This wasn't just about proving to myself I could handle a steep climb, but proving I could handle anything life threw at me. Reaching the lighthouse wasn't just about conquering a physical challenge; it was a symbol of my growing independence. Each step up the worn red staircase affirmed my ability to navigate this journey alone. The breathtaking view from the top, the endless expanse of blue stretching to the horizon, filled me with a sense of accomplishment and a newfound confidence that I could overcome any obstacle that came my way.

As I reached the landing and began the climb up the red staircase, worn smooth by countless footsteps, I savored the last bites of my mango ice cream. The cold, sweet mango swirled with a hint of nostalgia, a taste that took me back to carefree summer days as a child.

Standing alone in the beacon room, the sunlight warming my skin and the wind whispering secrets, I felt a sense of serenity I hadn't expected. The air was fresh, the view expansive – a tapestry of green fields and distant houses, the ocean stretching out to meet the horizon. Moments like this were why I chose solo travel. Here, amidst the vastness of the sky and sea, I felt a kinship with the lone adventurers in the video games that had always been my escape. All this time, I was projecting my desire for freedom and self-discovery onto Ash Ketchum...but maybe, just maybe, I could be the hero of my own story. My reverie was broken by the sound of footsteps – time to rejoin the group.

Next was the Kapurpurawan Rock Formation, a testament to the sculpting power of nature. Its white, hardened form felt both ancient and whimsical, like a giant sandcastle defying the elements. The smell of salt hung heavy in the air, the gentle crash of waves against the shore a soothing rhythm. I found a secluded spot, sat in a meditative pose, and let the cool breeze caress my face. The vast ocean stretched before me, its unending blue a stark contrast to the stark white of the rock. In that moment, I felt a profound sense of peace, a connection to something much larger than myself.

By the time we reached the Bangui Windmills, stomachs were rumbling. Hopping out of the van, most of the group retreated into the shade. "Too hot!" I heard someone complain. A grin spread across my face - finally, some time to myself. I had 20 minutes to capture the scene, and I intended to make the most of it. These windmills were massive! Standing beside them, I felt like a tiny ant next to a towering giant, their slowly circling forms dwarfing everything around them. The whirring of the blades was oddly soothing, a mechanical symphony against the endless blue sky. I experimented with angles, playing with the contrast between the stark white structures and the vibrant landscape. Time slipped by quickly.

Our final stop, the Bantay Abot Cave, was more about a souvenir photo amidst the crowds than true exploration.

Back in the van, the exhaustion of the day finally won over hunger. We continued the journey to Laoag City, bypassing the food options near Hannah's Beach Resort. The sprawling resort, with its vibrant water slides, thatched-roof cabanas, and the sounds of laughter, looked like a fun place to spend a leisure day. The quirky statues – Elvis Presley captured mid-song, Marilyn Monroe's iconic windblown pose – offered a touch of whimsy even from afar. Though we ended early, the return drive to Laoag City loomed. Still, a contentment unlike anything I'd known before lingered. Tomorrow held a new destination, promising even more to discover, and a newfound confidence that I could conquer any challenge, big or small.

Act 6: The Journey Home

The last day started with visiting the famous Baluarte Zoo. I'd always loved animals, so there was excitement... but also a pang of sadness. Seeing some of those magnificent creatures in cages tugged at my heart. Especially later, finding a room lined with mounted heads. Their silent plea lingered with me, making it impossible to stay. The Padre Burgos House National Museum was better, though even there crowds sometimes overwhelmed. *I found myself seeking moments of solitude, a quiet corner to process the conflicting emotions of the day.*

Still, the driver dropped us in Vigan City with its promise of a time capsule experience. With everything within walking distance, we agreed on a meeting time – freedom was in the air.

Lunch was Jollibee near the Ilocos Sur Capitol signage; a familiar comfort in this new environment. Snapping photos by the fountain, I felt a lightness I hadn't experienced in ages. Each day, the initial jitters of solo travel faded a little more. Maybe there was something to this, exploring at your own pace, being comfortable in your own company. *I realized that solitude wasn't loneliness, but a chance to connect with my own thoughts and desires.*

Next was a quintessential Vigan experience, a *kalesa* ride. I picked a cart with a brightly woven pattern, a small act of independent choice that felt surprisingly good. We clopped along cobbled streets, their history seeping up through the horse's hooves.

The Bantay Bell Tower sign caught my eye, and I couldn't resist exploring it. The quote by St. Augustine resonated; wasn't this trip about turning pages in my life's story? *I felt a sense of purpose, like I was finally writing my own narrative, one step at a time.* Then came *Calle Crisologo* itself. The architecture, the food stalls, the lingering scent of something sweet baking... it was pure magic. How lucky I was to stand here, a witness to this preserved slice of the past.

Excitement surged as I checked my watch. It was almost 2pm, time to rejoin the group. I practically skipped back to the van, eager to tell my family about this place. We piled in, ready for the long return to Manila. A brief stop at the tour office to settle up was routine, until the clerk asked, "Are you alone?" in a tone that seemed to echo around the cramped space.

"Yes," my reply felt small, the word catching in my throat.

"Next time, come with someone," she added with a pitying smile. Then, almost as an afterthought, "It gets lonely on the road, doesn't it?"

The kindness was fake, her assumption a punch in the gut. A surge of defiance rose within me, but I kept it silent. Filipinos, myself included, rarely confront strangers directly. Instead, my thoughts raced. *Lonely? Not at all.* I'd discovered parts of myself I never would have if I'd waited for company. *I was learning to embrace my own company, to find joy in my own thoughts and experiences.*

The van trundled onwards. Hours stretched into an eternity, the scenery blurring past. Now, the closeness of the van felt like more than just tired travelers. It was a reminder of the words that wouldn't fade away entirely. My quiet vanmates felt more like a reflection of the culture than a personal judgment. Yet, frustration lingered, battled by the growing realization of how much this trip had changed me.

I thought back to the anxious traveler who had boarded this van just a few days ago. I was still that person, but I was also someone new - more confident, more independent, more open to the world. This trip had been a catalyst for growth, a journey of self-discovery that I wouldn't trade for anything.

As Manila's familiar cityscape finally emerged, the journey felt far from over. My gaze fixed on the horizon, a flicker of uncertainty mixing with a strange sort of excitement. Home awaited, but it seemed like a different place now. A place where possibilities were endless, where adventure could be found just around the corner. Little did I know, a certain friend was about to prove that point.

Chapter 12

Climbing Cliffs, Climbing Fears

September 2016

My friend Tony was the kind of guy who'd buy you a plane ticket before telling you where you were going. The sort of whirlwind-in-a-polo-shirt who, after I'd helped him with a solo project, decided to repay the favor with an impromptu adventure. In my early days of travel, he contacted me to join him on a crazy trip across my hometown, Iloilo City.

He said it was an easy trip since I knew Hiligaynon, a local dialect. With my language skills, we could navigate my hometown effortlessly. We trekked from the city, through the outskirts, then deeper into rural places with hidden waterfalls and white-sand beaches. We even made it to Boracay, a paradise of powdery sand and crystal-clear water that felt like a world away from my usual cubicle life. It was an eye-opening experience, a taste of freedom and a first hint that maybe, just maybe, there was more to life than spreadsheets and lukewarm office coffee.

Back in Manila, those few days in Boracay felt like a distant dream. The daily grind had resumed, but the memory of that escape lingered, a tantalizing reminder of what was possible. Then, Tony struck again.

A few months later, while scrolling through Facebook and daydreaming about beach getaways inspired by a recent anime binge, a message from Tony popped up: "Hey, what's your passport number again?"

I choked on my tea. Okay, maybe a few drops escaped...but at least the fine china was safe. This was it. I hadn't yet fully adjusted to Tony's brand of spontaneous chaos, and the surprise trip announcement sent my mind reeling. Excitement battled with a familiar dread. Where were we going this time? And how much was this going to cost me? He always booked the tickets, which was great in the moment, but left me scrambling to play financial catch-up later. At least this time I'd have a few days' notice to brace my bank account for the impact.

Curious – and possibly a little terrified – I texted back. "Why the passport number?"

"Oh, we're going to El Nido Palawan tomorrow, flight is early morning, be prepared," he replied.

A wave of relief flooded through me. El Nido? That was the fancy place with the lagoons! But wait a minute... whaa? This was an outrageous surprise! My old swimsuit would have to do, but I didn't even own a waterproof camera. I had no time to complain. Frantically searching online, I found one and arranged a lightning-fast meetup with the seller at SM North Edsa. Then, I rushed home to throw everything into my suitcase, my mind still ablaze with the shock of the news.

Early the next morning, we met up at the airport, my suitcase hastily packed, and my caffeine levels through the roof. I was still my usual complaining self, griping about why he sprung this on me with so little notice. But we had no time for squabbles – it was time for some pre-flight pictures before boarding our Cebu Pacific flight.

We arrived in Puerto Princesa, Palawan, and after a quick

lunch, hopped into a van for the several-hour journey to El Nido. A German couple sat behind us, their chatter a constant hum. I tried to escape into my music, blocking out the noise as we made our way to our destination. Arriving in El Nido late in the after-noon, we hopped into a unique tricycle and headed to Tony's friend's place.

Tony, ever the planner, had already booked it for a few nights. "How cool is that?" I thought, marveling at our beachfront accom-modation. It turned out his friend, Josue, a true child of the tropics with his deep tan, owned this beachfront cottage business. No wonder Tony loved El Nido so much!

As we settled into our cottage, number 3, we noticed another guy in cottage #2, enjoying the ocean view. Tony, ever the social butterfly, couldn't resist his curiosity. "Why not go talk to him?" I suggested, busy unpacking my bags and prepping my clothes for the next day's adventures.

He wandered over, and I settled onto the hammock outside our cottage, a gentle breeze carrying the salty scent of the sea washing over me. I took a deep breath, savoring the moment.

Tony returned, a smile on his face. "He's a traveling writer," he said, a hint of awe in his voice.

"Interesting," I mused, "I wish I could be like him someday." The thought of wandering the world, documenting stories, and living a life of freedom resonated deeply.

Josue welcomed us warmly, offering us refreshing drinks and stories of the island's hidden treasures. I initially joined them for dinner, but a surprise late-night work meeting loomed. With a sigh, I excused myself after finishing my meal and hurried back to the cottage to connect online. Thankfully, there was Wi-Fi — being stuck without it would have been a disaster! Settling in, the irony of the situation hit me. Here I was, supposed to be on leave, yet tethered to my laptop "just in case." *Frustration simmered beneath the surface, a stark reminder that I couldn't fully escape the clutches of my professional life.* I had promised myself this would be a break, a chance to escape the city's relentless pace. But old habits die hard, and the fear of missing out on a crucial work opportunity gnawed at me. It was a stark reminder of the constant tug-of-war between my desire for freedom and the demands of my career.

Shortly after, Tony returned and settled in for the night while I tackled the meeting, my full attention on the screen. Eventually, by midnight, I was drained but victorious. Stepping outside, I took a deep breath of the calming beach breeze, letting it wash away the stress of the unexpected work session.

The Island Hopping Adventure

The sun beat down on my blue and green sando with its summery logo and my breezy floral shorts. We hopped onto a rickety tricycle, unique to El Nido, his friend at the wheel. After a quick breakfast, we were ready to set sail – our island hopping tour promising adventure around every corner. As we arrived at the busy dock, a thrill of anticipation chased away any lingering tiredness. I scurried after Tony, my earlier complaints about the heat forgotten. We wound through narrow streets, dodging vendors and other tourists, until a vast ocean vista opened up, dotted with boats and framed by a majestic mountain. This was Palawan, and it was breathtaking. "Island hopping day!" Tony bellowed with a grin.

We spent some time snorkeling here, snapping photos against the backdrop of incredible rock formations – perfect for those Instagram-worthy shots! The white beaches of El Nido stretched out before us, a reminder of this island paradise. Next up was the island with those strangely shaped rocks we spotted from afar. We explored the shoreline and found a lonely Mary statue tucked inside. It was a different kind of stop, but the unique formations made it interesting.

A short boat ride brought us to Tapiutan Island. The cool breeze whipped through my hair, carrying the scent of salt and the rhythmic sound of waves against the hull. The gentle rocking of the boat lulled me into a relaxed state, and laughter from other passengers created a sense of joyful camaraderie. Soon, Tapiutan

Island came into view, a lush green gem against the turquoise water.

Time seemed to slow as we ate on Tapiutan Island, the sound of the waves creating a soothing backdrop. We sprawled on the sand, watching other happy tourists play in the shallows. Their laughter drifted over us, adding to the sense of carefree joy. Our lunch was a delicious break before the adventure continued – freshly cooked seafood, juicy watermelon, and piles of rice fueled us up for what was to come.

Finally, it was time for Hidden Beach! "Get ready!" our guide announced, his voice crackling with excitement. "The only way to reach Hidden Beach is a deep dive – this hidden cove is a reward for those brave enough to take the plunge!" My heart hammered in my chest. With goggles in place, life vest secure, and a silent hope that my soul was still intact, I JUMPED! The ocean swallowed me, the roar of the water muffled as I plunged deeper. I kicked hard, following the dim shapes of other divers. My goggles fogged slightly, a trickle of water finding its way in. Up ahead, I spotted our guide. He grinned and with a powerful push, sent me hurtling towards shimmering light – the underwater entrance to the cove. For a heart-stopping moment, I was disoriented, then I burst through the surface into dazzling sunlight. And there it was – a natural wonder carved by the sea. The grotto stretched out before me like a giant piece of coral swept into the ocean. Towering stalagmites of stone surrounded us, like barricades between this hidden world and the vast ocean beyond. Inside, the water shimmered, sunlight dappling the smooth gray stones that sloped from a deep edge down to a shallow pool. Tiny fish darted around us as we swam and snorkeled, marveling at this hidden world. Our tour guide snapped a group photo, capturing our smiles against this incredible backdrop.

Adrenaline still coursing through me, we motored back to our cottage. The thrill of the grotto lingered as the boat rocked gently. It had been the perfect dose of excitement. The day's adventures replayed in my mind and a burning curiosity grew about what tomorrow held.

"Land Tour"

"What's our itinerary for today?" I asked Tony as I shuffled outside in my pajamas. He just sat there on a wooden chair outside our cottage, nonchalant-like. Typical.

"Land tour," was all he said before I headed back inside to change. A loose green-blue sando, my trusty blue beach shorts, and a pair of boat shoes – ready for whatever adventure, or misadventure, awaited. Another tricycle ride, Josue at the wheel, and we were off.

At first, we wound through tiny streets, houses blurring past. So, is this "land tour" going to be exploring some rural village? I could dig that... But then, we passed a swamp where water lilies bloomed and vines hung like curtains across the trees. Bird calls echoed – a proper jungle soundtrack.

The path turned to wobbly wooden tiles, each bounce sending a jolt through me. Was this eerie place going to be my final destination? All those jungle adventure movies with gruesome endings flashed through my head. Yet, there was a strange exhilaration too. This was nothing like the city, that was for sure.

Suddenly, the path ended. Was that it? All this buildup for a lame walk in the woods?

"Oh, we're just getting started," Tony quipped as he started climbing a rickety ladder. Up ahead, a giant wall of rock loomed, one of those crazy El Nido formations.

Are you serious? You expect me to climb that with no warning? A complaint formed in my head, but really, what choice did I have? And on an EMPTY stomach? Even a piece of pandesal would've been a lifesaver right then. With a sigh, I followed. Each creak of the wood echoed the pounding of my heart. Okay, so maybe this wasn't so bad... UNTIL I reached the top and faced a nightmare of sharp rocks and sheer drops. Complete panic.

Where in the world was Tony? This "land tour" was feeling

more like a death march. I couldn't find him anywhere. Panic fluttered in my chest, a flock of angry sparrows trapped in my ribs. *Are they messing with me?* I fumed, my voice barely a whisper against the wind. *He drags me out here, then vanishes into thin air?* I tugged at my blue beach shorts, cursing their lack of grip against the jagged rocks. And my shoes— flimsy boat shoes were no match for these treacherous slopes! Every sharp edge threatened to pierce through the soles, sending me tumbling into the abyss.

Then, a faint echo ahead. Tony's voice! A lifeline in the deafening roar of doubt that had filled my head. All I could focus on now were the rocks, the dizzying drop below, the wind whipping at my hair, and the last shreds of my rapidly dwindling courage.

My mind raced with a familiar torrent of self-doubt. What if I slip? What if I can't do it? What if this is how it ends – a city boy falling to his death in the middle of nowhere, wearing the wrong shoes and a stupid sando?

But then another voice cut through the fear. A voice that reminded me of the lessons learned on that solo trip to Ilocos, the lessons of resilience and self-belief. *Stop with the negative thoughts, Ray. Everyone is moving at their own pace, and no one's going to save you but yourself.* I took a deep breath, the crisp mountain air filling my lungs, a sharp contrast to the stale taste of fear in my mouth. *I can do this. I have to do this.*

With newfound resolve, I took a step forward, focusing on the path ahead. Then, the final challenge – a ridiculous open passage between rocks, spiky platforms my only footholds. Seriously, how was this even possible? After a moment to calm the panic, I focused, projecting my next few steps, one at a time.

I charged forward, ran like a kid chasing an ice cream truck, no time for fear, no thought but to make it.

I leaped onto the final platform, legs wobbly, heart still thundering. I MADE IT! Relief washed over me, stronger than any wave. That wasn't just about conquering a cliff. It was like all those doubts, all the times I told myself "I can't"... I just proved myself wrong.

A few more steps, and I caught up to Tony, soaking in the fresh air and the insane view. Turns out, going down was way easier – our brains are funny that way. It took a while for my legs to stop shaking, but the path from here seemed manageable. I looked out at the whole of El Nido, my stress vanishing with the breathtaking view. I even spotted the yacht from our island hopping yesterday! We snapped tons of photos, my hands still a bit unsteady. It was like this experience had ripped me open, then stitched me back together – a crazy mind trip, that's for sure.

We traced our way back down, the descent a welcome relief after the adrenaline-fueled climb. The adrenaline rush faded, replaced by a quiet satisfaction. I'd faced my fears, pushed my limits, and emerged stronger on the other side.

As the day wound down, we piled back into his tricycle and headed far, far away from the main road. The anticipation grew as the bumpy ride took us further into the countryside. Suddenly, the trees parted, revealing a breathtaking expanse of creamy white sand fringed by swaying palms. In the distance, a small fishing village hummed with life. This was Nacpan Beach, and it was everything I'd imagined and more.

After that life-altering hike, brunch on the beach felt like a reward. We spread out a blanket under the shade of the rustling coconut trees and devoured our meal, the sand like silk beneath us. As we sprawled on the sand, the conversation flowed effortlessly. It turned out Tony and Josue's friendship had blossomed years ago when Tony first visited El Nido, captivated by its charm. Their bond deepened over shared adventures and a love for the island's laid-back lifestyle. Josue, with his easygoing nature and infectious laughter, reminded me of the warmth and hospitality I experienced growing up in my mom's province. It was a joy to witness their camaraderie, a testament to the connections we forge in unexpected places.

We even spent some time with them taking pictures on Nacpan Beach's shores as we absorbed the wind and breeze of the ocean, talking about anything under the sun. The contrast between Manila's chaotic energy and El Nido's tranquil rhythm was stark. Here, time seemed to slow down, allowing me to breathe and appreciate the simple joys of life. The island's unhurried pace was a balm to my city-weary soul, a gentle reminder that there was more to life than deadlines and traffic jams. Even having grown up near beaches myself, Nacpan had its own magic. It was the simple joys, a different pace of life... it sparked something in me. I spent hours exploring the shoreline, feeling the gentle waves lap at my toes, the sun warm on my skin.

As the sun began its descent, we reluctantly left Nacpan Beach behind. Back at the cottage, there was just enough time for a quick shower and packing, bathed in the warm glow of the sunset. That evening, as we flew back to Manila, the island of El Nido shrank beneath us, becoming a tiny speck in the vast ocean. A bittersweet feeling swirled inside me – excitement to get home, but a lingering longing for the island's magic.

The adventure continued, and the lessons I learned in El Nido went far beyond island hopping and rock climbing. It was about facing fears, embracing the unknown, and finding strength in unexpected places. This trip had cracked something open in me. A hunger for more, a belief that there's always another hidden cove, another peak to reach... both out there in the world and within myself. It was a change I couldn't quite define yet, but I felt it, a thrill of anticipation for whatever lay ahead. El Nido wasn't the finish line. It was the launching pad.

Chapter 13

Japanese Vision, African Dreams

October 2016

My first day in Osaka began with a predicament that had become all too familiar – I was lost again. Wandering around the station, luggage in tow, I surveyed the typical maze of signs pointing every which way except where I needed to go. A lighthearted chuckle escaped my lips. If getting turned around in Japan's transit systems was an Olympic sport, I'd take the gold medal. From Tokyo to Nagano and now Osaka, this was clearly my hidden talent.

Finally, I emerged from the underground maze, blinking in the fading daylight. Unlike my previous fumbles, finding Kaito's apartment complex was a breeze – Google Maps to the rescue! As I walked, my phone flashed. Kaito had messaged, detailing instructions about the key and the apartment number. It would be stashed in a mailbox, and the key itself would have the word "GOAL" engraved on it.

The nondescript building came into view. I saw the Family-Mart, thinking I could grab a quick snack whenever I was hungry. But first, I slipped through the glass door and noticed rows of mailboxes lining the walls. I eagerly scanned until I spied the one Kaito mentioned – slightly ajar, another welcome bit of good fortune. I retrieved the key, a small beacon of hope after a long journey. The engraved word "GOAL" gleamed in the low light.

Then came the stairs, and at first glance, my heart sank. But wait! An elevator nestled in the corner – a glorious sight! I hustled my ecstatic luggage into the lift and hit the third floor. Apartment number 306, according to Kaito's message, was written on a small note tucked under the key.

Stepping onto the third floor, I noticed the vastness of the apartment complex. Other buildings peeked above the rooftops, and an open area stretched into the distance, offering a glimpse of even more residences. A cool breeze whipped past, a sharp contrast to the station's warmth. It was time to track down my temporary haven. Keys in hand, I scanned the doors until I found 306, the perfect match, conveniently located just steps from the elevator.

I immediately went inside as a light drizzle began to fall. Wide-eyed, I took in the apartment, feeling like I'd stepped into one of those YouTube home tours. The open doorway seemed to promise a cozy respite after my long journey. I carefully maneuvered my luggage inside and slipped off my shoes, leaving them respectfully in the designated area. The hallway stretched ahead, dimly lit. I flicked on a switch, flooding the space with light.

It mirrored those videos perfectly - every surface gleamed, not a speck of dust in sight. A single, elegant vase held a solitary lily on the countertop. There was the shoe area, a separate toilet and bath, and a large mirror with a faucet above the sink. The kitchen was tiny, boasting a small fridge. So small, in fact, that I had to crouch down to open it and see inside. It was empty, making me wonder what Kaito ate – did he always dine out?

As I stood up, a faint, but distinct scent floated in the air – that familiar blend of tatami and a hint of wood, the standard Japanese apartment smell. I looked to the left. Two equal-sized rooms lay ahead, separated by a sliding door that stood slightly ajar. My curiosity pulled me towards the first room. Kaito's space, I presumed. Before exploring further, I called out to him just in case he was taking a surprise nap, but I remembered he'd mentioned he'd be at work.

Gingerly, I slid the door open an inch, just enough to see inside. Shadows cloaked the space, the curtains drawn tight. Only a sliver of light snuck through, and as if staged, the beam fell upon a single object – a garment lying amidst the clutter on the floor, just behind the whiteboard. It was just a glimpse, a shadowy form bathed in unexpected light, but the intricate floral design on the fabric left no doubt – they were panties. Oddly, they seemed strangely out of place in the otherwise messy room.

A rush of confusion and a jolt of awkwardness shot through me. Instantly, I closed the sliding door. *What am I doing, snooping around? It's his space... Everyone has secrets.* I decided to keep this discovery to myself. Still, my mind raced. *What kind of person was Kaito? Was this a clue to a hidden side of him?*

With a shake of my head, I reminded myself to respect his privacy. Everyone's entitled to their own mysteries, even those who offer you a bed for the week.

Oh well, since I'm here, why not just enjoy the moment? I proceeded to my room and spread my belongings all over the tatami floor. The room was immediately welcoming – a traditional Japanese bed, a small table and chair beside it, and the familiar hum of a Japanese aircon. In the far corner, a sliding glass window offered a standard view of the surrounding apartment complex. Nothing extraordinary, just a sea of buildings and a few cars passing by, but the promise of fresh air was enticing. I slid open the window, and a clothes-drying rack jutted out, perfect for hanging laundry.

I stepped out onto the tiny ledge and gazed at the condominium complex. An ambulance wailed in the distance, and the familiar FamilyMart jingle drifted upwards. A light drizzle had stopped, and a cool breeze ruffled my hair. I closed my eyes and took a deep breath, savoring this moment of unexpected peace. I am always grateful for these simple experiences.

Then, my stomach grumbled, a harsh contrast to the tranquility. The FamilyMart jingle echoed again – lunchtime! It was time to fuel up before my afternoon adventures.

And with that, I launched into the whirlwind of my Osaka trip. I arrived on a Tuesday and spent the next few days exploring with gusto. My tightly packed schedule within the safety of the apartment complex left no room for a single encounter with Kaito. I'd wake up late around 10 am and wouldn't stumble back to the apartment until after 9 pm, always missing him – either he was at work or already sound asleep.

Saturday morning, and the frantic energy of packing buzzed through me. My phone was in one hand, the charger hopelessly tangled in the other, as I wrestled my backpack closed. Suddenly, a knock at the door startled me. Had I been that loud?

"Raymond? Are you there?" His voice was soft, hesitant, but warm.

A wave of relief flooded through me – Kaito! "Oh, Kaito, just a moment, yes I am here! Just getting ready for today."

I slid open the door, taking him in for the first time. "Hey, Kaito, nice to finally meet you." I bowed, hoping I remembered it correctly from the YouTube video.

Slightly taller than me and slender, his glasses hinted at a studious side I hadn't expected. Despite his semi-casual work attire and the suitcase-like bag, there was an air of relaxed charm about him. He returned the bow, a slight quirk to his smile. "My pleasure. So how's your stay so far?"

"Oh, it's been fun, I really enjoyed Japan," I replied.

"That's good to hear," Kaito said, his English a little hesitant but understandable. "And by the way, if you're free tomorrow at 9 am, I can show you around Osaka. That's what I usually do with my guests every Sunday."

"Sure, I am free tomorrow. You work on a Saturday?"

"Yes, we have work on Saturday. Okay, see you tomorrow!" He turned to leave, hoisting his bag and grabbing his umbrella.

"What an interesting guy," I mumbled to myself. "Japanese are really hard-working people, huh?"

With a renewed sense of adventure, I finished packing my things for my day out.

The next morning at 9 am sharp, I opened the sliding door, ready for whatever Kaito had planned. He stood there, a small map clutched in his hand, a hint of nervousness in his usually calm demeanor. "Good morning, Raymond-san," he said, his English carefully pronounced. "Are you ready for today?" "Definitely!" I replied, excitement bubbling up. "Where are we headed first?" A shy smile spread across his face. "A special place," he replied, his eyes twinkling behind his glasses. "I think you will like it."

He led the way, and we soon found ourselves at the bustling Osaka station. The sheer number of platforms and crisscrossing train lines overwhelmed me, but Kaito seemed completely at ease. He consulted his map briefly, then confidently pointed towards a specific line. "This one," he said, a touch of pride in his voice.

The train ride was filled with the rhythmic clickety-clack of the wheels against the tracks, a soothing soundtrack to the ever-changing scenery outside the window. I stole glances at Kaito, curious about the secrets he was keeping. He seemed to sense my curiosity and offered a gentle smile. "Don't worry," he said, his voice barely audible above the train's rumble. "We will have a good time today." His words, though simple, reassured me. I knew I was in good hands. We exited the station, and with a short walk, the world transformed. Gone was the gentle hum of the city. Before us stood the vibrant red gate – the entrance to the shrine.

We continued our exploration, and soon, I spotted a cluster of barrels bearing intricate Japanese symbols lining the side path.

"What are those?" I asked, curiosity piqued.

"Barrels for *sake*," Kaito replied, his pronunciation a bit hesitant. "They age it here for many years..." He trailed off, then added with a shy smile, "It's like wine, but made from rice." "Souka (*I see*)," I murmured, taking it all in.

As we neared the heart of the sanctum, the pebbles beneath my feet grew larger, their clatter echoing against the ancient walls. Stepping into the inner sanctum, a gray-stoned rabbit statue immediately caught my eye. Kaito glanced at it too, and we walked closer.

"You leave coins as an offering to the gods," he explained, gesturing towards a large steel offering box, "and touch the shiny marble rabbit statue for healing."

"You rub the part of the rabbit that corresponds to what you need healed," he added, his voice barely a whisper.

Their traditions felt surprisingly familiar, reminding me of my Catholic upbringing – the statues, the offerings. Yet, there was a distinct beauty in the rituals here, a quiet reverence that resonated with my own spiritual curiosity.

Finally, we reached an area adorned with countless small bags hanging from weathered beams. A small gate and a cement block filled with pebbles stood before it.

"You pick three pebbles marked with symbols," Kaito said, dipping his hand into the pebbles. He held up a placard displaying various symbols. "Then, you put them in a bag, seal it, and hang it here. They say it will make your wish come true."

"Ah, wishes for 300 yen," I chuckled to myself.

It would probably take all day to find the right pebbles, and others were struggling as well. Before leaving, we decided to try our luck with the shrine's fortunes near the exit.

Kaito grabbed an omikuji box, his eyes gleaming with anticipation. "Shake it until a stick falls out!" he instructed, demonstrating with a vigorous rattle. A numbered stick clattered out. "This tells you where to find your fortune!" he exclaimed. He eagerly scanned the numbers on the stick, his face a mixture of excitement and nervous anticipation. Then, with a triumphant grin, he unfolded the corresponding paper. "Very lucky!" he boomed, his voice filled with elation. "This is the best fortune you can get! It says incredible luck awaits you today!"

My turn came next. With a mix of nervousness and excitement, I rattled the box, the wooden slats clacking against each other. Finally, a stick tumbled out, landing with a soft thud at the bottom. Kaito helped me decipher the cryptic markings, leading me to the corresponding paper. As I unfolded it, my heart pounded in my chest. "Lucky!" I exclaimed, relief washing over me. While not as impressive as Kaito's "very lucky" fortune, it was a positive sign nonetheless, and I couldn't help but feel a surge of optimism for the rest of the day.

Afterwards, we headed out of the shrine, hunger leading the way. The aroma of various street foods filled the air, a mix of savory meats, sweet treats, and the sharp tang of spices. We decided to sample our way through the culinary landscape, starting with savory fried treats on skewers. Juicy yakitori, still sizzling from the grill, was followed by delicate tempura vegetables that practically melted in my mouth. Next up was a refreshing serving of edamame, perfectly steamed and sprinkled with a touch of salt – a simple yet satisfying snack.

But the main course was the star of the show: a sizzling okonomiyaki, a savory pancake filled with cabbage, meat, and seafood. The aroma filled the small restaurant, mingling with the chatter of customers and the rhythmic clanging of spatulas against the grill. Kaito, ever the gracious host, even let me try my hand at flipping it. It was a hilarious experience, as I struggled to maneuver the large spatula and keep the pancake intact. Despite my initial clumsiness, the okonomiyaki cooked through beautifully, and we devoured it with gusto, laughing together at my fumbling attempts.

With full bellies, we wandered into an open stadium where families picnicked on the sprawling lawn. Kids chased each other, their laughter echoing through the warm afternoon air. A friendly sports game raged inside the stadium, the cheers of the crowd a distant rumble. A giant panda mascot waddled onto the field, waving enthusiastically at the children. I couldn't resist snapping a photo – a perfect snapshot of Japanese family life.

The afternoon passed in a blur of sunshine and laughter. As dusk settled, the city lights began to twinkle, casting a magical glow over the urban landscape. Kaito suddenly pointed at an orange sports car zipping through the intersection. "I could buy one," he mused, a mischievous glint in his eye. I just chuckled along, amused by his unexpected display of ambition.

We eventually found ourselves in a narrow alleyway, a stark contrast to the earlier crowds. Locals filled the small restaurants, their voices a low hum against the backdrop of sizzling food. The mouthwatering scent of grilled meat drew us into a cozy niku shop, a Japanese barbecue haven tucked away in the alley. "I don't drink beer," I said to Kaito, "but I wouldn't mind joining you at the bar if you're going. I can always order a fruit drink, right?"

The bar was a world apart from the vibrant energy of Shinsekai. Dim lights cast long shadows across the polished wood of the counter, and the air hummed with low conversation. As Kaito and I settled onto the stools, a sense of intimacy filled the space. It felt a little like hiding in plain sight.

The bartender, a man with a neatly trimmed beard and a welcoming smile, greeted Kaito like an old friend. Their conversation flowed easily in Japanese, too fast for me to follow every word. Yet, even without translation, a shift in Kaito's demeanor was clear. Gone was the playful guide from earlier. In his place sat a man with a weight on his shoulders, the looseness of a few drinks beginning to ease it away.

Kaito ordered another round, and this time, I accepted the bartender's suggestion of a sweet, fruity concoction. The tang balanced the warmth of the unfamiliar alcohol warming my cheeks.

"You know," Kaito began slowly, a pensive frown replacing his usual grin, "I've been to some European countries. The way they drink beer there... it's so different from here."

He talked about cobbled streets in Germany, the lively crowds at English pubs, the taste of a beer he'd loved somewhere in France. It wasn't just the descriptions that painted the picture – it was the wistfulness in his voice, the slight slur of his words.

Travel stories flowed into tales of a different life, one that hinted at a purpose deeper than tourism. "I want to go back to Africa," he confessed, eyes flickering in the dim light. "I want to finish what I started there."

A mosaic of questions formed in my mind, but the answer to the most pressing one remained unspoken. What had he left unfinished on another continent? *Although he didn't elaborate, I had a feeling he was a volunteer on a mission to help others.* The bartender refilled our glasses, an unspoken gesture of support for whatever story Kaito needed to tell.

As we walked back to the apartment, the cool night air cleared my head a bit. "So, what other places have you been?" I asked Kaito, eager to hear more about his adventures.

He perked up, a familiar spark returning to his eyes. "Oh, many places! Southeast Asia, South America... even a few countries in the Middle East."

At the apartment door, I extended my hand. "Thank you, Kaito. This was... incredible."

His smile had a hint of melancholy. "Anytime," he replied warmly. "Get some rest. You have more adventures ahead tomorrow, I'm sure."

With a final wave, he disappeared down the hallway, leaving me alone in the familiar silence of our shared apartment. It was late, but sleep seemed miles away. Thoughts swirled about my first day's adventures – the temple, Shinsekai, that hilarious okonomiyaki incident. Even stronger than those memories, though, was Kaito's confession at the bar, heavy with unspoken dreams.

"I want to go back to Africa," he'd said, the dim lights casting long shadows across his face. "I want to finish what I started there."

What had he left behind? What mission remained unfinished? I closed my eyes, scenes of the day flickering behind my eyelids. The image of Kaito faded away, replaced by a vast unknown landscape – a vision of Africa, perhaps, where a piece of his purpose awaited.

Kaito's words, his unwavering determination to chase his dreams, sparked a similar yearning within me. His unfinished business in Africa was a stark reminder of my own lack of direction. My future seemed a wide-open expanse in comparison, a canvas waiting to be painted, but filled with too many possibilities. What did I want? What was my purpose?

A comforting tiredness finally enveloped me as my thoughts softened, leaving space for a silent wish for Kaito and a surge of my newfound determination. His spark of passion was contagious, igniting a flicker of hope within me that perhaps, one day, I too would find my own Africa, a place where my purpose would become clear. I may not have all the answers yet, but I knew one thing for sure: My journey was far from over.

Chapter 14

The Southern Air Temple

March 2018

My anxiety gnawed at me like the mountain fog. Did I mess up again? It was already 5:30 pm, and not a single bus in sight. Was the timetable wrong? I frantically searched Google, cross-checking it against the schedule. Everything SEEMED right, so where was the bus?

Perched high on this mountainside, the cold wind whipped through me with a vengeance. Thirty minutes passed, then 6 pm. Still no sign of the ride to the station. I sat at the bus stop, shivering, as darkness clawed its way up the slopes.

Just as I was about to lose it completely, a figure appeared – a girl joined me at the bus stop. She huddled in the corner, eyes glued to her phone. I figured she was waiting for the same bus, but she didn't acknowledge me. I didn't blame her. Nobody wanted to be stuck here with a stranger radiating anxiety and defeat.

At 6:15 pm, I couldn't take it anymore. A walk back towards the Center began, already planning the expensive Plan B – stay the night. But a stubborn voice whispered, *what if the bus came?* It felt like a ridiculous test of travel skills.

Despite the fading light, I returned to the bus stop. Another 15 minutes, I swore. Another silent prayer for a miracle. Japan this was not. Here, schedules were unreliable and miracles seemed unlikely. Oh well, another travel fail to add to the collection...right? Inside, it stung. Plans, crushed. The thought crept in — *Was this all for nothing? Was my solo adventure just a pointless escape, a distraction from the real problems I faced back home?*

The watch ticked to 6:28 pm. Resigned, I stood up to walk back to the Center. Just then...

...The sudden sound of a small car made me jump. It pulled over near the desolate bus stop where me and the girl waited. Just as I was about to give up hope, the driver stepped out and shouted, "Station! Station!"

My heart pounded. "You're going to the station?" I asked, barely above a whisper.

"Yes, yes! Going to the station, only 100 NTD!" He gestured towards both of us.

Without hesitation, I dashed towards the car, the other girl trailing behind me. We piled in, her with another foreigner in the back, me claiming the front seat. As the car finally lurched forward, a wave of relief flooded me. What just happened? Had I finally caught a break? The scenery whizzed past, a blur of unfamiliar sights. Fortune truly did favor the bold! I couldn't believe it.

But let's rewind a bit...how did I even end up stranded at a mountainside bus stop in Taiwan? The thing is, this trip wasn't even the original plan...

<Flashback Starts Here>

My journey started in Taipei, where I fueled up with brunch before heading to the main station. It was a long, winding trip — first the sleek high-speed rail, then a bus that snaked its way up the mountainside towards Fo Guang Shan. The views were fantastic, and by the time I arrived, even a fancy mall bathroom before boarding the bus felt like a hilarious, yet necessary, adventure.

Stepping onto the grounds felt like entering another world, a place where spirituality and beauty were perfectly intertwined. The main attraction – a massive temple complex – beckoned from the heart of Fo Guang Shan. But first, I wanted to explore the smaller structures dotting the landscape.

As I marveled at my surroundings, I saw monks in their orange robes walking serenely by. Their shaved heads and flowing garments were a striking sight. "This is just like Avatar: The Last Airbender!" I smiled. The realization that the cartoon drew inspiration from Eastern religions made Fo Guang Shan feel even more special. This wasn't just a beautiful place – it was a glimpse into a world of profound tradition and spirituality.

I ventured into a sprawling hall filled with vegetarian cafes and restaurants – even a Starbucks! The air buzzed with the chatter of tourists and locals alike, a mix of languages I couldn't understand. The smell of incense mingled with the aroma of freshly brewed coffee and exotic spices, creating a sensory symphony that both soothed and invigorated. The space felt like a luxurious hotel lobby, with high ceilings, gleaming chandeliers, and polished marble floors. I could have easily gotten lost in the grandeur of it all.

Onwards to what I called "The Buddha Museum!" Here, a giant, majestic Buddha sat enthroned in the center, the museum entrance is below it, flanked by towering temple halls. It was a walk I'll never forget, the path winding through manicured gardens and ornate archways. The scene was simply breathtaking.

The sight of it filled me with anticipation. The giant Buddha overlooking the terrace, the playful pagodas – it was all so visually striking, and a part of me wanted to capture those moments. But there was also a sense that this place held something deeper, something to be experienced, not just documented. Even the monk statues sparked a touch of Avatar's otherworldly beauty!

Entering the Buddha Museum, a waft of woody, floral, and earthy scents followed me inside. Large, clear signs stated "No phones or cameras allowed," and I felt an immediate sense of respect. This was a place for stillness and reverence, a stark contrast to the usual buzz of daily life. The clatter of dishes from the nearby cafe and the hushed murmurs of other visitors faded into the background as I entered the dimly lit halls.

Mr. Google's mention of 48 underground palaces intrigued me, but my immediate goal was simple: find the Golden Buddha. As I shuffled along the smooth, cool golden pathways, the sheer scale of the place hit me – the vastness explained by the supposed 48 underground levels! The maze-like corridors twisted and turned, each corner revealing a new statue or artwork. A wave of awe washed over me, mingled with a sense of disorientation. I was lost, both physically and metaphorically, in this labyrinth of faith and beauty.

Lost in this maze, a question echoed in my mind: What am I doing here? I should be in Japan, exploring bustling cities and ancient temples. Yet, fate had rerouted me to Taiwan, to this mountainside sanctuary. Was there a reason? A purpose? A part of me felt drawn to the tranquility of this place, a longing for a connection to something bigger than myself. Perhaps this was what I needed - a moment of stillness amidst the chaos of my life.

Ever since I had questioned the teachings of my own religion growing up, and after my encounter with Pat, I had become more open to exploring the teachings of other faiths. This journey, I realized, wasn't just about me anymore – it was about understanding the diverse ways people connect with the divine.

As I wandered through the halls, the serene faces of the Buddha statues seemed to watch over me, each one a silent reminder of a life lived with purpose and devotion. Their presence felt ancient, powerful, as if they held secrets of lifetimes lived before mine. What would my story be? Would I leave a mark on the world? The thought both humbled and inspired me. Perhaps this journey wasn't just about exploring a new country, but also about discovering my own dharma, my own purpose in this life.

Finally, I arrived at a spot where people removed their shoes before a final door. This had to be where the Golden Buddha resided. The smell of shoes and the like wafted by as I gave my shoes to the nearby taker. Then, the wooden sliding door opened, revealing an entirely new world.

A big Buddha statue dominated the center, bathed in a soft, golden light. Just then, two priestesses in red and white robes caught my attention, patiently gesturing me forth. In turn, they handed me two red, electronic candles – an offering for the Buddha, it seems! With no sound permitted, I traversed the floor towards the center, mindful of each step.

Reaching the statue, I gazed upon it with reverence before placing the candle as an offering. Afterwards, I turned my back. Cushions were arranged in rows for quiet meditation, and I found one off to the left. Incense swirled around me, adding a mystical quality to the air. I could feel the presence of something far beyond my understanding, like it was right in front of me, watching over me.

For twenty minutes, I let the world outside fade away... This was more than just a beautiful place – it was a space that resonated with a different kind of energy. My birthday felt profoundly right, spent in this unexpected sanctuary.

Back outside, I stood in front of the Buddha statue once more. What next? I'd seen the shrines, marveled at the monk figures... it was time for the final part of my adventure. My watch said 4 pm, leaving just enough time.

Off I went, back to the main hall of Fo Guang Shan, which took some time. I even peeked at the famous vegetarian Starbucks, but the line...yikes! My water bottle would suffice.

More walking brought me to the western area from where I came from, what they call the Great Buddha Land. First it was a long walk, traversing many passageways under the Chinese roof carved upward in red, taking so many turns. On my last turn, Suddenly, I saw them – rows upon rows of golden monk statues. Each step revealed more, until finally, I reached a wide clearing where they all converged, surrounding another majestic Buddha. My amazement was off the charts!

As I continued taking pictures here and there, at the end of the endless statues, I found stone chairs. One Asian girl sat in the far corner, and as I absorbed the view, she glanced at me. There was a hopeful glint in her eyes, a silent request for a photo in front of the majestic Buddha. I smiled and captured the moment for her, and she returned the favor. A brief conversation followed, where she mistook me for Vietnamese. "No," I grinned, "I'm Filipino!" Her laughter echoed amidst the golden statues as she went on her way. I stayed for a moment longer, savoring the unexpected connection, and a sense that I was not truly alone, even in this foreign land.

Little did I know that my path had led me to one of the highest points of the grounds. The statues encircling me formed a protective barrier against the steep drop. Below, a breathtaking tapestry of Taiwan's countryside unfolded: vibrant rice fields, charming rural architecture, stretching towards the distant horizon. The wind carried a clean, crisp chill as I inhaled deeply, savoring the serenity. This unexpected vantage point filled me with awe and gratitude.

My rerouted trip, initially filled with uncertainty, was now overflowing with blessings. This experience was incomparable, a testament to the unique beauty of every journey. A silent prayer of thanks rose in my heart - to the environment, to the statues, or perhaps to an unseen force. Whatever it was, this adventure felt miraculous. I rose from the stone chair and descended the path, back towards the maze of golden figures. I felt watched, as if something spiritual was keeping an eye on me, guiding my path.

The late afternoon light cast long shadows. Though the Buddha statues seemed identical, a sudden shift caught my eye – a distinctly feminine form, a touch of grace I hadn't noticed before. I bowed in respect, a silent farewell before continuing towards the entrance.

Twilight painted the sky in hues of orange and purple as I

whispered my final goodbyes near the gates. The car that had rescued us earlier was waiting, its engine humming a comforting tune. As I climbed in, a wave of gratitude surged through me for the unexpected kindness of the driver and my fellow passengers.

The ride back to the city was filled with comfortable silence, punctuated only by the occasional shared glance and a murmured comment about the passing scenery. Though strangers just hours before, the shared experience of uncertainty and unexpected rescue had forged a quiet bond between us. A testament to the power of human connection, even in its most understated forms.

As the car pulled into the station, I thanked the driver profusely, my gratitude a mix of relief and genuine appreciation for his kindness. I exchanged a few words with the other girl, a shy smile replacing her earlier apprehension. With a wave goodbye, I rushed towards the platform, eager to catch the next bullet train back to Taipei.

Back in Taipei, the neon lights and bustling crowds felt jarring, an unwelcome intrusion into the tranquility I'd found on that mountainside. Yet, as I collapsed onto my bed in the hostel, exhaustion washing over me, I couldn't help but smile. Fo Guang Shan had etched an unforgettable mark upon my heart, a reminder that even amidst the chaos of life, there are places of serenity and unexpected connection waiting to be discovered.

The next morning, as I sipped my coffee and planned my remaining days in Taiwan, I felt a renewed sense of purpose. I was no longer just a tourist; I was an explorer, a seeker of truth and meaning. And I knew, deep down, that this journey was far from over. Little did I know that fate had a surprise in store for me, an unexpected encounter that would unlock secrets from my past and forever change the course of my life.

Chapter 15

The Rainbow Village

In March 2018, Taichung, Taiwan, my disbelief in chance encounters was about to be hilariously challenged. Picture this: me, glued to Google Maps, desperately trying to find Rainbow Village, and *bam!* I bump into a girl on the sidewalk.

At a quick glance, she was cute, but honestly, I had bigger concerns. Like avoiding getting lost in a maze of quiet neighborhood houses. Still, I mumbled a quick "sorry" – she didn't even wince. I didn't have time for distractions and moved along.

Moments later, on a different alleyway, Google was stubbornly recalculating. I look up and – boom! There she was again, a flash of white against the weathered walls – that cap was unmistakable. For a split second, a flicker of amusement danced in her eyes before she vanished into the maze of houses.

We're both walking the same way, meandering through this tiny alleyway. The sun's starting to dip below the rooftops, and I'm getting slightly panicked. Minutes tick by, and she catches up to me, glances down at my phone for a brief moment, then overtakes me as she walks purposefully ahead.

The scent of lavender teased my nose, a delicate whisper

carried on the breeze. A flash of purple brushed my field of vision as she glided past, her voice a soft melody of unfamiliar syllables.

"That's weird," I mutter to myself. This isn't exactly a bustling metropolis; you don't just run into the same person twice in one alley, especially when you're both glued to your phones!

So, on a whim, I decide to roll the dice. Forget the directions for Google Maps for a minute – maybe she knows the way!

Rushing to catch up, I blurt out, "Hello, do you mind if I ask if you know Rainbow Village around here?"

"Yes, I'm actually going there," she replied.

Okay, score! But then, the awkwardness sets in. Should I walk with her? Should I stay behind? What if she thinks I'm a weirdo for following her through the deserted alleyway? But long shadows danced on the brick walls. The chirping of crickets filled the air, the only sound besides the occasional distant bark of a dog.

I sneaked a peek at my phone again (out of habit more than anything) and caught her eye. She arched an eyebrow playfully. "Are we there yet?" she teased, then glancing down at her phone for a second, her expression unreadable. A playful glint still lingered in her eyes, but now it was tinged with something else – curiosity? Maybe a hint of mischief?

"Uh...not exactly," I stammered, shoving my phone into my pocket. "Just, uh, admiring the local architecture." This came out way too high-pitched, and I mentally facepalmed.

She chuckled, a light, melodic sound. "Don't worry, I get it. These side streets can be confusing."

We continued walking, the silence a little less oppressive now. My brain scrambled for a conversation starter that wouldn't come across as cheesy. Finally, I blurted out, "Traveling solo is impressive! It's not something you see very often, especially for someone your age."

"It's no big deal," she said with a casual shrug. "I'm actually staying nearby with my family."

"Oh, cool! So you're Taiwanese then?" I asked, mentally kicking myself for not picking up on any accent.

"Nope," she replied with a sly smile. "I'm from Japan. My dad has a business here, so I tagged along for the vacation."

I stopped in my tracks, dumbfounded. Of all the people I could've bumped into, it had to be a Japanese girl? Here in Taiwan? The world felt incredibly small at that moment.

Snapping out of my surprise, I realized she was walking ahead. Eager to continue our conversation, I hurried to catch up. As we rounded a corner, the alleyway came to an abrupt end, swallowed by a tangle of weeds and vines. It was as if the path itself had decided to play a part in our bizarre encounter.

No time to lose, we split up to inspect the vicinity. She goes to the left of the street and I go to the right.

Heart pounding, I push through the thick undergrowth and stumble into a small clearing. A path cuts through the tall grass, leading to another street. I called her over, my voice breathless with hope.

From afar, I saw a burst of color – vibrant, chaotic, unmistakable. Could this be it? The wetlands stretched between us and our goal, a muddy obstacle course, dotted with pools of murky brown water.

Her eyes widened. "What are we going to do?"

"Do we have a choice?" I grinned. Without waiting for her answer, I took off, dodging and weaving through the mud. She followed, laughter echoing behind me as we evaded muddy puddles and searched for solid ground.

It's like we agreed to be children again, running amok across the grassy wetland. The squish of the mud, the scent of the earth – it was pure, reckless joy.

When we reached the finish line, panting and mud-splattered, we both gasped, "Whoa, that was fun!"

Turning to face our prize, we were speechless. Finally, it was here! The Rainbow Village exploded before our eyes, a symphony of color. Sun-bleached blues swirled into fiery oranges, lime greens danced with bubblegum pinks, and deep purples collided with vibrant yellows. Every house, every wall, every inch of concrete was a canvas for Huang Yong-Fu's wild imagination. We grinned at each other. What are we waiting for? Let's go!

We explored the village, our cameras clicking away, capturing the explosion of color and whimsy. Every corner revealed a new surprise – a grinning cat, a swirling dragon, a kaleidoscope of flowers. We were like kids in a candy store, wide-eyed and giddy with delight.

Eventually, we found ourselves in the center of the village. As I gazed around, a middle-aged Taiwanese man materialized beside us, a wide smile on his face. He'd been sitting in the corner, as though waiting for our arrival. "Photo? Photo?" he chirped, gesturing at us.

Almost in a trance, I handed him my camera. He gently pushed me towards the center mural, its vibrant colors swirling around me. *What? I didn't sign up for this!* A wave of panic flooded through me. Being the center of attention was my worst nightmare! Everyone was staring!

I caught a glimpse of the girl, already mesmerized by the man's enthusiasm. With a sigh of resignation, I found myself drawn into the impromptu photoshoot. I just followed her lead, managing a weak smile as the man barked instructions. 1. 2. 3. "Say cheese!", and "Another one". "There you go!"

He gave my camera back, and we stumbled away, a little dazed. This definitely wasn't in the plan, but hey, at least we had some hilarious photos to remember it by.

In one of the narrow alleys, we stumbled upon a small child posing for a photoshoot with her parents. They were so focused, they didn't even notice us as we passed by.

"Kawaii," I muttered under my breath, the Japanese word for 'cute' slipping out without thinking.

The girl beside me froze, her cheeks turning bright red. *Oops.*

Did she realize? I hadn't meant to let on that I understood Japanese, at least a bit.

Trying to play it cool, we pressed deeper into the village, snapping our own photos. As the last light faded, the crickets began their evening chorus, a vibrant soundtrack to the explosion of color around us.

"Did you know that only one person painted this whole village?" she said, her voice filled with awe. "It used to be an old military camp, back in the war days. It's crazy to think that just one man's vision and creativity saved it from being torn down."

"Yeah," I agreed, nodding in amazement. "It's a beautiful place. It's really inspiring how one person's art can have such a huge impact."

"Definitely a story worth sharing," I said, thinking about my own blog and the power of storytelling.

A comfortable silence settled between us as we continued our walk, the colorful murals a blur in the fading light. The scent of night-blooming jasmine filled the air, a sweet contrast to the day's earthy aromas. The sound of laughter and music drifted from a nearby bar, a reminder of the vibrant energy that pulsed through this city even after dark.

"I'm hungry," she said, breaking the silence. "Are you up for some dinner?"

"Definitely," I replied, my stomach rumbling in agreement. "I'm not very familiar with the food here. Maybe you could recommend a good spot? You know, since you speak Cantonese..."

A playful smirk spread across her face. "Let's just say my Cantonese is a work in progress," she said, a hint of mischief in her eyes. "But I know a great noodle place nearby. Follow me!"

We dashed through the darkening alleys, the cool evening air a welcome relief after the day's heat. Her steps were quick and confident, and I had to hustle to keep up.

The aroma of star anise and ginger drew us into a hole-in-the-wall noodle shop, its windows fogged from the steam rising from countless bowls. Inside, the air buzzed with the chatter of locals, the rhythmic clack of chopsticks on porcelain, and the sizzle of dumplings hitting hot oil. We squeezed into a small corner table, our knees bumping as we settled in.

The conversation flowed easily as we devoured steaming bowls of Taiwanese beef noodles. Then the waitress appeared, bearing what looked like two cooked eggs. I stared blankly. Had she ordered these? A mischievous glint appeared in my eye as I glanced at her.

"What are those?" I asked innocently, feigning ignorance.

She chuckled, a hint of amusement in her eyes. "They're boiled eggs. It's a common topping for noodles here. Don't you like them? They're really good! They add a nice savory flavor and a bit of texture to the noodles. You can crack it open and crumble it over your soup, or you can just eat it on its own after you finish your noodles."

With a playful smile, she launched into a mini-tutorial on the art of the noodle egg, becoming a professor of yolky lore. She explained the different textures based on cook time, her voice taking on a mock-serious tone that made me laugh. A soft-boiled egg, she explained, would provide a burst of creamy richness, while a hard-boiled egg offered a more substantial, protein-packed bite. I couldn't resist capturing her in this moment, enthusiasm radiating from her as she lectured, so I snapped a few photos and a short video, hoping to document her adorable professorial persona.

Feeling lighthearted, we moved on to other topics: Taiwan, her father's business, and her impressions of the country. Taiwan seemed as exotic and exciting to her as Japan was to me. We discovered a shared love for exploring hidden gems and the thrill of getting lost (in a good way) in new places. This connection made the conversation flow effortlessly, and the way she asked questions at my sharings, the way her eyes lit up when she talked about her travels, the way we effortlessly navigated the bustling night of Taichung – everything about her drew me in. I found myself wanting to know more, to spend every waking moment with her, to unravel the mysteries hidden beneath her infectious smile.

"Have you seen much of Taichung yet?" I asked, fishing for ideas for my remaining days in the city.

"A bit," she replied, twirling a strand of noodles around her chopsticks. "I've been to the National Museum of Natural Science, and of course, I couldn't miss Rainbow Village. It's amazing what one person's art can do, isn't it?"

"Absolutely," I agreed. "It's inspiring, actually. Did you know it was almost demolished?"

Her eyes widened in surprise. "No way! Really?"

"Yeah, it was a former military dependents' village," I explained, my voice filled with the excitement of a newfound google expert. "It was slated to be torn down, but this one veteran named Huang Yong-Fu started painting the houses to save them. And it worked! People fell in love with his artwork, and now it's a tourist attraction."

She leaned in, her eyes sparkling with interest. "That's incredible. It's like a fairy tale."

A blush crept up my neck. "Thank you," I stammered, feeling a warmth spread through me that had nothing to do with the restaurant lights. The warm glow of the restaurant lights cast soft shadows, highlighting her features. Her delicate frame seemed out of place amidst the bustle of the noodle shop, yet she carried herself with an air of quiet confidence. Her porcelain skin seemed to glow in the dim light, and her smile, a gentle curve against her lips, was the most adorable thing I'd seen all day. She had an infectious laugh, and her eyes sparkled with curiosity and intelligence. A strange warmth bloomed in my chest, and I realized – I was completely smitten.

Suddenly, the clatter of my spoon hitting the floor shattered the moment. We both lunged under the table in unison, a silent comedy routine playing out beneath the worn wooden surface.

Our heads bumped with a soft "thunk," and I emerged to find her already stifling a laugh, her eyes sparkling with mischief.

"I got the spoon first!" I exclaimed, a grin spreading across my face.

As we emerged from under the table, smiles lingering on our faces, I fumbled for my phone. "Excuse me," I stammered, a blush creeping up my neck. "I need to use the bathroom."

"Go ahead," she chirped. "Take your time."

I retreated to the tiny bathroom, staring at my reflection in the cracked mirror. What was wrong with me? My heart pounded erratically, and a goofy grin wouldn't leave my face. This unfamiliar feeling swirled inside me – like a cauldron of melted chocolate, overly sweet and decidedly not something I usually craved. Why was I even thinking of chocolate?

Glancing at my watch, my heart skipped a beat. *7:50 pm!* The last train to Taipei was at 9 pm!

Charging out of the bathroom, I nearly knocked over a surprised waitress.

"What happened?" she asked, a puzzled smile on her face.

"Oh no!" I blurted out. "I totally forgot– the last train is at 9pm! I have to run!"

"I see," she said calmly, stirring the last dregs of soup. "Well, let me finish, and we can walk back outside."

A surge of adrenaline coursed through me as we hurriedly exchanged social media accounts and raced out of the noodle shop. This was the moment I learned her name: Kaya. It suited her perfectly. A flicker of disappointment lingered – the evening had ended too quickly. But there was a flicker of anticipation too – I had her contact information now, a lifeline to a new connection.

"I will meet you again in Japan someday..." I said tentatively, my heart pounding with hope.

"Heh, sure. Just let me know," she replied, a hint of amusement in her voice.

As our paths diverged, she headed back to her local accommodation, and I raced to the bus station, a desperate hope fueling my steps. Had I remembered the time correctly? Every second ticked by with agonizing slowness as I willed the bus to appear.

Finally, at 8 pm, I found myself under a flickering streetlight, fingers crossed, eyes scanning the darkened road. A flicker of movement – headlights rounding the corner, the bus lumbering towards me. Relief and fatigue battled within me.

My phone buzzed – Kaya had added me! A smile threatened to break across my face as we exchanged messages, sharing tidbits of our lives and promising to stay in touch. Time seemed to blur as I typed, my fingers moving of their own accord.

My goodbyes were half-hearted. Could this connection continue, even across the distance of miles and time zones? Deep down, I desperately hoped so. Boarding the bus, I found a seat and made it back to the station in the nick of time – a stroke of luck considering the train to Taipei had been delayed. Exhaustion clung to me like a second skin as I finally settled into a seat on the train.

As we parted ways that night, I couldn't shake the feeling that this unexpected encounter had been more than just a chance meeting. It was a spark of hope, a reminder that trust, once broken, could be rebuilt. Kaya's genuine warmth and kindness had chipped away at the walls I had built around my heart, and for the first time in a long time, I felt a glimmer of trust in another person.

In my hostel, I collapsed on my bed, the events of the day replaying in my head. To be honest, these unfamiliar feelings were overwhelming. It felt like a fever dream – stars, trains, laughter, and that warmth that lingered even now. Was I really coming down with something?

The answer came with a wave of nausea and a shivering chill. I curled into a ball beneath the covers, trying to ignore the throbbing in my head and the growing sense of disorientation. As I drifted into a fevered sleep, my thoughts clung to Kaya and the strange connection we'd formed. *"To be honest, I don't know what's happening with me. It's the first time that I felt like this. I feel like I have a fever of some sort, that I am floating in the clouds, counting the starry skies, waiting for the land of the rising sun, like a blazing daydream."*

The next morning, I woke up hoping the strange symptoms had vanished. A quick glance in the mirror dashed those hopes. My eyes were bloodshot, and my skin had a sickly pallor. That's when it hit me: I actually had a fever.

"Ahhhh, where did I get this?!!"

Chapter 16

Whiteout

March 2019

The first snowflake landed on my window like a star fallen from the sky, a teasing glimpse of the winter wonderland that awaited. I was on the train to Sapporo, heading north towards Niseko, where Japan's legendary powder snow promised an unforgettable adventure. My desire to witness both snow and *Sakura* seasons during a single trip stemmed from my belief that it would provide a unique and extraordinary experience.

Outside, the snowscape gradually smoothed out, the once-jagged drifts blending into a seamless white canvas. The rhythmic clickety-clack of the train wheels lulled me into a trance.

"Ladies and gentlemen, we're approaching the underwater tunnel connecting us to Hakodate," a voice announced over the intercom, jolting me from my reverie.

The world went dark. Outside my window, the vibrant landscape vanished, swallowed by a strange, inky blackness. A faint fluorescent hum filled the tunnel, the only sound competing with the rhythmic thrum of the train. Pressure built in my ears, a subtle tingling sensation reminding me of the immense weight of the sea above.

How long had I been suspended in this strange darkness? Minutes? Hours? Just when I started to feel a creeping sense of unease, a flicker of light appeared in the distance. It grew steadily brighter, a beacon guiding us out of the watery abyss.

Then, with a jolt, we burst into sunlight. I squinted against the sudden brightness as my phone chirped, the signal miraculously restored. Peeking out the window, I gasped – a blanket of pristine white stretched as far as the eye could see. With each passing mile, the snow deepened, a breathtaking canvas unfolding before me. It felt magical, a new world revealed after the tunnel's transformative darkness. The rest of the journey was painted in shades of white and wonder.

After spending a few days exploring the vibrant city of Sapporo, it was time. Niseko, the powder snow capital of the region, was calling. The city emerged from the darkness, a vibrant tapestry of neon signs reflecting off the snow-covered streets. J-pop tunes drifted from storefronts, mingling with the crunch of my boots on the icy pavement. When I finally arrived, a thrill shot through me. Night cloaked the resort, but towering ski lifts cut through the darkness like lighthouses, guiding adventurous souls. It was a force I could almost taste in the wind, an echo of the mountains.

I messaged my Airbnb host, Shingo, to let him know I had arrived. Luckily, his place was nearby. Ten minutes later, his black car pulled up, and he stepped out with a friendly smile. "Are you Raymond?"

"Yes, I am," I replied, relieved to have finally arrived. Introductions were a fumbling mix of English and my broken Japanese, but his warmth shone through. As we drove, we got acquainted. Upon arriving at his cute, cozy home, we signed the usual terms, and they had a check-in process where I had to provide my passport – standard procedure, but thrilling after such a long journey.

Afterwards, his wife, with her graceful movements and gentle smile, glided through the guesthouse like a whisper of silk. She greeted me warmly and showed me around. My room was upstairs, shared with four other guests, mostly Japanese. A young Japanese woman with bright red cheeks led me through the maze of converted rooms – bathroom, dining hall, and the heart of the place: a cozy lounge with sprawling windows overlooking the snow-covered yard. I sank into the plush carpet, the warmth of the crackling fire a welcome contrast to the smooth, cool wood of the exposed beams. On a side table, a collection of miniature Zen gardens and colorful kendamas tempted me to play. Weariness finally claiming me, I slept soundly amidst the quiet of the guesthouse.

The next morning, I woke up earlier than everyone else, the crisp mountain air a welcome change from the stuffiness of the dorm room. I hurriedly packed my bag, fidgeting with my gear, barely able to contain a grin. I recalled Shingo telling me to be ready at 8 am for the pickup to the snowfield. As I peeked out my room window, the first rays of sunlight glinted off the pristine snow, painting the landscape in a breathtaking palette of white and gold.

I went downstairs to the lounge, where Shingo's wife was preparing breakfast. "Kindly please wait for the breakfast, onegaishimasu," she said in soft Japanese. "Hai so desune," I smiled back, then settled at my chosen table. Moments later, she emerged from the kitchen, carrying a tray laden with colorful bowls. It was a typical Japanese breakfast spread, each dish displayed like a miniature artwork on its own porcelain plate. Rice, gleaming and perfectly cooked. Soup, its aroma savory and inviting. An array of small plates and saucers, each promising a different flavor experience. The breakfast tray was a kaleidoscope of colors and textures: glistening white rice, steaming miso soup, and an array of tiny dishes each holding a different jewel-toned delight. It looked too beautiful to eat, like a miniature art exhibit on a porcelain canvas.

As I savored the first bite, I felt her gaze linger from the kitchen doorway. Did she secretly want feedback? Was I doing it right? I caught her eye and gave an enthusiastic "Oishi!" A warmth spread across her face.

When I was about to finish my food, I heard another footstep that came from the door. It was Shingo, his familiar black beanie perched on his head. A puff of cold air followed him in as he entered the room. "Ohayo gozaimasu, Raymond-san," he greeted with a smile. "Be ready in a few minutes, we're about to head out." He moved with a practiced ease, gathering his things and checking his gear. A quick glance outside the window revealed a bluebird sky – perfect conditions for a day on the slopes.

I dashed through the door, Shingo's black car a fading speck against the snow. As we drove, Shingo told me about how he and his wife had grown tired of the hustle and bustle of Tokyo and longed for a simpler life surrounded by nature. "Niseko called to us," he explained with a faraway look in his eyes.

Soon, a sprawling warehouse and a snowy landscape filled my vision. Shingo dropped me off, a warm smile on his face. "Enjoy your stay, Raymond-san!"

He waved goodbye as I stepped out into the snowy paradise, the crunch of fresh powder beneath my boots a symphony of excitement. This was it – the start of my own Niseko adventure.

The scene unfurled like a movie set. Gondola cables hummed overhead, skiers whooshed past in a blur of color, and the skating rink shimmered with laughter. I inhaled the sharp, sweet air, my lungs burning with the cold. A giant warehouse loomed ahead, its snow-laden roof promising untold possibilities. This was the heart of it all.

Inside, voices bounced off the high ceilings, mingling with the tang of hot chocolate and the damp scent of drying gear. But as I scanned the rental counter and the lockers, a pang of loneliness hit. A sea of unfamiliar faces, all rosy-cheeked and bundled in colorful gear, surrounded me. *Was I the only Filipino here?*

Just then, a mother's voice, rapid-fire Tagalog. Two grinning boys wrestled into ski boots nearby. Relief flooded through me, followed by a wave of gratitude. I wasn't alone after all.

"You'll need a helmet too," the mother said, her gaze falling on my bare head. Gratitude warmed me more than any fleece jacket as I followed her advice.

Back outside, helmet strapped on, I fumbled for my phone. Was it time to meet Astrid? A flicker of blonde caught my eye. Could that be...?

Suddenly, laughter burst forth, a joyful cascade that echoed through the crisp mountain air, a melody that chased away any lingering doubts. A tall woman with sun-streaked hair swirled towards me. "Raymond?" Her smile was like a ray of sunshine cutting through the biting wind. The corners of my own mouth twitched in response, and a laugh bubbled up from somewhere deep inside. "I saw you earlier! Let's do this!" Before I could reply, she was striding off, a blur of energy against the snowy backdrop.

As I hurried to keep up, a wave of relief flooded through me. The advice, the familiar voices — these were small kindnesses, reminders that even in this vast white wilderness, I wasn't truly alone.

Meeting Astrid felt like encountering a kindred spirit. She patiently explained the basics of snow skating, her words sparking that childlike excitement I hadn't felt in years. Despite being a total newbie, I couldn't wait to hit the slopes.

We took it slow at first, me wobbling along while she effort-lessly swooped and glided on her snowboard. Once I found a semblance of balance, we tackled the first path, carving our way through the fresh powder. Then, it was time for the real adventure — the chairlift to the second base of the mountain.

The chairlift swayed gently, carrying us higher into the snowy sky. "So..." I began, "Couchsurfing, huh? Guess I really lucked out."

Astrid shrugged, a strand of blonde hair escaping her beanie. "Mostly curiosity," she admitted. "And a serious need to get out of my apartment." Her grin was contagious, easing any lingering nerves.

As we rode the chairlift, Astrid reminisced about her time working on a vineyard in New Zealand, her eyes sparkling with the memory of sun-drenched grapes and endless skies. "Niseko's different," she said, "but the mountains have a way of making you feel small and alive at the same time, don't they?"

Her words resonated with me. I gazed out at the vast expanse of snow, the trees dwarfed by the towering peaks. A sense of awe mingled with my lingering nerves.

"You'll be fine," Astrid assured me, her voice carrying over the wind. "Just trust your instincts and remember to breathe."

She let out a whoop of joy as we floated above the treetops. "This never gets old," she shouted, her voice filled with a childlike glee that was infectious.

At the second base, the crisp air hit me like a jolt of adrenaline. We were higher now, the view even more breathtaking. I tightened my grip on the snowskate paddles, a mix of exhilaration and fear coursing through me. Astrid, ever the pro, carved graceful turns ahead. I struggled to keep up, my balance precarious, but the thrill of gliding through fresh powder was undeniable.

A gust of wind nearly knocked me off my feet, but Astrid reached out a steady hand, a reassuring smile on her face. "Easy there, speed racer," she teased. "We'll get you there."

We reached the next ride, a gondola this time, its violet cabin a bright spot against the blinding white landscape. As we ascended towards the mountaintop, I peered out the window, my heart pounding with anticipation. But as we reached the peak, the wind howled, and snowflakes whipped past the windows like tiny bullets. The slope below was steeper than I had imagined – a sheer drop that made my stomach lurch.

"Whoa, this is... intense," I stammered, my voice a mere whisper against the howling wind.

Astrid threw back her head and laughed, a sound as bright and clear as a bell. "Don't worry, you've got this! Meet me at the snow café in an hour, yeah? A hot chocolate should warm you up." Her confidence was infectious, but a knot of fear still twisted in my gut.

As Astrid strapped on her snowboard, she paused, a playful grin on her face. "Hey, have you ever built a snowman before?"

The unexpected question caught me off guard. "Uh, no. Not in real life, anyway," I admitted, a wave of childhood longing washing over me.

"Well, then," she said, her eyes twinkling, "let's fix that!"

Laughing, we rolled snowballs, transforming the pristine white into a lopsided Mr. Snowman. An orange plastic bottle became his nose, twigs his arms. I even sacrificed my scarf, adding a touch of personality to our creation. It was a ridiculous, childlike moment, but it filled me with a warmth that melted away the earlier fear. Astrid snapped a few photos of me, my goofy grin a stark contrast to the dramatic backdrop of the swirling blizzard.

"This is awesome!" I shouted, my voice barely audible against the howling wind.

After a final farewell to our faraway snowman, Astrid strapped on her board and disappeared down the slope in a flurry of snow. I watched her go, a mix of admiration and relief swirling within me. It was time to face my own fears, albeit at a slightly less breakneck pace.

As I explored the area, the blizzard intensified, swirling around me like a ghostly dance. I pulled out my camera to vlog, but the wind howled so fiercely, it drowned out my voice. *Well, that's not going to work,* I thought, a wry grin tugging at my lips. Defeated, I retreated indoors, seeking refuge in the warmth of the lodge.

With renewed determination, I battled through the blizzard. A lone red cabin, smoke curling from its chimney, offered a beacon of warmth. Exhaustion gnawed at me, but I pushed on, finally collapsing against the cabin's rough wooden door with a sigh of relief.

Inside, the crackle of the fireplace thawed my frozen limbs as I gratefully sank into a plush armchair. The cozy atmosphere was a stark contrast to the wild storm raging outside. I spent a blissful thirty minutes inside, savoring the warmth and the scent of burning wood. But eventually, duty called. With a touch of regret, I left the warmth of the cabin, my gaze falling on Mr. Snowman, still standing watch over the blizzard-swept summit. *We'll meet again, my friend,* I thought with a chuckle.

I approached the violet gondola, its bright color a welcome sight against the monochromatic landscape. *Time to meet Astrid at the café,* I reminded myself, a nervous flutter rising in my stomach. The gondola ride down was a visual feast. All around me, Niseko stretched into infinity, a canvas of pristine white. I felt a profound sense of awe, mixed with a twinge of vulnerability. *This place holds power,* I thought, *both beautiful and terrifying.* It was a reminder that I was just one tiny figure in a vast, indifferent world.

Stepping out of the gondola, I rushed to our meeting spot, but Astrid was nowhere to be found. Minutes ticked by, and a knot of worry tightened in my stomach.

Where could she be? I wondered, scanning the crowd for a flash of her blonde hair.

Not wanting to miss her, I decided to explore the rest of the resort. As I wandered, a secluded practice slope caught my eye – skiers of all levels were gliding down the gentle incline, their laughter echoing in the crisp mountain air. A spark of mischief ignited within me. *Hey, how hard could it be?*

The snow escalator looked deceptively easy. *Step on, glide to the top. No problem,* I thought, brimming with false confidence.

Except... I didn't see that dip in the snow. Suddenly, my legs were doing the splits, skis flying in opposite directions. A sharp pain shot through my right knee.

"Ow! A little help here?" I yelled, my voice barely a squeak against the wind. With a jolt, the escalator whirred to a stop. A stern-faced instructor materialized, a flurry of Japanese words swirling around my embarrassed face. I fumbled for my translator app. All I caught was "lessons required...no unauthorized persons..."

Slinking away with a bruised ego, I spotted Astrid striding towards me, her blonde hair a beacon amidst the snowy chaos. Her grin was infectious.

"Ready for the real deal?" she asked, her eyes sparkling with excitement.

I nodded, my bravado masking the fear that still lingered.

We decided to head back down to the base level of the ski resort. The only way down was a much steeper route, and I wasn't sure I could handle it. Astrid assured me it would be fine, but my feet were already shaking with nerves. *I imagined everyone else taking off smoothly, carving effortless turns. If I didn't get the hang of this, I'd end up tumbling headfirst into an unguarded canyon!* The mountain felt untamed, and a surge of fear gripped me.

We counted down and took off. My heart pounded as if it would burst from my chest. As the slope steepened, my legs turned to rubber. All I could focus on was turning, turning. It was working, but barely — each swerve felt like a last-ditch effort against gravity's relentless pull. The wind whipped past, stealing my breath, tears streaming sideways from my eyes. My knees screamed in protest, the muscles in my thighs threatening to give out.

And then the speed became terrifying. Below, a blur of figures moved like ants. My feet trembled uncontrollably, as if they belonged to someone else. I was a runaway missile hurtling towards... towards... a small child! Bright blue jacket against the white chaos. *Time fractured — the child wasn't moving, just staring up the mountain.*

Instinct took over. *There was no time for brakes, no time for anything. Just a primal need to protect, to not cause harm.* All the lessons, all the technique melted away. *I had to fall.*

The impact was a shock, a silencing of the world. And then...

cold. So much cold, seeping under my jacket, my boots, the blessed helmet. For a moment, the only sound was my ragged breath. Then, a flurry of snow and I think I heard Astrid's voice from afar.

"Hey! Can you move? Say something!"

I blinked, and the world slowly reassembled. Pain surged back as I tried to sit up. But I was alive. *The child... I hadn't seen...*

A wave of relief surged through me. I must have missed them entirely. *As I closed my eyes, I knew for a moment that time halted as I feel the miniscule cold breeze entering underneath my cheeks. Few seconds later, I found myself buried, head first in the snow. Phew, I am still alive. Good thing the Filipina mom told me to rent a helmet, or else I could have found myself with a broken neck.*

I noticed one of my right skis was thrown a few feet in front of me. The impact must have been very strong. As I was planning to get the ski, Astrid materialized beside me. She removed her helmet and screamed,

"Hey are you okay? I saw you head first in the snow, I thought you're a goner. "

"You will know if you have a broken leg right?" I asked hesitantly.

"Yes of course, you won't have the chance to walk or even stand," she replied.

"I guess that's another lucky accident for me," I grinned.

Since we were near the starting point, we decided to just walk on our snowy boots.

"You were amazing back then, you didn't flinch and your speed was phenomenal! I couldn't even catch up with you," she said. "Did you purposely do the brakes because of someone?"

"Yeah, I didn't want anyone to get hurt because of me."

"Ah, I see, so it makes sense why you ended up head first in the snow," she chuckled.

"I wouldn't say I am 100% okay, there's a bit of pain in my legs, must be a small ligament tear, but I'm glad it didn't tear apart or else my adventure would have halted here in Hokkaido."

We came back to the same starting warehouse and gave back the snow equipment I borrowed earlier.

We went to the 2nd-floor canteen to have a warm drink in one of Japan's high-tech vending machines. Hot & Cold drinks for your preference.

"Whoa, that's an experience I won't soon forget," I said, sipping on a steaming hot chocolate.

"Heh, for sure, you don't see someone flying every day," Astrid chuckled, warming her hands around a cup of coffee.

"I remember! Do you know if this place is near here?" I showed her a photo of a snowy Japanese village.

"From the looks of it, it's on the other side of this mountain. It's gonna be a long walk before we even reach that place. With your current situation, you might need to slow down."

"Oh well, there's always gonna be next time."

"Yeah, take a rest with your feet for now, you can always visit the place in the future."

Sipping hot chocolate in the warmth of the second-floor canteen, I felt a deep sense of gratitude. The snow-dusted peaks of Niseko glittered in the afternoon sun, silent witnesses to my adventure. I thought back to the fear that had gripped me at the summit, the exhilaration of gliding through fresh powder, and the bone-jarring impact that had briefly silenced the world. I remembered the warmth of the cabin, the laughter shared with Astrid, and the unexpected kindness of strangers. Niseko had been a symphony of contrasts: fear and joy, pain and laughter, isolation and connection. It was a place that had tested me, humbled me, and ultimately reminded me of the indomitable spirit that resides within us all. I knew that this experience, with its bruises and laughter, would forever hold a special place in my heart, a reminder that even in the face of fear, there is always beauty to be found, connections to be made, and a whole lot of fun to be had.

A few months later, a WhatsApp message from Astrid appeared on my screen, a photo of the snowy Japanese village I'd longed to visit, captured through her lens. I may not have made it there myself, but seeing it through the eyes of a friend who had been there with me in Niseko filled me with a warmth that transcended distance. It reminded me of the profound connections that can blossom in the most unexpected places.

Chapter 17

Beneath the Shooting Star

March 2023

The taxi door clicked shut, and a rumble of hunger echoed the hollow feeling in my stomach. The familiar logo of the Filipino fast food chain just steps away beckoned, but I knew mere chicken couldn't compare to the excitement—and nerves—churning within me. I stepped onto the bustling sidewalk, a lone traveler in a sea of yoga mats and oversized backpacks. The sun beat down, but a shiver ran down my spine. This wasn't the beach, this wasn't my plan.

Lost in the swirling crowd, a girl's voice cut through the noise. "Wow, there's so many people!"

I glanced up to see a petite young woman with a bright green backpack, her eyes wide with a mix of excitement and apprehension. Beside her stood a tall guy with oversized glasses, a bemused smile playing on his lips.

"Hello, is this the festival assembly place?" I blurted out, hunger momentarily forgotten.

They instantly looked at me and with a chorus, "Yes".

"I'm Raymond," I offered, extending my hand.

"Maya," the girl chirped, shaking it enthusiastically.

"Leo," the guy added, a hint of a smirk playing on his lips.

And just like that, my solo adventure became a shared one. The rumbling of my stomach, now competing with a flutter of anticipation, reminded me of the fast food joint just steps away. But as I joined Maya and Leo on the curb, a strange sense of belonging began to take root. Maybe this unexpected detour was exactly what I needed.

"First time?" Leo asked, glancing at me with a touch of amusement in his eyes. I gave a tentative nod. His question hung in the air as Maya shot us both a curious look. "First time too," she chirped, then added with a twinkle in her eye, "You guys headed to the festival as well?"

The word "festival" still felt new, strange. Fire dancers, yoga, people from all corners of the globe – it wasn't the beach, but maybe it was exactly the kind of unexpected adventure I needed after all. A quick glance around revealed other foreigners milling about amidst the early morning locals. This crowd held a different kind of energy, a palpable sense of belonging.

Maya and Leo both mentioned Instagram as their source of discovery for the festival. When they turned to me, I couldn't help but chuckle. "You won't believe it. Facebook," I admitted. "Actually, total birthday impulse decision. Funny story... this whole trip wasn't the original plan. Change of plans due to, uh... health issues."

Their eyes widened with curiosity. "Change of plans?" Maya prompted, her voice gentle.

I took a sip of my green matcha tea, trying to find the right words. "Yeah, it was supposed to be an epic birthday dive trip. Imagine this... a beach in Batangas, a wetsuit, the whole scuba diving experience. That was the plan." A wistful smile tugged at my lips. "But sometimes, life throws you a curveball... an ulcer flare-up."

A flicker of surprise crossed Leo's face, followed by a look of understanding. Maya's gaze softened. "Ouch. That sounds rough, especially right before your birthday. I've always wanted to try scuba diving, though!"

Her comment sparked a new thread of conversation. "Me too," Leo chimed in. "Where in Batangas were you going? What kind of reefs is it known for?"

Instead of dwelling on the missed opportunity, I found myself describing the dive sites I'd researched. The promise of vibrant reefs, the possibility of sea turtles... Sharing what I'd planned made the experience feel a little less unrealized.

"It's definitely on my bucket list still," I admitted. "But for now, I'm trading scuba gear for yoga mats, and that's okay." A glance around the growing crowd made me smile. "This festival looks like a whole different kind of awesome."

Maya's enthusiasm was contagious. "Speaking of awesome, any of you know what the fire dancing situation is like here? First-timer needs details!"

Leo grinned. "They did mention some big finale on the website... maybe it has something to do with that?"

I took another sip of my matcha, the slight bitterness a grounding force against the anticipation bubbling within me. "Well, there's only one way to find out. Festival newbies unite!"

The Journey Begins

The bus finally lumbered to life after a thirty-minute wait, its engine roaring in protest as it pulled away from the station. Inside, it was a different story. Every seat was full, so I ended up on the floor, feeling the hot metal vibrate through my jeans. "So much for my birthday, right? Sitting on the floor," I muttered, trying to make light of the situation.

Leo, who was perched on a slightly elevated step, chuckled. "At least you have the floor, my friend. I'm practically hanging on for dear life!"

At first, the disappointment gnawed at me. But then, I closed my eyes and took a deep breath, letting the rhythm of the bus lull me into a meditative state. The rumble of the engine became a mantra, the cramped space a cocoon. I drifted off to sleep, embracing the unexpected detour.

Hillside Haven

Four hours and one numb leg later, we finally arrived. My stomach rumbled in protest, reminding me I hadn't had a proper meal since breakfast. Thankfully, the festival was all about nourishment. I tracked down the food stalls, the tantalizing smell of spices guiding my way. Plant-based delights filled the trays - crispy vegan *longganisa*, smoky "corned beef" hash, all bursting with surprising flavor, a testament to the creativity of the vegan chefs.

The festival grounds sprawled over a hillside, a chaotic maze of activity. While everyone else dispersed, buzzing with a mix of excitement and confusion, I found myself wandering, seeking a moment of tranquility amidst the bustle.

I saw Maya and Leo again, now with a few new friends. They introduced me to Vito, the quiet one with a spark of mischief in his eyes, and Joaquin, who exuded a calm, grounded energy. We chatted for a bit, then set up our tents for the night before separating to explore the festival on our own.

I stumbled upon a scenic spot overlooking the mountains. Vito was already there, quietly observing the view. I handed him my camera to take a photo, and he nodded, the shutter clicking softly.

As we stood there, a flash of color caught my eye. Two women were setting up a makeshift stall under a nearby tree, crystals glinting in the afternoon sun, incense filling the air with a heady fragrance. I looked at Vito, and without a word, we both knew what the other was thinking. *Energy reading?* Why not? We approached the women, curiosity piqued.

The Tarot's Whispers

"Do you read energy?" I blurted out, startling the woman closest to me. Her eyes widened, then quickly regained her composure.

"I do," she replied, her voice low and calming. "If you'd like a reading..."

I hesitated. The desire for guidance warred with that voice in my head – trust your own intuition. But curiosity won out.

She gestured towards a blanket spread on the ground. "Sit. Let me see..." Her hand reached for mine, her touch surprisingly strong. A jolt of energy shot through my arm, making me shiver.

Her gaze seemed to bore into my soul. "Pink. Your aura... it's pink. A rare color for a man. Tenderness, yet..." – she paused – "a core of bright yellow. Willpower."

The words echoed strangely familiar. Was this woman the real deal? Her fingers traced my palm, her touch surprisingly gentle as a flicker of doubt surfaced. Questions bubbled up within me, about my path, my potential... but the urge for deeper connection over-whelmed them.

"Tell me more," I urged. "And about... that yellow?"

She closed her eyes for a moment, her brows furrowed in concentration. When she looked back at me, there was a new glint in her gaze. "Your kindness... it radiates outwards, a soft warmth. People are drawn to it, but some might see it as weakness." The words hit uncomfortably close to home. Hadn't my mother always warned me, 'Don't let people take advantage of your good nature'?

"But the yellow... it burns beneath the surface. Like sunlight trapped in amber. It's your drive, your determination. When you set your mind to something, nothing can hold you back." She traced the lines on my palm. "See here? This line... it speaks of ambition, but also... a touch of loneliness."

I felt a lump rise in my throat. Always the achiever, always striving... was my pursuit of success pushing others away?

She took a deep breath, her voice softening. "The pink and the yellow, they're at odds sometimes. Your task is to find balance. To use that powerful will to protect your gentle heart."

"And the cards?" I asked, needing the concreteness of the tarot to ground the whirl of emotions.

She laid out several cards with deliberate care. Flashes of imagery – a winding path, a crossroads, the image of someone shedding an old skin. "A shift is coming," she said, her voice low. "It might feel disorienting at first, but it leads to a brighter place. Trust your intuition, and don't be afraid to embrace the changes this festival might bring."

I left the energy reading feeling both empowered and unsettled. The woman's words had resonated deeply, but they also left me with a lingering sense of unease. Was my kindness truly a weakness? Could I find a way to balance my gentle heart with my ambitious spirit? These questions swirled in my mind as I made my way towards the soothing sounds of music emanating from the yoga area.

Yoga's Embrace

The yoga class was already in full swing as I arrived. I unfolded my mat and slipped into a space near the back, grateful for the anonymity it offered. The scent of incense mingled with the damp earth and exotic flora of the jungle surrounding the mountaintop festival grounds. The setting sun cast long shadows across the yoga mats, creating a mesmerizing interplay of light and darkness. The instructor's voice, a soothing balm amidst the festival's chaos, guided us through a series of poses. Each stretch, each twist, felt like wringing out the tension that had built up inside of me. The energy reading lingered at the back of my mind, the woman's words echoing alongside the beat of my own heart.

I glanced towards the front of the class and spotted Maya and Leo, their bodies moving in unison with the instructor's cues. Their presence brought a smile to my face, a reminder of the unexpected connections I had made on this journey.

The class intensified. Sun salutations flowed into warrior poses, each movement demanding strength and focus. Sweat dripped down my forehead, blurring my vision. My muscles ached, protested, but something stubborn within me pushed harder. The instructor's cues for "warrior pose" resonated with the energy reader's words. *Yellow burns beneath the surface.* Was this what she meant? Could I channel this strength, this fire, without losing my gentle nature?

With every breath, I seemed to shed another layer of doubt. My body, pushed to its limits, became a tool of self-discovery. I wasn't merely seeking answers anymore; I was forging something new, a resolve born of physical exertion. The exhaustion that swept over me as we moved into *savasana* was more than just fatigue – it was a release, a cleansing.

As I lay there, my breath finally slowing, I realized something profound. The festival had opened cracks within me, exposed hidden anxieties. But it could also be a crucible, a place to transform those fears into something stronger. Maybe this wasn't just about finding balance, but about discovering how my inner fire and gentle spirit could work together, propelling me forward.

Cacao Ceremony: A Ritual of Intention

As the last strains of sitar music faded, I rolled up my yoga mat, a sense of calm washing over me. But the energy reader's words still echoed in my mind. *Was my kindness a weakness?* It was time to explore this newfound energy, and what better place to do so than at the heart of the festival – the fabled cacao ceremony.

I'd heard whispers about this ceremony, its origins rooted in ancient rituals. The promise of connection and manifestation resonated with the raw emotions churning within me. As the sun began to dip below the horizon, we gathered in a circle. I spotted Maya and Leo seated across from me, their faces glowing in the soft candlelight.

A woman with a gentle smile and eyes filled with ancient wisdom welcomed us, sharing the stories of cacao, its use in setting powerful intentions. The woman carefully poured the steaming cacao into earthenware mugs, the rich aroma filling the air. She began a low chant, her voice a rhythmic pulse that seemed to sync with the beating of my own heart.

My heart pounded as I held the earthenware mug in my hands. Her words – "Drink with purpose, with a full heart" – became my anchor. I closed my eyes, focusing on the desire for clarity that had brought me to this festival. "Openness," I whispered, letting the intention settle deep within me. The cacao was thick, earthy, with a hint of bitterness that mirrored my own anxieties. *Would I be brave enough to truly shed those old fears?*

The music started, a pulsing rhythm that seemed to emanate from the earth itself. Something shifted within the circle. An unspoken invitation. Feet shuffled hesitantly, then bodies began to sway. I let the warmth of the cacao course through my veins, a counterpoint to the lingering self-doubt.

A Moment of Vulnerability

As the music swelled, a sudden wave of self-consciousness enveloped me. What if my awkward dance moves betrayed my inner turmoil? What if I couldn't let go, couldn't truly embrace this moment of vulnerability?

I glanced around the circle, seeking reassurance. My eyes met Vito's, and a silent understanding passed between us. A gentle smile touched his lips, as if he knew exactly what I was going through.

"What are you so scared of?" he asked, his voice a low rumble.

"Other people judging me," I admitted, surprised by my own honesty.

A gentle smile touched Vito's lips. "Hey, we all feel that way sometimes. But remember, you're not alone in this." He nudged me playfully with his elbow. "Besides, you're a good guy, Raymond. Don't let anyone tell you otherwise."

A surge of emotions pulsed through me like a riptide. Gratitude for the unexpected detour that led me here. Anxiety about the changes the energy reader had foretold. A yearning for deeper connection, for acceptance, for belonging.

I stepped into the circle. The music surged, my movements awkward at first, then finding their rhythm. Around me, bodies swayed and dipped, lost in the shared experience. We were strangers, yet connected by this raw, primal energy. It was exhilarating, liberating. Under the darkening sky, amidst the flickering lights, I felt a piece of my carefully constructed armor begin to crack.

Fire Dancing: A Symphony of Sparks

The anticipation crackled through the crowd as dusk settled over the festival. If there was one event everyone gathered for, it was the fire dancing. My pulse quickened, a primal thrill mixing with the residual warmth from the cacao ceremony. This was it – the spectacle that drew people to festivals like these, a glimpse of something ancient and mesmerizing.

As part of the ritual, a few newbies were chosen to carry torches and circle the wooden pyre, lighting the flames. Maya, who'd been standing next to me, was one of the chosen ones. Watching her carefully carry the torch, her face illuminated by the flickering light, filled me with a sense of shared excitement and anticipation.

A hush fell as the pyre blazed to life. The fire dancers emerged, their bodies silhouetted against the flames. A sense of awe enveloped me, the heat of the flames mirroring the intensity of emotions churning within me. I was mesmerized by the raw power and grace of the dancers, their movements a hypnotic dance of light and shadow. I took out my phone to capture the mesmerizing scene, snapping photos and videos, my smile growing wider with each frame as I shared the visual feast with my mates.

The fire dancing finale was an explosion of energy, a symphony of sparks and whoops from the crowd. It was a shared experience, a moment of collective wonder that transcended the boundaries of language and culture. As the last embers dwindled, the energy of the festival shifted. The rhythmic pulse of electronic music beckoned from the disco area.

Serendipitous Encounters

The festival grounds were a kaleidoscope of sights and sounds.

Vendors hawked handmade crafts and organic snacks, while musicians played a symphony of global rhythms. The air was thick with the smell of incense, exotic spices, and the sweet aroma of blooming flowers.

I found myself swept up in the creative spirit, joining the arts club and twirling around the dance floor with a blue lightsaber. The energy was infectious, and I danced until my feet ached, laughed until my sides hurt, and lost myself in the moment. But as the hours passed, a yearning for stillness began to creep in.

Feeling a pang of hunger, I took a detour to grab some dinner and found myself sharing a table with a man with an Indian accent wearing a wolf headdress, and another man with long, dark curls and sun-kissed skin.

The wolf-man introduced himself as Raj, a tech-savvy programmer with a passion for drones. The curly-haired man was Kael, a fellow Panay Island native. We shared musings about the festival and our lives, the conversation flowing easily. Raj's knowledge of drones and Kael's insights into island life opened up new worlds of possibility. It was a reminder that even amidst this chaotic celebration, genuine moments of human warmth and unexpected connections could be found.

A Streak of Light

Later that night, drawn by the solitude, I hiked back to the hilltop. Vito and Joaquin were already there, some asleep, others quietly gazing upwards. I joined them, lying back on the cool grass and letting the vastness of the cosmos consumed me.

For a moment, there was only silence, broken only by the chirping of crickets and the distant hum of the festival. I felt a sense of peace settle over me, a stark contrast to the vibrant chaos below. Then, a streak of light blazed across the darkness.

"I just saw a shooting star!" I whispered excitedly, nudging Joaquin awake.

"Huh, really? Where?" he mumbled, rubbing his eyes. "I wish I could have seen one too."

I couldn't help but smile at the magical coincidence, a feeling of awe and disbelief. A shooting star on my birthday – it felt like a sign, a cosmic wink, a reassurance that I was exactly where I was meant to be.

Reflections Under the Stars

Some of the boys eventually returned to the hilltop, and we all found ourselves watching the night sky like soul friends, connected by this shared experience. "So Raymond," Leo's voice broke through the quiet reverence, "what do you think of your first festival experience?" The faces of my new friends – Leo, Vito, Joaquin – turned towards me, expectant.

I paused, taking in their eager expressions. I'd never had this kind of experience before, where people genuinely seemed to care about what I had to say. It was a warmth that spread through my chest, a feeling of belonging that I hadn't realized I was craving.

"It's different," I admitted, searching for the right words. "Magical, even. Coming here, not knowing what to expect... it's shaken things loose, in a good way." Their smiles were warm, understanding. "Have you seen Maya?" I asked, suddenly realizing I hadn't seen her since the dance floor.

Leo shrugged. "Last I saw her, she was headed towards the main stage. You know Maya, always the life of the party."

We spent the remaining hours under the vast night sky, swapping stories, laughter echoing into the darkness. At one point, the conversation turned to astrology.

"So, what's your sign?" Joaquin asked me, his voice barely a whisper.

"I'm an Aries," I replied, feeling a bit self-conscious. "What about you guys?"

"Sagittarius," Leo chimed in. "Pisces," Vito offered softly. "Capricorn," Joaquin said.

As we discussed the traits associated with each sign, I found myself spouting off information I'd gleaned from books and online articles, feeling a bit like a walking encyclopedia of astrological knowledge. My friends listened patiently, their eyes twinkling with amusement. It was a hilarious experience, realizing how much I had absorbed about a subject I hadn't even considered myself particularly interested in before.

As the first hints of dawn began to paint the sky, a bittersweet feeling settled over me. This magical night was coming to an end, a fleeting moment of joy and connection that would soon become a cherished memory. The festival had filled my heart with light, but it also cast long shadows, reminding me of something I'd been avoiding. The shooting star, a symbol of hope and new beginnings, now seemed like a farewell, a gentle nudge towards the next chapter of my journey – a chapter I wasn't ready for.

I stayed in Manila for a few days after the festival, trying to hold onto that lightness. But the pull to go home to the province grew stronger. When I finally made the trip, Raychel greeted me at the door with her usual excitement - tail wagging, that familiar spark in her eyes.

But something felt different. She seemed tired in a way I couldn't quite name.

I told myself she was just getting older. That it was nothing.

I was wrong.

Part Three

Awakening

"Your vision will become clear only when you can look into your own heart. Who looks outside, dreams; who looks inside, awakes."

- Carl Jung

Chapter 18

Endings, Beginnings, and Everything In Between

January 11, 2023.

I'd been counting the days since the vet visit - the one where I'd nodded yes, where I'd watched her give Raychel that new 3-in-1 tablet. "It's safe," the vet had assured me, her smile warm and confident. "Much easier than the old treatment."

I'd hesitated. Something felt off. But Raychel had taken it so easily, without her usual resistance, and I'd convinced myself that was a good sign. Maybe I was just being paranoid.

The tablets were supposed to help. Instead, I'd been watching my dog die in slow motion ever since.

That morning, I'd heard something - not with my ears, but somewhere deeper. *'You've taken care of me all these years. Now it's time to take care of yourself the way you took care of me.'*

I thought it was just me being sentimental. Maybe projecting.

I didn't realize I was hearing goodbye.

The Vet Visit

Raychel, our tiny Japanese Spitz, always knew when an adventure was brewing, her excited yips and tail-chasing spins signaling the change in routine. Today's adventure was a vet visit, a rare outing from Mom's balcony fortress.

The new vet, all smiles and gentle reassurances, suggested we try a new 3-in-1 tick and flea preventative, a small, chewable tablet. I hesitated, recalling past struggles with other vets and Raychel's stubborn refusal of anything forced into her mouth. But she surprised me again, accepting the tablet with an unsettling ease. A seed of doubt was planted, but I pushed it aside, trusting the vet's expertise.

With the appointment over, we decided to make the most of our day out. Plaza Molo bustled with life, the cheerful chaos a stark contrast to the sterile clinic we'd just left. Passersby cooed over Raychel's fluffy white coat and perky ears, their admiration momentarily eclipsing my lingering anxiety. I even snapped a few photos of her by the fountain, the same spot where a painful incident with my father had occurred years ago. As I watched her pose, her tail tentatively wagging, the weight of worry lifted. Perhaps those chewable tablets weren't so bad after all?

A Night of Loss

That night seemed normal. She even gobbled down all her dog food, happy to be part of our family dinner. I headed back to my room, work looming...

Hours later, a piercing shriek ripped through the silence. It was my mother's voice, choked with panic. "Raychel! Raychel!!"

Adrenaline surged through me. I jumped from my chair and raced to the dinner area, my heart pounding in my chest. A chilling silence hung in the air as my eyes frantically searched the dimly lit space. Shadows danced ominously on the walls, the only movement in the otherwise still room. Then I saw her. Raychel lay crumpled on the floor, her small body unnaturally still.

I dropped to my knees beside her, my voice a hoarse whisper as I called her name. Her eyes, normally sparkling with mischief, were dull and lifeless. A cold dread settled over me as I gently touched her, hoping for any sign of life. But her body was limp, her warmth fading with each passing second.

My stepfather appeared beside me, his face pale with alarm. He immediately started performing CPR on Raychel, his face contorted with effort. In the midst of the chaos, he paused, looked up at me, and with a nervous chuckle said, "Never thought I'd be doing this...and getting dog saliva all over my face!" The unexpected humor in such a dire situation momentarily broke the tension, reminding me that even in the darkest of times, life can find a way to surprise us.

But the moment of levity was fleeting. Despite our desperate efforts, Raychel remained unresponsive. The weight of reality crashed down on me, crushing any lingering hope. My mom's sobs echoed through the house, a haunting melody of grief. I fumbled for my phone, my hands trembling as I dialed the vet's number. The unanswered ringing felt like an endless torture, each unanswered tone amplifying my despair.

After an eternity, Raychel finally stirred. A flicker of hope ignited in my chest, but it was quickly extinguished. Her movements were uncoordinated, her eyes glazed over, her head listing to one side. A wave of nausea hit me as the realization sank in: she wasn't okay.

We tried to convince ourselves it was just a temporary setback, a minor reaction to the medication. But deep down, I knew the truth. This wasn't a minor setback. This was the beginning of the end.

A Second Loss

I carried Raychel, her fragile body cradled in my arms, back to the familiarity of my room. Whispering words of comfort and reassurance, I settled her on the bed, hoping against hope that she would somehow bounce back. But even as I stroked her soft fur, a chilling certainty crept into my heart. This was more than a simple reaction to medication. This was something far graver.

Exhaustion weighed heavily upon me, but sleep remained a

distant dream. How could I rest while Raychel fought for her life, her every shallow breath a painful reminder of her vulnerability?

Just as a fragile peace began to settle, my mother's voice pierced through the quiet, thick with sorrow. ""To, your Aunt B... she's gone." The words hung in the air, heavy and suffocating.

My world lurched on its axis. Aunt B, a pillar of strength and love in our family, had passed away. The news sent shockwaves through me, a second devastating blow in a matter of hours. My cousins had lost a second mother, a source of unwavering support and guidance. A sense of despair engulfed me, the weight of two immense losses threatening to crush my spirit.

As I sat beside Raychel, my hand gently stroking her fur, I could hear the muted sounds of my mother's grief echoing from the living room. My stepfather's voice, a low murmur of comfort, offered little solace. "Everyone goes at some point," he said, his words hanging heavy in the air.

The coincidence of it all – Raychel's sudden illness, Aunt B's passing – felt like a cruel twist of fate. But as I looked into Raychel's dimming eyes, I knew that she needed me now more than ever. In that moment, amidst the chaos and sorrow, a fierce determination ignited within me. I would fight for Raychel, no matter the odds.

Raychel's Struggle

The next day, we returned to the vet, the air heavy with dread. The doctor's diagnosis was swift and devastating: Raychel had suffered a seizure triggered by a rare reaction to the tick and flea tablets. Her kidneys were showing signs of damage, and her age wasn't on her side. The vet's words, delivered with a somber tone, echoed in my mind: "Kidneys don't regenerate like the liver."

Guilt gnawed at me like a parasite. I had put my trust in the vet, allowed those seemingly harmless tablets to be given to Raychel, and now she was paying the price. Anger surged within me, a burning rage against the vet, the manufacturer of the tablets, even myself for not questioning the decision more thoroughly. But in that moment, I knew that anger wouldn't help Raychel. Instead, I resolved to channel my frustration into action, vowing to ask the doctor to report the incident to the drug manufacturer and ensure that other pets wouldn't suffer the same fate.

Initially, Raychel's condition seemed to improve. We embarked on a regimen of vitamins and supplements, carefully monitoring her every move. My work was put on hold as I dedicated myself to Raychel's care, following her around like a doting parent, ensuring she ate and stayed warm. For a few days, it seemed like she might recover. A glimmer of hope flickered in my heart.

Then, the rains came. Days of relentless downpour chilled the house, and despite my best efforts, Raychel caught a cold. The illness hit her weakened body hard. Her appetite waned, her energy dwindled, and her once bright eyes grew dull. The hope I had clung to so desperately began to fade.

A Difficult Decision

Days blurred into a routine of vet visits, each one a painful reminder of Raychel's dwindling health. The medication, the supplements, the vet's assurances - none of it seemed to be enough. Raychel grew weaker with each passing day, her once vibrant spirit fading like a dying ember.

Then came the morning when the vet, her face etched with a familiar sorrow, pulled me aside. "The bloodwork results are in," she said, her voice barely a whisper. "Raychel's kidney damage is severe... far beyond Stage 4. The tablets likely triggered it, and her age isn't helping."

A cold knot formed in my stomach, my worst fears confirmed. "What are her chances?" I managed to ask, my voice choked with emotion.

The vet's eyes softened with empathy. "Slim," she admitted. "We've done everything we can, but her body is shutting down."

The news hit me like a physical blow. I felt the air leave my lungs, my legs threatening to give way beneath me. The vet's words echoed in my mind, a relentless drumbeat of despair. But even in that moment of profound grief, a flicker of resolve remained. I would not give up on Raychel. Not yet.

Carrying her frail body home, IV drip in hand, a numbing acceptance settled over me. It wasn't a surrender, but a recognition of the inevitable. I knew that our time together was growing short, but I was determined to make every remaining moment count. I would shower Raychel with love, comfort, and the dignity of a peaceful passing.

A Glimmer of Hope

Back at home, I transformed our living room into a sanctuary for Raychel. A soft cushion became her bed, a salt lamp provided warmth, and her favorite toys lay scattered around her, silent witnesses to her struggle. I watched over her tirelessly, administering her medications, changing her IV drip, and coaxing her to eat. Despite the odds, her condition seemed to stabilize, offering a fragile hope that she might defy the vet's grim prognosis.

The next morning, Mom prepared to leave to witness Aunt B's casket arrival in the province. It was a poignant reminder of the double loss looming over us. As Mom said her goodbyes, Raychel, sensing the farewell, roused herself from her bed. With a wobbly determination, she stood on her unsteady legs and stumbled towards Mom, her tail barely offering a weak wag. It was as if she understood the finality of the moment, a silent goodbye between two souls deeply connected. This unexpected display of strength, a final act of love for her human companion, filled my heart with a bittersweet blend of hope and sorrow.

Later that day, a wave of emotion overwhelmed me, and I reached out to my sister overseas. My voice cracked as I tried to update her on Raychel's condition, the unspoken truth of our impending loss choking my words. "What happened?!" she asked, her voice thick with concern. "Nothing," I lied, "she's just sleeping right now." But the tears that streamed down my face betrayed my words. The nagging feeling that our time with Raychel was fleeting grew stronger with each passing moment.

Then, on January 29th, a ray of hope pierced through the gloom. Raychel, from her cozy nest in the living room, barked at me – a weak, raspy sound, but a bark nonetheless. It was the first time she had vocalized in days, and it filled me with a surge of joy.

I allowed her to move around as she pleased, her halting, unsteady steps a testament to her fighting spirit. She even managed to make a mess on the floor – a small, disgusting victory that brought a bittersweet smile to my face.

Despite the mounting workload and the looming deadline for a project at work, I kept a vigilant eye on Raychel. Every small improvement, every wag of her tail, felt like a gift. For a brief moment, it seemed like she might defy the odds and recover.

The Final Hours

But the reprieve was agonizingly short-lived. As evening approached, a chill crept into the house, a harbinger of the approaching storm. The distant rumble of thunder echoed the growing unease in my heart. Raychel shivered despite the warmth of the salt lamp. I moved her back to her cushion, changed her IV drip, and hurried to the kitchen to prepare her food.

A symphony of clanging pots and whirring blenders filled the air as I cooked dinner for the family, my mind constantly drifting back to Raychel. I was juggling multiple roles – caregiver, breadwinner, and now, a heartbroken pet owner facing the inevitable. The weight of it all felt crushing.

Suddenly, a faint sound cut through the noise. It was a whimper, a sound so unlike Raychel's usual barks that my heart stopped. I rushed back to the living room, a sense of dread washing over me.

Raychel was struggling to breathe, her tiny body wracked with tremors. Her eyes, once filled with life and mischief, were now wide with panic. The IV drip was flowing too fast, her paw swollen where the needle was inserted. My mind raced, desperately searching for a solution, but I knew there was none. This was it. The end.

I fumbled for my phone, my hands shaking as I hit record. I needed my sister, miles away, to witness this final goodbye, to share in the heartbreak that was about to unfold. The video was shaky, a blur of Raychel's labored breathing and the fading light in her eyes. But it captured the essence of the moment, the raw, unfiltered agony of losing a beloved companion.

Setting the phone aside, I knelt beside Raychel. Time seemed to distort, each agonizing second stretching into an eternity. Memories cascaded through my mind, a bittersweet torrent - the day we brought her home, a fluffy ball of energy; the countless walks in the park, her joyful leaps and playful barks; the quiet nights curled up together, her warmth a comforting warmth against my skin.

As if from a distant dream, a memory surfaced—a whispered conversation in the hush of the night, a friend sharing their own experience of loss, their voice filled with quiet wisdom: *When the end comes, put your hand on their heart, be grateful for all you shared, tell them as they slip away...*

Tears streamed down my face, hot and relentless, blurring my vision as I reached for Raychel's tiny paw. Her once-warm fur felt cool against my skin, her heartbeat a faint flutter beneath my fingertips. A sob tore through me, a raw, primal sound that echoed the shattering of my heart.

"Raychel," I choked out, my voice barely a whisper. "My sweet girl, my constant companion... thank you. Thank you for eleven years of unwavering love, of boundless joy. Forgive me... for the vet visit, for not protecting you. I should have known better."

My words tumbled out in a rush, a desperate attempt to convey a lifetime of love and gratitude in those final moments. "Thank you for choosing me, for loving me unconditionally. I will never forget you, my sweet Raychel."

With a final, desperate squeeze of her paw, I felt her life force ebb away. The tremors ceased, her labored breath stilled. The room fell silent, save for the relentless ticking of the clock. 7:45 PM. The same time as her first seizure. Was it fate? A cruel coincidence? In that agonizing moment, the questions seemed meaningless. All that mattered was the vast, empty space where my heart used to be.

A New Day, A Final Farewell

My stepfather fell silent, the weight of the situation sinking in. Without another word, he gently lifted Raychel's small body and carried her to the backyard. I turned away, unable to bear the sight of her being lowered into the earth beneath the guava tree.

The living room, once a haven of warmth and comfort, now felt cold and empty. Stained blankets, discarded IV bags, and the lingering scent of vitamins – all remnants of our desperate fight against the inevitable. Mechanically, I began to clean, the repetitive motions a way to numb the pain.

Work emails piled up, unanswered and forgotten. I knew I should log in, but my spirit felt broken. Emergency leave – it was the only option, the least I could do for myself.

As the night wore on, I scrubbed the living room until it was spotless, erasing all physical traces of Raychel's presence. It was a futile gesture, a desperate attempt to regain control in a world that suddenly felt chaotic and unpredictable. But even as I worked, I knew that nothing could erase the memories of my beloved companion. She would forever live on in my heart.

Waking up the next morning felt surreal. The house was eerily quiet, the usual pitter-patter of Raychel's paws replaced by the rhythmic *tick-tock* of the wall clock. Each tick felt like a hammer blow to my heart. A hollow ache pulsed within me, a constant reminder of the void she had left behind. I glanced towards the backyard, where the pale sunlight illuminated the guava tree under which she now rested. I couldn't bring myself to go near it, the pain of confronting her final resting place too raw and overwhelming.

"Hi Doc. Raychel's gone," I texted the vet, my fingers numb as they tapped out the words.

"Okay, sir," came the curt reply. The mundane exchange felt jarring against the backdrop of my overwhelming grief.

As I prepared to leave, my stepdad emerged, his eyes mirroring my own sorrow. "Where are you going?"

"To the vet," I replied, my voice a hollow echo. "To finish this."

He nodded silently, understanding passing between us in that shared moment of grief. The drive to the vet was a blur, my mind replaying scenes from Raychel's life in a bittersweet loop, each memory punctuated by the sharp cracks of fireworks exploding in the distance. It was a fiesta, a celebration of life, but here I was, grieving for the life that had just ended. *Life moves on, doesn't it? Even when your world stops.*

Shared Grief and Unspoken Understanding

The young vet greeted me with a look of genuine sorrow. "We're so sorry for your loss," she said, her voice soft and compassionate.

Guilt gnawed at me. "Doc, I think I failed her. I changed the IV drip, but it must have been too fast. I didn't notice..."

"It's not your fault," she insisted gently. "Some owners, in their desperation, speed up the drip hoping it works faster. Don't blame yourself."

But I couldn't shake the feeling that I had somehow contributed to Raychel's suffering. "But... remember what you said? Her creatinine levels... her kidneys..."

"Her kidneys were failing," she confirmed, pain etched in her eyes. "That, combined with her age... her body simply couldn't handle it."

Sorrow replaced guilt. There was nothing I could have done. "But Doc... before she died, she was restless. In pain, maybe? Her eyes..."

"Her failing kidneys put immense strain on her heart, causing imbalances," she explained softly. "It was a system failure, one organ failing after another."

The vet's voice grew quieter, almost hesitant. "We were grateful for you," she added, her gaze dropping to the floor. "You handled this better than some..."

Her words hung in the air, heavy with unspoken meaning. The implication was clear: some pet owners, faced with the loss of their beloved companions, lash out, blame, even sue. But seeing the vet's vulnerability, the shared grief etched onto her face, something shifted within me.

I paused, struggling to find the words. "Then... maybe I understand a bit..." A pause. "Why you became a vet. Sometimes, the worst losses... they push us in directions we didn't expect."

Her eyes met mine, glistening with unshed tears. "To tell you the truth, sir," she confessed, her voice trembling, "that's why I'm here. I had a dog... couldn't save him. It felt like... a way to keep trying, even when I failed the first time."

Empathy flooded through me. In that moment, we were not just a grieving pet owner and a veterinarian. We were two souls bound by a shared experience, a deep understanding of the profound love and loss that comes with caring for another living being.

"You're always welcome to visit," she said softly. "To talk, anytime."

I nodded, a silent understanding passing between us. In the face of death, we had found a strange solace, a connection forged in the crucible of grief.

The Journey Home

I stepped outside the vet clinic, the weight of the past few days pressing down on me. The sun beat down on the bustling streets, but its warmth felt distant, unable to penetrate the chill that had settled deep within me. I hailed a jeepney, the familiar rattle and jostle of the ride a jarring contrast to the numbness that had taken hold of my senses.

As we rumbled through the city, my gaze drifted towards Plaza Molo, a place filled with bittersweet memories. It was here, just nineteen days ago, that Raychel and I had taken our last walk together. The vibrant colors of the plaza seemed muted now, the laughter of children playing a distant echo. Life, in its relentless march forward, continued around me, oblivious to the gaping hole in my heart.

My phone buzzed, a message from my sister flashing across the screen. Her words, filled with love and sorrow, confirmed my worst fears. She, more than anyone, had known Raychel as a playful pup, a constant source of joy and companionship. Now, that light had been extinguished.

A wave of bleak humor surged through me as I stared at the Molo Plaza Church. First, the incident with my father years ago, and now, Raychel's last walk—this same place seemed to bookend so much loss in my life. Was it a cruel twist of fate, or simply a series of unfortunate coincidences?

Another buzz from my phone interrupted my thoughts. "Tato, I've read your post. Seeing how much you loved Raychel... I remember, even when I was little..." The message was from my younger cousin.

Tato. The nickname, given to me by Aunt B, jolted me, a bittersweet echo of her voice. A sudden urge to connect with family, to share in their sorrow and find solace in their memories, overwhelmed me. I made my way to my cousins' house, a haven of warmth and familiarity in the midst of the storm.

We talked for hours at my cousin's, memories of Raychel and Aunt B intermingling with tears and laughter, a bittersweet symphony of grief and shared love. Then, heavy-hearted, I returned home, retreating to the solitude of my room. The front door creaked open, a sound that once heralded Raychel's excited barks, now filled with an eerie silence.

My mom entered, her face etched with exhaustion. Her eyes, red and swollen from days of weeping, darted around the living room, searching for the familiar sight of Raychel curled up on her cushion. A tremor passed through her body as she realized the space was empty, the silence deafening.

I emerged from my room, my heart heavy with the knowledge I had to impart. As our eyes met, the unspoken truth hung in the air, a suffocating presence. "Mom," I began, my voice trembling, "Raychel... she's gone."

After a moment of stunned silence, my mom looked up at me, her eyes glistening with tears. "At least she can rest in peace now," she whispered, her voice barely a breath. The words hung heavy in the air, a mix of resignation and a desperate attempt to find solace in the face of overwhelming grief. The timing of their deaths, both on the same day, the 29th, seemed too uncanny to be a mere coincidence. Raychel had clung to life for nineteen days after her initial seizure, as if waiting for Aunt B's spirit to guide her on her journey. Now, both were gone, leaving an aching void in our hearts.

Finding Meaning in the Numbers

My mind, still reeling from the events of the past few days, sought refuge in the familiar patterns of numerology, a practice I had discovered in 2017 during a particularly turbulent period of my life. It was during a trip with friends that numerology had revealed itself to me, its seemingly mystical connections resonating with a truth I couldn't deny. Now, in the face of overwhelming grief, I turned to it once more, seeking solace and understanding.

The number 11, a symbol of intuition, spiritual awakening, and new beginnings, kept appearing in my life. Both Raychel's initial seizure and Aunt B's death had occurred on January 11th. Raychel then held on for another nineteen days, her final day falling on the 29th—2 + 9 = 11, the same day Aunt B's body arrived in the Philippines for her funeral. These coincidences felt too significant to ignore.

My life path number, according to numerology, is also 11. This realization felt like a cosmic confirmation, a message that this chapter of my life was ending, and a strange, uncharted one was beginning. It was as if Raychel had agreed to this divine plan, her passing a sign for me to move forward, to embrace the unknown.

I know it sounds wild, but things got even stranger. While scrolling through YouTube, I stumbled upon a video of a dog psychic. Her words, spoken with gentle conviction, struck a chord deep within me:

"Animals offer us an opportunity to understand family in a way that we wish we could understand our own families. By being present for them in their final stage, we're getting to experience being of service, we get to experience unconditional love, we get to experience uncomplicated love and we're not just receiving it, we're being it. By being present when they're going to the rainbow bridge, we're actually gifting the entire universe. Is it painful? Yes. Is it beautiful? Yeah. And it is also really perfect."

Those words, a balm to my wounded heart, brought a sense of peace that I hadn't felt since Raychel's passing. Looking back, it seemed as if she had been trying to communicate with me all along, sending subtle messages through her illness and her unwavering love. Her fragility during those nineteen borrowed days had taught me more about sacrifice, perseverance, and unconditional love than I could have ever imagined.

This trial by fire, these last few weeks, had pushed me to my limits. The exhaustion of caring for Raychel, the grief of losing both her and Aunt B on the same day, the uncanny numerological connections – it all felt like a test of my resilience. Yet, through it all, a transformation occurred within me. I had learned from Raychel, from her resilience in the face of adversity. Her passing had cracked open my heart, allowing me to feel a depth of emotion I had never known before. And in that newfound vulnerability, I discovered a strength I didn't know I possessed.

A Twist of Fate

In the months that followed, as I navigated the murky waters of grief, another unexpected blow landed – I lost my job. A recent raise and a positive performance review had lulled me into a false sense of security. The abrupt dismissal, a cold email citing vague reasons, left me reeling. Just a few months ago, I had been planning trips to Japan, dreaming of a future fueled by my career. Now, those dreams seemed distant and uncertain.

As I sat in my room, staring at the brown butterfly that had mysteriously appeared on the ceiling the day of my termination, a wave of disorientation overwhelmed me. Was this a random occurrence, or was the universe trying to tell me something? The butterfly, its delicate wings a stark contrast to the harsh reality of my situation, seemed to beckon me towards an unknown future.

Ms. Kris, my ever-optimistic friend, had tried to offer comfort, reminding me of the brown butterfly. "It's a sign of financial luck, Eaglet!" she texted, her words brimming with unwavering belief.

I couldn't help but chuckle at the irony. But her words, spoken with such unwavering belief, planted a seed of hope in my heart.

Maybe this wasn't the end, but rather a new beginning. Maybe the universe, in its infinite wisdom, had cleared a path for me, a path that would lead me to a new purpose, a new passion. It was time to leave the familiar behind and embrace the unknown, to trust in the journey, and to believe that even in the darkest of times, there is always a glimmer of hope.

The Next Chapter

While I knew the pain of losing Raychel and Aunt B would never truly fade, I also recognized that life was urging me forward. The coincidences, the numerological signs, the unexpected job loss – they all seemed to be pointing me in a new direction. It was time to start a new chapter, to take the lessons I had learned from my losses and use them to create a life that was more fulfilling, more meaningful, and more aligned with my true purpose. But what that purpose was, I had yet to discover.

Chapter 19

Seekers of Truth

February 2020

Why do I have to suffer? Why this tragic childhood? Why is my life so hard?

"It's essential for your growth," she'd said, her voice a calm island in the storm of my thoughts.

"But why me?" I demanded, the bitterness rising in my throat.

"You have something unique – your experience." Her words were cryptic, but they held a kernel of truth that both terrified and intrigued me. On February 14th, 2020, that kernel sprouted into an undeniable pull towards Ayahuasca, a sacred brew made from Amazonian plants, used for centuries by indigenous tribes for healing, spiritual growth, and connecting with the divine.

Preparing for the Journey

My journey took place in Cavite, the quiet of a rural farm replacing the relentless noise of the city. Arriving, I encountered a mix of strangers, bonded by a yearning for something more. Metaphysical theories were exchanged under the fading afternoon light.

For a week leading up to the ceremony, I followed a strict diet, abstaining from meat, alcohol, and any substances that could interfere with the medicine's effects. I also refrained from sexual activity, a practice meant to conserve and focus my energy. These preparations, both physical and mental, were designed to create a receptive state for the profound experience that awaited me.

After setting up camp, the time came for additional rituals to prepare for the Ayahuasca journey. First came Kambo, a secretion from the giant monkey frog, applied to small burns on the skin. Its pungent, acrid smell filled the air as the shaman explained its traditional use in Amazonian tribes for cleansing and strengthening the body and spirit. Then came Rapé, a powdered tobacco snuff blown into the nostrils through a long pipe. The sharp, earthy scent of the Rapé cleared the sinuses and heightened the senses.

These rituals, steeped in ancient wisdom and connection to nature, stirred a sense of wonder within me. I marveled at the interconnectedness of all living things, the power of plants and animals to heal and transform. It was important to remember that Ayahuasca was not just a recreational drug, but a sacred medicine deeply rooted in Indigenous traditions. It was with reverence and respect that I approached this experience, mindful of the potential risks and the profound benefits it could offer.

Setting Intentions Under the Stars

As 6 PM approached, we gathered in the vast open grass field. Yoga mats were laid out, a small black bucket beside each, with the shamans a respectful distance ahead. The anticipation was palpable. I watched as the shamans circled the field, their drumming creating a rhythmic pulse that seemed to sync with the beating of my own heart.

Most people clustered near the front. Not me. I craved space, a sense of solitude, so I settled at the back. Methodically, I laid out my yoga mat and, one by one, my crystals: protective allies. Finally, the Moldavite – its potent energy a beacon in the deepening twilight. Prayers whispered, intentions set – *I want to understand my purpose in this lifetime and heal from my past traumas – I was ready.*

Unexpected Companions

"What's all that?" A voice startled me. A man had settled to my right, close enough to touch. His eyes scanned the colorful stones.

"Crystals," I explained. "A kind of protection, since this is my first time..."

"Amazing!" He seemed genuinely excited. "I'm new to this whole spiritual thing. Truth is, I came because my neighbor did a retreat like this, and now his business is booming!"

I raised an eyebrow, a smirk playing on my lips. "Well, this isn't exactly a business seminar," I thought to myself. Aloud, I simply asked, "Meditation?"

"Nope," he replied, wide-eyed innocence radiating from him.

Bold. This guy had guts, leaping headfirst into the unknown.

A friendly face peeked in from my left. "Can I sit here?" A woman with kind eyes settled beside me as the front filled up.

"Sure," I smiled.

"Did you hear about the drumming earlier?" I asked. "What was it all about?"

"It's a protection spell," she explained. "The shamans are encircling this space to keep it safe from outside interferences."

She seemed knowledgeable and, like me, sensitive to energies. But she admitted to feeling a bit worried; she hadn't followed the strict pre-ceremony diet.

As the shaman's voice cut through the night, we fell silent, the air thick with anticipation.

The Call of Ayahuasca

"Greetings, seekers," the shaman began. "Tonight, we embark on a journey assisted by the sacred medicine..."

Eyes closed, I followed his guided breathing, feeling a strange energy surge through me as the tempo shifted into those rapid, rhythmic breaths. The air crackled with a palpable intensity. With each breath, I felt a tingling sensation spreading through my body, culminating in a strange, electric buzzing in my hands. It was as if my body was awakening to a new level of perception, a heightened sensitivity to the energy that flowed through me and around me.

"Now, for the main ceremony," the shaman continued as I opened my eyes. "You will be called by name..."

The wait was nerve-wracking, but the background music was soothing. My leg bounced with nervous energy as I watched others approach the altar, their faces masks of serene anticipation. As others went ahead, I closed my eyes again, trying to maintain composure. *What if I have a bad trip?* I wondered. *What if I see something I can't handle?*

"Raymond." My name, a summons. I stood, making my way around those already in trance-like states.

The altar, the shamans – I sat, a spectator. The shaman's weathered hands, etched with the stories of countless journeys, held the cup with a reverence that sent a shiver down my spine. The scent of the brew hit me full force – earthy, vegetal, with a hint of something bitter and metallic. It was unlike anything I'd ever encountered, a complex aroma that spoke of the forest floor, damp earth after rain, and ancient, moss-covered stones.

Those three words hung in the air, heavy with meaning. Intention. *I want to understand my purpose in this lifetime and heal from my past traumas.* Focusing on this yearning, I whispered a silent prayer to the cup, imbuing the brew with my desires.

Then, I drank. The liquid was thick and viscous, coating my throat with a bitter, earthy taste that lingered on my tongue. But beneath that bitterness, there was a hint of something else – a warmth that spread through my chest like a long-forgotten memory. It was the taste of my grandmother's herbal remedies, concoctions brewed from roots and leaves to soothe childhood ailments. The unexpected comfort of that memory eased a knot of tension in my shoulders. Perhaps, I thought, there was healing power in this strange brew after all.

With a silent prayer, I settled back into my spot, the vast night sky a canopy above. Worrying thoughts swirled, *This is it, no turning back now.* But I pushed them aside, focusing on my breath – a mantra urging me inwards.

Into the Vortex

Thirty minutes passed. Then, the visions began. A swirling vortex of neon geometry pulsated and morphed before my eyes, a symphony of cool, electric colors against the backdrop of the infinite night sky. Circles, squares, triangles – a perfect, impossible dance that held my attention captive, each shape humming with an otherworldly vibration.

Suddenly, a jarring sound pierced the trance – a phone ringing! The shaman's instructions echoed in my head...silence...yet it persisted. Half-conscious, driven by a desperate need for quiet focus, I stumbled to my feet. The sound...it seemed to be coming from the tents. The shaman and others watched, their faces blurry and indistinct as I pushed past them. Something felt off...

Then, halfway to the tents, I froze. My companions' eyes...they were on the vibrating phone beside my still-unconscious neighbor. That ringtone...it was his. Embarrassment mixed with the lingering after-effects of the Ayahuasca as I shuffled back to my mat, the phone mercifully silencing itself.

Shaking off the interruption, I refocused my energy, determined to dive back into the depths of the experience. After the shapes, a new sensation: my soul rising, soaring into darkness. A feeling of weightlessness washed over me as I ascended, the pull of gravity replaced by a sense of exhilarating freedom. Upwards, ever upwards, I felt myself accelerating through a tunnel of nothingness, each movement a silent whoosh.

A glimmer of white light pierced the blackness, beckoning me closer. Yearning took over, and I shot towards it like a comet, my astral self merging with the light in a blinding flash of unity. In that moment, my physical body felt heavy and rooted, fused with the earth, with all that existed.

Tears of pure joy welled up, a relentless stream overflowing, each drop carrying a lifetime of pent-up emotions. My eyes became waterfalls, my face submerged in a flood of overwhelming love and gratitude. Simultaneously, my chest thrummed – a deep, heart-pounding rhythm mirroring the outpouring of tears. *This is what pure, unfiltered love feels like,* I marveled.

Then, amidst the torrent of emotion, a shift. Voices, faint and distant, reached me as my vision blurred. The darkness had turned to light. I soared through a white tunnel, still weeping tears of joy. Finally, I emerged, weightless and free, into a vast expanse of pure white light.

Communing with Mother Ayahuasca

Time and space dissolved. I drifted in a boundless expanse, the heart of the cosmos. Yet, I wasn't alone. A luminous orb of energy shimmered before me.

"Are you...Mother Ayahuasca?" I inquired mentally.

"You may call me as you wish, child. Welcome home." Her voice, gentle yet resonant, filled the expanse of my being, connecting us in a timeless embrace.

Overwhelmed with love, I whispered, "It's true then. All the stories..."

Her radiant presence filled the void. My physical body rested on Earth, but my soul communed with her in this surreal, liminal space.

"So many questions..." My voice trembled. "Why all the suffering? Why the tragic childhood? Why is my life so hard?"

"It's essential for your growth," she soothed. "You have something unique – your experience."

"But why me?" I protested, tears flowing freely. "Why this burden?"

"Your burden is your gift," she reassured. "It is what makes you strong, what allows you to connect with others who are suffering. You have the power to turn your pain into purpose."

I felt my heart lifted, enveloped in her energy. A warmth radiated through me, dissolving knots of tension and pain. My heart returned, lighter, brighter, filled with a forgotten joy.

"Ah, such innocence and joy... How did I forget?" I marveled.

"It was intentional," she replied. "You had to forget the baggage of your past, to fulfill your mission."

"Mission?" I asked, confused.

"The time will come when you'll know," she said. "Remember, you already have in you what it takes. We are just waiting for your command."

"We have met. You can always call me, as I am now part of you," she added.

I basked in her presence, feeling a profound sense of peace and understanding settle over me.

Facing the Shadows

Moments later, a chilling darkness seeped in from my right. The man who'd been so ecstatic earlier...his energy had soured. Malicious tendrils snaked from his closed eyes and mouth, slithering towards me, threatening to devour my light. A cold dread gripped my heart, my breath coming in ragged gasps as the shadows closed in.

Then, from my left, the same sickening shadow erupted from the woman, turning towards me with a hungry malice. Trapped between these tendrils of darkness, I thrashed my head back and forth, a desperate resistance against the encroaching void. It felt like drowning, suffocating – the shadows were relentless, closing in on all sides.

Just as I was about to be consumed, a voice echoed – not from outside, but from within. Mother Aya's voice, a resonating force within my own heart. Tears streamed down my face as she spoke, her tone laced with urgency yet unwavering in its support.

"Raymond, remember your strength! You've overcome so many things in your life, hardship, doubt, loneliness. Don't let this darkness, this fear, defeat you. You've come so far on this journey. Don't give up now!"

Her words sparked something within me. A defiance, a surge of protective energy fueled by the battles I'd won in the mundane world. The darkness was inches away. Instinctively, I raised my soul-hands high. A beam of pure white light shot forth, blinding in its intensity. This light blasted outwards, pushing back the tendrils of shadow. The inky cloud recoiled, its tendrils dissolving like smoke under a fierce wind. Silence returned, thick and heavy, but the immediate threat was gone. My companions remained asleep, their forms peaceful once more, the darkness purged from their immediate vicinity.

Curious, I dared a momentary glimpse through my physical eyes. My hunch was correct: they'd turned away, locked in their own private struggles. And there, up ahead... a fellow seeker stood, arms raised high, their silhouette a stark contrast against the lingering shadows – a priest, a warrior, or perhaps, just a soul facing his own demons.

A Cosmic Dance

I closed my eyes again, settling into a cross-legged position. Mother Aya's words echoed in my mind as I returned to that timeless, boundless expanse, adrift in the cosmos.

My eyes flickered open. Just a glimpse of my surroundings... and then her voice, startling in its suddenness. "Do you see their light?"

"Yes," I whispered, awestruck.

"Each will contribute to this land, their communities. You were brought here for a reason," she said, her voice imbued with a profound certainty.

Then, the strangest thing. My hands, my arms, began to move as if guided by some unseen force. They undulated in a mesmerizing wave, like a vibrant festival ribbon twirling in the wind. It was a graceful yet primal dance, my limbs weaving through the air in time to the rhythmic drumming that pulsed like a heartbeat through the night. For almost thirty minutes, my body became a conduit for some unknown energy, the effects of the Ayahuasca still reverberating through me

Finally, the movements ceased. I opened my eyes and saw the lead shaman still sitting before me, in the same spot he had been throughout the ceremony. A beam of pure white light descended from the starry sky, connecting him to the cosmos - and to us. It felt as if he was a conduit, focusing the energy of the heavens. Overwhelmed, I bowed low, a gesture of respect and gratitude. He met my gaze, returning the bow, a silent acknowledgment of the profound night we'd shared.

As I basked in the afterglow of the experience, Mother Aya's voice whispered in my mind, gentle yet firm. "You have a choice, Raymond," she said. "You can follow your dreams of travel, exploring the world and expanding your horizons. Or you can embrace the path of the healer, sharing your wisdom and compassion with others. The choice is yours."

I closed my eyes once more, pondering her words. The shaman's face, serene and wise, remained imprinted on my mind. The decision was not an easy one, but I knew that whatever path I chose, it would be guided by the profound experiences of this night.

Mother Aya spoke again, her voice filled with warmth and encouragement. "You will find those who believe in you, who will support your journey. Trust them, trust your heart, and the universe will guide your path."

I nodded, my heart filled with a newfound sense of purpose.

The Veil Lifts

Hours passed. It was nearly 11 p.m. when I finally stretched out, surrendering to the journey's end. As the intensity of the experience ebbed, a profound exhaustion settled into my bones. My eyelids felt heavy, my body yearning for rest.

I opened my eyes. Moonlight bathed the world in silver, but the sky... it seemed warped, a veil drawn around the moon. A disorienting feeling, a dissolving of the familiar. Then, a panicked voice in my head: *Who is that person to my left? And that one to my right?*

Glancing back up at the moon, a profound confusion engulfed me: Who am I? Where am I? Why? I sat up, the faces around me now those of strangers. This place... it held no meaning.

And yet, amidst the fear, an unshakeable knowing arose: *I am here for a reason.* Identity, memories, the world I knew — all seemed to have melted away, but this deep conviction remained. I would discover that reason, find my purpose anew.

I lay back down, surrendering to the final echoes of the Ayahuasca journey. When the effects finally faded, a realization dawned: Ego Death. The 'self' designed to protect us, to define us, had temporarily dissolved. A terrifying, yet exhilarating experience that stories couldn't do it justice. It was a profound reminder that we are not just our bodies or our egos, but something far more vast and interconnected.

Emerging from the Darkness

Now, I sat up, watching others. Some were still lost in trance-like states, others already gathered in small circles, sharing whispered words. Me? A smile I couldn't erase was plastered across my face. My crystals, those anchors of protection, lay undisturbed. At least I hadn't caused a scene! And thankfully, no purging either... though I had heard some less fortunate retching sounds earlier.

Still smiling, I let the rhythmic music wash over me until 11:30 pm. The shaman's voice cut through the night: those whose journeys had ended were free to retreat to their tents and rest. I lingered, savoring the last moments of this unique atmosphere, the music, the night. Around 1 am, a soft drizzle began. Most of us were awake by then, and we made our way to our shelters. Sleep came easily. Lying on the earth, feeling connected to it, was the most rejuvenating experience - pure bliss after the mental storm.

Morning sunlight pierced my tent at 8 am, jolting me awake. The memories of the night flooded back — too vivid, too profound, to be dismissed as mere dreams.

Following voices, I found a small hut where everyone had gathered. What a shift from our quiet group the night before! Now, stories tumbled out, laughter filled the air.

"Your energy remains receptive, go slow," the lead shaman advised, now dressed casually. We swapped stories over peanut butter toast, each recounting their unique journey.

Sharing Stories and Finding Connections

As I munched, I spotted the guy who'd been beside me last night.

"Finally awake!" He grinned. "I had a rough time. Your crystals helped, though. It's like those glowing stones were the only guiding light in my struggles."

"Glad they served you, but what happened?" I asked, intrigued.

He grimaced. "A bad trip. Multiple ones, actually. So many limitations revealed...blockages I had to face before I could move forward."

"That sounds intense," I said, suspecting there was more to his story.

"In one of those dark phases, I saw a faint light, a single beam. It led me towards your crystals." He paused, a flicker of awe in his eyes. "They were glowing."

"Well, it's my first ceremony," I confessed. "I put them there for protection, hoping they'd be a source of light...kind of a reminder."

He just smiled, spreading peanut butter on his toast.

The morning was lighthearted. Games, shared stories – it felt like a family reunion. The communal breakfast of peanut butter toast fueled laughter and conversations about the night's events. Some shared profound insights and emotional breakthroughs, while others confessed to challenging or even frightening experiences. The air buzzed with a newfound sense of camaraderie, a shared vulnerability that transcended the usual boundaries of social interaction.

In the afternoon, the woman with kind eyes who'd been on my

left during the ceremony approached. She stood nearby, then finally worked up the courage. "Can we chat for a minute?"

"Sure," I said, intrigued. "You noticed me last night?"

"Yes." She paused, her eyes searching mine. "You were sitting, talking...but who were you talking to?"

"Oh, that...I think I was talking to Mother Ayahuasca. Or maybe just myself, hard to tell after a night like that!" I chuckled, remembering the surreal nature of my experience.

"That's strange. Sounds like Light Language," she mused.

We found a quiet spot away from the group and delved into a deep conversation about spirituality, energy, and the interconnectedness of all things. It felt as if we were old friends, picking up a conversation that had been interrupted lifetimes ago.

"What's your Life Path number?" she asked suddenly, her eyes sparkling with curiosity. "Let me guess – 11?"

"How did you know?" I was genuinely startled.

She smiled, a knowing glint in her eyes. "We recognize our own. I'm an 11 too. An old soul, just like you."

"Looks like we're the crazy weirdos," I laughed, feeling a sense of kinship with this kindred spirit.

Our talk stretched for hours, exploring all things spiritual and esoteric. We shared our hopes, our dreams, our fears, and our vulnerabilities. In that sacred space of connection, I felt seen, heard, and understood in a way I never had before.

The Journey Home and Beyond

Finally, it was time to go. Coincidentally, the man who'd been beside me during the ceremony was heading in the same direction, becoming my unexpected travel companion.

As the bus carried us back to the city, he turned to me, his eyes still sparkling with a touch of the wonder from the night before. "I can't believe what we just experienced," he said, shaking his head in amazement. "It was like nothing I could have ever imagined."

"I know," I agreed, a smile spreading across my face. "It's hard to put into words, isn't it?"

"Absolutely," he replied. "But I think it's changed something in me. I see the world differently now."

"Me too," I said, gazing out the window at the familiar landscape rushing by. "It's like a veil has been lifted."

We chatted about our shared experiences, comparing notes and laughing at the absurdity of some of the visions we had encountered. It felt like we had known each other for years, a bond forged in the crucible of the ceremony.

"I'm so grateful for the light you brought to my journey," he said, his voice filled with sincerity. "In some of my darkest moments, it felt like the only thing guiding me forward."

"I'm just glad it was helpful," I replied, touched by his gratitude. "I think we all need a little light sometimes, especially when things get tough."

As the city skyline came into view, a deep sense of gratitude filled my heart. I had been given a glimpse of a world beyond the mundane, a world of infinite possibilities. And I knew, without a doubt, that this was just the beginning of my journey.

The Ayahuasca had opened my eyes to a deeper reality, a world of interconnectedness and hidden meaning. I had glimpsed the profound wisdom of the ancient traditions and the healing power of plant medicine. But I also recognized the potential for misuse and cultural appropriation, and I knew that anyone considering this path should approach it with respect, humility, and a willingness to learn.

The effects of the ceremony lingered for days, a subtle yet persistent vibration humming beneath the surface of my everyday life. I felt more attuned to the energy around me, more aware of the subtle cues and synchronicities that seemed to guide my path. The experience had deepened my meditation practice, allowing me to connect more fully with my inner self and the world around me. I realized that we are all interconnected, part of a larger cosmic tapestry, and that even in the face of immense suffering, there is always the possibility for growth, healing, and transformation.

Although I didn't come back to Ayahuasca after that ceremony, while most people say to take it yearly, I decided to follow and heed the advice from the trip itself, to only come when I need it. Essentially, it changed my outlook in life, and I have a deeper degree of understanding about my external world and why people do what they do.

I carried the echoes of that night within me, a reminder that even in the darkest corners of our souls, there is always the potential for light.

Chapter 20

The Initiation

October 2023

My heart hammered against my ribs, each beat echoing the frantic thoughts that raced through my mind. *"Raymond, I will not let you die here,"* Marcus declared, his voice firm yet laced with a surprising concern.

My lungs burned, each gasp for air a struggle. My body trembled, waves of anxiety engulfing me with a force I couldn't comprehend.

"I...I don't feel well," I managed to tell Marcus. Fear trembled in my voice, an echo of some primal terror.

Worried, he promised to find the teacher. *"Just hold on,"* he said before rushing off.

As the other students milled around, awaiting the orientation, I fought to regain control. *Deep breaths, the techniques I'd learned....nothing helped.*

Years earlier, a friend had mentioned this thing called 'Vipassana Meditation', a free 10 day retreat nestled in the forest. The name stuck in the back of my mind, forgotten until last year, when a sudden urge for change had me searching for alternatives - especially birthday plans. Work got in the way then, but destiny, it seems, had other plans. After a jarring layoff earlier this year, I stumbled across a podcast where the speaker mentioned 'Vipassana' as his life's turning point. *That was it - the sign I was waiting for.* With nothing holding me back, I finally made the decision to go.

The journey to the retreat began with a shared van ride alongside the female students. Sparks of connection flickered amidst the hushed anticipation as we embarked on this shared adventure. Laughter, whispered conversations, and the rustling of bags filled the van, creating a palpable buzz of feminine energy. I, however, felt strangely detached, as if observing the scene from a distance, a silent spectator in a play about to unfold.

Upon arrival, the separation of men and women added to the sense of venturing into the unknown. When we arrived at the retreat center, the women were ushered towards their quarters, leaving me to face the stark silence of the men's area. The energy shifted abruptly, like a door closing on a world I was no longer a part of.

The retreat center nestled in the heart of the forest, a tranquil oasis amidst the urban chaos. Sunlight filtered through the leaves, painting a dappled pattern on the forest floor. The air was rich with the scent of damp earth and wild orchids, a delicate fragrance that both calmed and invigorated.

I felt a sense of both trepidation and hope, like a traveler stepping onto a new continent, unsure of what lay ahead but eager to explore. And as I entered the men's area, my first impression wasn't reassuring: A buzz-cut, tattooed figure with an air of stern authority greeted me, making me wonder if I'd accidentally joined a boot camp instead of a spiritual retreat. His brown skin and imposing presence sent a shiver down my spine, an unwelcome echo of my father. Taking my place in the signup line, I sized up my fellow participants. A tall Caucasian, a compact Asian man, an older Filipino gentleman...only four of us? This was going to be...interesting.

The four of us stood awkwardly, our filled-out forms a flimsy shield against the unknown. Marcus, our 'full-time manager,' cast a cursory glance at the paperwork before sorting it with an air of practiced indifference. Marcus's voice, sharp and clipped, reminded me of my father's tone when he was displeased.

"Plenty of time before orientation at six," he said. He paused, his gaze sweeping over us with a hint of assessment. "Now, we need to collect those distractions - phones, laptops...you won't be needing them." It was phrased as a statement, not a question.

Numbly, we surrendered our devices, watching them disappear into nondescript pouches. Our lifelines to the familiar, severed in a matter of seconds. As I watched my phone vanish, a wave of nausea washed over me. It wasn't just the lack of connection; it was the fear of being truly alone with my thoughts, the ones I usually drowned out with mindless scrolling.

"Right, let's get you settled."

The trek to our quarters was daunting. The ground crunched beneath our feet, a harsh mix of dirt and stones, each step a jarring reminder of the physical discomfort that likely lay ahead. Twenty-eight meters from the cafeteria, then a steep, crudely-constructed stairway - two meters of crumbling concrete leading down into...what?

Two container houses. These were to be our home for the next ten days. Bleak. Unwelcoming.

We stepped into the first.

"Make yourselves at home," Marcus said, his tone softening slightly. He swiftly assigned us rooms: the Asian and Caucasian men on the left, the older Filipino gentleman given the task of ringing the morning bell, and me placed on the right, closer to Marcus's own quarters.

"Orientation at six upstairs. Rest for now," was his parting instruction.

The moment he left, my restless nature took over. Bags dropped, I went exploring. The other container house seemed empty. Behind ours, a designated washroom area – functional, but with a surprising touch of beauty. Banana trees, their broad leaves rustling in the breeze, transported me back to childhood summers spent in the province, a simpler time filled with laughter and carefree exploration. A newfound curiosity bubbled up inside me, especially about the man named Marcus. From the moment we met, his buzz-cut hair, brown skin, and stern demeanor had given the impression of a strict disciplinarian, yet there was also something intriguing about him. His curt instructions left me wondering: What exactly does a manager do here? Is he our teacher, or is there someone else? I wondered why someone like him would free up ten days to attend such a retreat and help other men. What experiences had led him down this path? Was he seeking the same solace and transformation that I was? *Or was the universe playing a cruel joke, sending me a distorted reflection of my father, the very figure I sought to escape?*

Eager to find out more, I headed back to the cafeteria upstairs. As I approached, the black netting that served as walls offered a glimpse of the inside. I could see Marcus hunched over the table, intently reading something. The net was attached to a steel rod, acting as a beam for the entire structure, and a faint metallic scent hung in the air.

"Hi Marcus, I have a question, if you don't mind?"

He looked up, his expression as stern as ever. He nodded once, signaling me to continue.

"Uhh, I'm wondering if you are our Teacher for this batch?" I asked nervously.

"No, it's not me. I'm the manager," he replied curtly. "You will meet the Teacher later. Anything else?" He seemed eager to return to his manual.

Disappointed but undeterred, I went outside and closed the net-like door. Just then, I spotted another figure, a slim-bearded man who looked lost, on the other side of the cafeteria. I approached him. "Are you looking for the men's area?" I asked.

"Yes," he muttered, his eyes scanning the unfamiliar surroundings. "I seem to have taken a wrong turn."

I pointed him in the direction where Marcus resided.

Feeling a small sense of accomplishment, I headed back to our washroom to take a quick bathroom break. The air here was different – clean, sharp, invigorating. A sense of peace settled over me as I washed my hands and splashed my face with cool water. But as I stepped back outside, my eye caught sight of a sign: "Course Boundary." A strand of barbed wire snaked away from it, encircling the entire area. We were free to roam, it seemed, but only within these carefully defined limits.

Nearby, a row of hangers, empty save for a few stray cloths, indicated this was the laundry area as well. Lost in the beauty of my surroundings, I jumped as footsteps broke the silence.

The other men from my group were approaching. They spotted me, then after a short while, introductions followed.

"Raymond, from the Philippines. First time doing Vipassana," I offered, extending my hand.

"Ethan, from Toronto," the man said, clasping my hand with a firm grip. "Nice to meet you."

"Alec, from Melbourne," the Australian chimed in, his eyes twinkling with amusement. "Welcome to the jungle, Raymond."

I chuckled nervously. "Nice to meet you both. So, what should I expect?"

We fell into a comfortable rhythm, sharing our past experiences with the retreat. Ethan and Alec had both completed a 10-day retreat in their respective countries. Their stories were filled with a mix of challenges and insights, fueling my curiosity and apprehension.

Ten minutes later, another set of footsteps approached. The

older Filipino gentleman, hesitant at first, was drawn into our conversation.

"Sir," I began, "we were just discussing our backgrounds with Vipassana. Is this your first time, or...?"

"Oh, many times," he replied, a touch of pride in his voice. "My longest was a 30-day course."

"Wow, impressive!" Ethan exclaimed, while Alec shared his own experiences in Australia.

The Filipino gentleman's tales of Vipassana's history in the Philippines linger in our minds. A sense of awe settled over us, knowing we were part of something with deep roots. After parting ways, I retreated to my room, my attempt at a brief nap thwarted by restless anticipation.

With hours until orientation, I took a leisurely bath, savoring the feeling of cleanliness after the journey. Back in my room, as I straightened my few belongings, my excitement was palpable. Another attempt to catch a bit of sleep failed miserably. *Was this normal pre-retreat jitters, or something more?*

Silence hung heavy in the air. The other men seemed to have disappeared; maybe to explore, or perhaps seeking a quiet corner to find their own center before the official start. Unable to simply wait, I took another stroll through the washroom area, venturing a little further toward the trees.

The rhythmic chirping of unseen insects filled the air, a constant backdrop to the rustling of leaves in the gentle breeze. My smartwatch buzzed with a health reminder — a jarring intrusion into the quietude. A casual check of my vitals sent a shock of alarm through me: heart rate elevated, blood pressure spiking. Despite deep breathing exercises, the numbers refused to budge. Confusion and a creeping sense of unease took hold. *What on earth was wrong?*

Time seemed to both drag and disappear as I nervously paced by the washroom. I distracted myself by studying the posted schedule - a glimpse of the regimented days to come.

Suddenly, footsteps. Marcus burst through the doorway, glancing around. Were more students expected? He spotted me, clock-watching and jittery.

"Raymond, you alright?" he asked.

"I don't know!" I admitted, adding a touch of drama. "Hours without my phone...it feels...wrong."

"The orientation hasn't even started yet," Marcus said, a hint of amusement in his voice.

I went back to my room, hoping to catch a quick snooze. *Two hours to go.* I fought a losing battle with my racing heart, finally achieving a slightly calmer 85 BPM – just as the clock demanded I change for the orientation.

"Seriously?" I groaned to myself. *Finally calmed down...and now I can't sleep.*

As I dressed, a figure with long hair caught my eye outside the window. I'd noticed him earlier, dismissed him as staff...could he be another late arrival? No time to ponder; I steeled myself and headed upstairs.

I hurried back to the cafeteria. The orientation hadn't begun, but Ethan and Alec were already deep in conversation, the soup's warmth a stark contrast to the chill of my anxiety. The Filipino gentleman sat nearby, lost in his bowl of...soup? Porridge? My nerves rendered even the simplest details fuzzy. I checked the hot water dispenser, but it seemed like it was empty, so I headed to the kitchen, a few miles away from our cafeteria. There, a tall, broad-shouldered man with a gentle smile approached me and asked if I needed anything. I told him I might need some hot water for my tea. He agreed to deliver it to the cafeteria so I could wait there.

I returned to the cafeteria, my anxiety a knot in my stomach. The forest symphony seemed muted now, the chirping birds a distant echo to the frantic drumbeat of my heart. I went back to find any nearby seat and ate my porridge, afterwards I turned towards Ethan and Alec talking until Ethan noticed me shivering.

"Are you okay, Raymond? You look anxious," Ethan said, his

voice barely above a whisper. He glanced around, as if checking for prying ears, before adding, "This is normal, you know. The first day is always the hardest."

Yeah, it's been like this since the late afternoon. I don't know what's gotten into me," I replied. "My breath hitched in my throat, each inhale a shallow gasp. My fingers tingled with a numb coldness, and a cold sweat beaded on my forehead."

"Hey, have you heard of that Andrew Huberman guy?" Ethan asked, breaking the tense silence. "Neuroscientist dude on YouTube. He's got this breathing thing for anxiety – really helped me when I had a bad panic attack a while back. Want me to show you?"

"Worth a shot," I said, grateful for the distraction. "Huberman, right? I've seen some of his stuff."

He demonstrated the technique, and though familiar, the rhythmic inhales and exhales did offer a sliver of calm. After our conversation, the tall man appeared with the hot water. As I filled my water bottle and steeped a chamomile tea bag, I hoped the calming properties would ease my nerves.

Mustering my courage, I took a few more deep breaths before joining the group heading outside for the orientation. *This might make me look weak, I thought, but sometimes you've gotta take care of yourself first.*

As the sound of voices drifted from the other cafeteria, signaling the start of orientation, desperation clawed at me. My anxiety, a relentless knot in my stomach, refused to loosen its grip. I spotted Marcus returning from the quarters and rushed towards him.

"Marcus," I blurted out, "I'm still not okay. Something's wrong, and I don't know what to do."

He listened intently, concern etched on his face. "This isn't unusual, especially for first-timers. Let me talk to the Teacher. I'll signal you when it's time, okay?"

"Thank you," I managed, my voice barely above a whisper.

Marcus hurried off on some unknown errand, while I made my way towards the female cafeteria where the orientation would be held. Snagging a seat near the back door and focused on my breathing. *It didn't help.* My heart hammered, a relentless drum-roll against my ribs. All around me, the room buzzed with conversation, fellow students forging new connections. I, however, was struggling for any semblance of calm.

Five minutes stretched into an eternity. A sudden jolt, then a gentle touch on my back. "You okay? Your energy...it's radiating out from here," It was the long-haired student I'd seen earlier, his brow furrowed with worry.

"Honestly, no," I confessed. "This started this afternoon, and I can't seem to shake it..."

Our conversation was abruptly halted. Marcus surged through the back door, the sudden burst of noise barely registering over the ongoing chatter. His eyes found me instantly.

"The Teacher will see you now," he announced. "I explained your situation." He gestured towards the exit.

Uncertainty gnawed at me. Taking a deep breath, I steeled myself and headed towards the small white houses known as the 'White Hall', the Teachers' residences.

Two chairs sat on the porch. I sank into one, my heart still pounding. A moment later, the Teacher emerged. His eyes were a startling blue, a vivid counterpoint to his fair skin. His weathered face bore the marks of countless hours spent in meditation. Yet, there was an unsettling stillness about him. His face remained a serene mask, devoid of any discernible emotion. His eyes, though fixed on me, seemed to gaze through me, as if I were a mere apparition. He remained perfectly still, not a single muscle twitching, his presence as unyielding as a mountain.

Finally, the silence became unbearable. My voice, when it finally came, was a strained whisper: "Hello, sir. I...I was asked to see you. I'm suddenly feeling very unwell. Anxious... my heart's racing, blood pressure skyrocketing...I've never experienced this before." I felt a tremor in my voice, betraying my unease.

The Teacher listened patiently, his gaze steady as I poured out my story. The rhythmic chirping of crickets filled the air, a soothing counterpoint to my racing thoughts. I inhaled the damp, earthy scent of the forest, a grounding fragrance that anchored me to the present moment. His voice, when he finally spoke, was low and resonant, each word imbued with a sense of calm authority.

"The suffering, the inner turmoil...it will be uprooted," the Teacher said. "By stepping onto this path, by signing that paper, you declared your willingness to break free, to transform. That, in itself, is a profound act of courage."

The Teacher's words pierced through the fog of my anxiety, offering a glimmer of hope. Yes, I remembered that feeling - the desperate need for something different, anything to quiet the internal storm. But could I truly break free from the past? From the resentment I still harbored towards my father, a man whose shadow seemed to follow me even here, in the form of Marcus with his stern expression and brown skin?

"Teacher," I confessed, "honesty compels me to admit...I'm still terrified. I'm not sure I belong here, not sure I'm strong enough. I need...support to make it through."

His brow furrowed with concern, and for a moment, the stern exterior softened. "What you feel is natural, especially with your history of anxiety. This intensity often strikes at the start." He paused, his voice gentle yet firm, like a guiding hand in the darkness. "But know this: you are in a safe space, surrounded by those who understand. There is no shame in needing support."

Breaking free... The words echoed in my mind again, a tantalizing promise. Earlier, when I explored the grounds, I had noticed a barbed wire fence encircling the entire area. It seemed to symbolize both the limitations I sought to escape and the necessary container for my transformation. But what does freedom even mean for me? Am I running towards something, or away from everything I've ever known? Could this retreat, this surrender to the unknown, be the key to unlocking the life I yearned for? The life of my dreams, whatever that meant to me.

"The suffering," he began, his voice barely above a whisper, "the inner turmoil...it will be uprooted. "By stepping onto this path, by signing that paper, you declared your willingness to break free, to transform. That, in itself, is a profound act of courage."

A weight lifted from my shoulders. I wasn't being judged for my weakness, but understood. The anxiety hadn't completely vanished, but a spark of hope now flickered alongside it.

"Before coming here, I prided myself on my spiritual knowledge, my self-care routines," I admitted. "Now...I realize how little I truly know."

His gaze remained steady as he replied, "That willingness to acknowledge your own limits is a powerful step. It's the first step on a long path, but a necessary one."

The Teacher paused, his eyes reflecting a glimmer of something I couldn't quite define. "Now, let me teach you a simple technique – a preview of tomorrow's teachings. It's called Anapana. The word itself comes from Pali, an ancient Indian language, and translates to 'mindfulness of breathing.' By focusing on the sensation of your breath at the nostrils – you'll begin to train your mind in a new way. Don't force it, simply observe. Notice the coolness of the air entering your nose, the warmth leaving as you exhale. We'll do it together for a few minutes. Close your eyes if you wish, and allow yourself to sink into the experience."

I'd done countless breathing exercises before, but this felt different. The focus on my nostrils, the gentle rhythm...it quieted my racing thoughts with surprising ease. Five minutes passed. Opening my eyes, I found the Teacher watching me.

"So?" he asked gently. "How do you feel now?"

"Calmer," I admitted, surprised by the shift. "The anxiety hasn't completely vanished, but... it's not so overwhelming anymore."

A small smile flickered across the Teacher's face. Then, he turned away, his gaze fixed on the gathering crowd just visible from the edge of the White Hall's porch.

"Looks like you're needed," he said. *The orientation must be starting.*

"Thank you, Sir," I murmured, a genuine sense of gratitude replacing my earlier panic. With a final bow, I turned and headed back towards the female cafeteria. The buzz of voices grew louder with every step.

As I slipped inside, the big, tall man from earlier, who had helped me with the hot water, was speaking. I made my way to the back, where the rest of the men were already assembled. Their welcoming smiles, the warm glances – it was a balm to my anxious soul. *"This is going to be okay,"* I thought, a flicker of hope igniting within me.

Then, it was down to business: the rules, the expectations, the structure that would shape our next ten days. The speaker explained the importance of noble silence, the segregation of men and women, and the surrender of all electronic devices and reading materials. Our days would be structured around a rigorous schedule of meditation, beginning at 4:30 AM with the sound of the gong. We were to abstain from any outside spiritual practices and commit to completing the entire ten days, no matter how challenging it became. A wave of apprehension rippled through the room as the gravity of our undertaking sank in.

A short break followed. At 7:15 PM, it was time for the first Dhamma Talk – a video discourse by S.N. Goenka. He explained the principles of Vipassana, what to expect over the next ten days, and the importance of maintaining the practice. It was an enlightening hour, filled with ancient wisdom and promises of transformation.

Afterwards, we retreated to our quarters, the official start of noble silence looming over us. No talking, no interaction – a battle of the will unlike any other. As I lay in bed, the silence of the dormitory amplified the echoes of S.N. Goenka's words in my mind. *The path ahead was shrouded in uncertainty, but one thing was clear: this retreat would be a test of my resilience, a journey into the depths of my own being.* I drifted off to sleep, unsure of what the next ten days would bring, but with a newfound resolve to embrace the challenges and uncover the truths that lay hidden within.

Chapter 21

The Mission I Cannot Fail

Day 1:
The harsh clang of the gong ripped through my sleep at 4 AM. It was a rude awakening, the sound echoing through the dormitory like a physical blow, a harsh reminder of discipline and the day's routine ahead. My eyelids felt heavy, each blink a struggle against the weight of yesterday's emotional turmoil. My body ached, my mind still swirling with the anxieties that had driven me here in the first place.

Meditation? Right now, all I craved was the comfort of sleep, a chance to bury myself under the covers and forget everything.

Thirty minutes later, the insistent clanging of the triangle chime signaled the start of the day. It was the middle-aged Filipino guy's assignment every morning.

A silent battle raged within as the sun began to seep in. I knew the importance of starting the day right, of following the established routine. But the pull of sleep was overwhelming. *Just a few more minutes,* I bargained with myself, pulling the covers up tighter. Yet, a pang of guilt jabbed at me - the commitment I had made, the expectations I had set for myself. With a sigh, I dragged myself out of bed and sank onto the mattress, closing my eyes and focusing on my breath.

The world outside intruded in the form of footsteps, their steady rhythm drawing me back from the depths of my meditation. It was Marcus, peering in through the curtain. His hand gestured urgently towards the cafeteria – a silent but insistent reminder that breakfast was about to begin.

I stifled a laugh, the corners of my mouth twitching despite my best efforts. The image of us all gesturing wildly, like a troupe of mime artists, was too absurd to ignore. *No talking, no contact, no distractions...it's no wonder people leave early,* I thought. *But I had a reason for being here, and I was determined to see it through.*

Finally ready, I headed out. Empty grounds...of course. I rushed upstairs, breathless by the time I reached the cafeteria. To my surprise, some of the guys were nearly finished eating!

"Oh no! I've got to hurry. This is embarrassing!" The internal scolding did little to speed up the process of shoving food into my mouth. The breakfast – plain porridge with some ginger and tofu, plus some wheat bread and peanut butter – was a vegan affair. Guys around me, including Ethan seated beside me in our designated corner overlooking the garden through the net-like covering of the cafeteria, were already clearing their plates.

"They won't wait," a panicked thought flashed through my mind. *"But the group meditation's not until 8 am! I have time..."* This battle waged on in my head as I tried to savor my meal amidst mounting pressure.

So many thoughts were buzzing through my head it was like an internal conversation. *So, talking to myself for the next ten days it is, huh? This is gonna be...interesting.* My gaze landed on a spider dangling above my head – I'd grown accustomed to spiders as a child in my mom's province, so its presence held more fascination than fear: *another tiny companion for my enforced solitude, Mr. Spidey.*

When I finally stood, I was the last one in the cafeteria. "Ah well, not like we can socialize anyway...might as well go for a walk." I inspected the cafeteria, noting the teacher's talk sign-up list, the daily instructions, and the rows of chairs and unused utensils.

As I walked around the grounds, I noticed Ethan emerging from the opposite side, also strolling around. Though our eyes remained downcast, I could feel Ethan's presence beside me, a shared rhythm in our footsteps, a silent acknowledgment of our parallel journeys.

With time to spare before the 8 am meditation, I headed towards the dishwashing station with my plate and utensils. Ethan converged on the same path, his heavy footsteps echoing behind me. The rules of noble silence kicked in: eyes downcast, avoiding any acknowledgment. It felt like a strange dance, searching for a non-existent coin on the ground. *Oh, the irony.*

Once he was gone, I made my way to the dishwashing station, then back to my table to meticulously dry my utensils.

With time to spare before the 8 am meditation, I set out to explore my surroundings for the first time since the 'noble silence' began. A quick check of the schedule posted near the Manager's room revealed free periods between 6:30-8 am, 12-1 pm, and 5-6 pm for free time/tea time and a light fruit dinner. Laundry and showers...well, that could wait. I'd bathed yesterday, and between the limited activity and my minimalist packing, my clothes would last a few days.

A trip to the washroom revealed a few of the guys already tackling their laundry. Others, I noticed, were perched on patches of grass uphill as if seeking out their own solitary spaces within the retreat's boundaries.

A glance at the hallway clock – almost 8 am! The gong, ringing for the second time today, confirmed it was meditation time. Its sharp, resonant tone jolted me, a visceral reminder of the discipline and focus demanded by this place. My heart pounded with a strange mix of excitement and nerves as I hurried towards the

Meditation Hall. Its interior was starkly simple – gleaming tiled floors reflecting the harsh overhead lights. Rows of blue, square-size cushions lined the floor, inviting us to surrender to their embrace. At the front, a small stage, elevated a bit, held two chairs and a television in the center, where we would gather each night to watch the Goenka talks. I joined the queue at the back, a consequence of arriving late on Day 0, and claimed my designated spot.

We reunited with the girls again, their presence a gentle reminder of the shared humanity in this silent endeavor, but they were on the right side of the hall and the boys were on the left. Two teachers, a man and a woman, sat in front of us, their serene presence radiating a sense of calm and authority.

The female teacher's voice, a soothing contralto that resonated through the hall, began the instructions. "Today, we will begin the practice of Anapana, the observation of the natural breath." Her words were simple, yet they carried a weight that settled over the hall like a comforting blanket. She guided us through the technique, reminding us to focus on the sensation of the breath at the nostrils, to observe the subtle nuances of each inhale and exhale without judgment or manipulation.

As I closed my eyes and turned my attention inward, the chaos of my mind gradually subsided. The coolness of the air entering my nostrils, the warmth as it flowed out... each sensation became a point of focus, an anchor to the present moment. *But could I sustain this for an entire hour? No movement, no distractions, just me and my breath. The thought sent a shiver of apprehension through me.* It was a struggle at first, my mind rebelling against the imposed stillness...

When the session ended and I opened my eyes, a wave of tranquility washed over me. The world seemed sharper, more vivid, as if a veil had been lifted from my perception. The anxiety that had plagued me for days was still present, but it felt more distant, less potent.

It was on one of those early days, after a particularly filling lunch of lentil stew and rice, that I noticed the Teacher Talk sign-up sheet posted near the cafeteria. They were scheduled daily from twelve noon to one PM, offering a chance for one-on-one sessions with the teacher to ask questions or seek clarification on the technique. A mix of curiosity and trepidation stirred within me. I decided to observe for now, unsure if I was ready to voice my questions or concerns in such a private setting.

Day 2:

As the second day unfolded, a familiar pattern emerged: meditation, meals, and the soothing voice of Goenka during the evening Dhamma Talks. During meals, I noticed subtle gestures of consideration—a shared glance of understanding when someone accidentally dropped a utensil, a gentle nod of encouragement as another struggled with the unfamiliar vegan fare. Though no words were exchanged, a quiet understanding seemed to bloom in the shared silence.

These men, strangers just days before, were now companions in silence, each of us facing our own inner battles and seeking solace in this shared experience. It filled a void I hadn't even realized was there—perhaps a longing for a healthier sort of male community, one without competition or bravado.

The retreat was divided into distinct realms—the female area, hidden behind a curtain of dense foliage and a steep, sun-drenched hill, felt like a distant world. The only sounds that reached us were the muffled echoes of their gong and the occasional bird call carried on the breeze. Yet, the gong's resonating clang, echoing through both realms, served as a reminder that despite our physical separation, we were all united in this shared pursuit of inner peace. While walking through the grassy hill one day, I saw a female participant in the distance. Our eyes met for a fleeting moment, a silent acknowledgment across the divide. This made me think that even from afar, someone could sense your energy.

My senses sharpened, attuned to the rhythm of the retreat.

The rustling of leaves, the chirping of birds, the distant hum of insects—all became part of the symphony of silence that surrounded us. I could even distinguish individual footsteps now: Ethan's a hiker's crunch of pebbles, the long-haired dude's a gentle sway in the wind, each one a unique signature in this symphony.

Amidst this heightened awareness, the mask I wore so effortlessly in the 'real world' was starting to crack during those meditation sessions. The more I delved into the practice, the more aware I became of the subtle ways I presented myself to others. The cheerful facade, the carefully crafted persona I used to deflect attention from my anxieties...it was all starting to crumble under the weight of introspection. The silence was forcing me to confront the raw, unfiltered truth of my being, and it was both terrifying and exhilarating.

Day 3:

Three days passed, each one a relentless cycle of waking, meditating, eating, and meditating again. It was on this day that anxiety began to creep back, demanding my attention. A wave of unease crashed over me, a cold dread that settled in the pit of my stomach. As I realized this was a battle to be faced alone, the fear was palpable, yet a defiant resolve grew within. There was no choice but to confront the darkness that threatened to consume me.

The afternoon meditation session felt different that day. A familiar disquiet, a whisper of unease, began to stir within. As I settled onto my cushion and closed my eyes, a subtle tremor rippled through the earth, vibrating up through the floor and resonating deep within my bones. I opened my eyes, startled, but everyone else remained focused in meditation. Taking a deep breath, I closed my eyes again, determined to delve deeper into the practice.

After around 30 minutes, I was able to silence my mind from all the noise and entered a meditative state. I focused on my breath, trying to anchor myself in the present moment, but the sensation persisted. It began as a subtle tingling in my hands, then spread like wildfire throughout my body. Soon, the solid ceiling above me seemed to ripple and dissolve, its once-familiar texture transforming into a shimmering, iridescent veil. The boundaries of my body dissolved, and I felt myself expanding, merging with the space around me. A gentle vibration coursed through my being, as if every cell in my body was humming in unison with the universe. The solid ground beneath me seemed to give way, replaced by a boundless expanse of pure energy. I was no longer a separate entity, but a shimmering thread woven into the tapestry of existence.

In a deep state, my consciousness soared, as if flying through the roof of the hall. A question arose unbidden: "Who am I? Who are we?" A flood of visions, uncontrolled by my will, unfurled before my mind's eye. A monk in orange robes ascended a mountain, sunlight crowning the peak. Then, scenes I'd never witnessed but somehow recognized: the Taj Mahal, Mayan temples, pyramids in their dozens. Had we journeyed from these places, converging here once more? The thought sent shivers down my spine.

Then I entered another plane, my anxiety a phantom lurking in the shadows. It was like I was walking a tightrope, the abyss of uncertainty yawning below. *One misstep, I thought, and I'll plunge into the chaos.* Then came the visions of my father, not as I knew him, but as a raw, exposed nerve. His face contorted in silent agony, his eyes hollow with despair. I felt his desperation washing over me, his yearning for understanding seeping into my pores, the crushing weight of isolation pressing upon my shoulders. It was as if I were peering into his soul, witnessing the torment that raged within.

Tears streamed down my face, not from sadness, but from the overwhelming empathy that flooded my being.

Pa, I understand. The words echoed in my mind, a silent plea for forgiveness for my past ignorance. *Then he merged with me, and I had this feeling that his blood flows through me, like I have a mission that I cannot fail.*

The meditation ended abruptly, leaving me shattered and disoriented. *What had I just experienced? Had my consciousness transcended dimensions, briefly touching upon the threads of interconnected existence?* The questions lingered, a tantalizing enigma wrapped in the aftermath of a profound, unsettling journey.

During lunch, I found myself fixated on a tiny spider spinning its web in the corner of the cafeteria. Its delicate movements, the intricate patterns it created, held a strange fascination for me. It was as if time itself had slowed down, each strand of silk a testament to the patient persistence of life. Lost in this miniature world, the clinking of utensils and the hushed movements of my fellow meditators faded into the background. The days themselves started to melt together, the boundaries between past, present, and future blurring into a disorienting haze.

My turn for a private audience with the Teacher finally came. I described the experience in detail – the way the solid ceiling seemed to ripple and dissolve before my eyes. The Teacher listened patiently, then offered a dismissive wave of his hand. "Imagination," he said, his voice calm but firm. "In Vipassana, we focus on observing reality as it is, without getting caught up in thoughts, emotions, or visions. These experiences may arise, but they are not the goal. The true focus is on understanding the impermanent nature of all things." Disappointment consumed me. *Was this all my vivid experience amounted to – a mere figment?*

Yet, there was a flicker of validation amidst the dismissal. When I spoke of the intense physical sensations, the way my body seemed to break down into a million vibrating particles, the Teacher's demeanor shifted.

"Bhanga," he acknowledged, a hint of respect in his voice. "Yes, that is the dissolution of the illusion of solidity, an important stage in the Vipassana practice."

The door closed behind me. It was strange, this mix of validation and dismissal. I'd glimpsed the profound, but he'd brushed aside the details that didn't fit the neatly packaged narrative of the practice. Suddenly, I felt a flash of rebellion. *I didn't need his approval, nor his rigid definitions.* For the next few days, I'd skip the 'Teacher Talks' altogether.

Day 4:

On the fourth day of our silent retreat, a profound weariness settled upon me. The familiar aroma of peanut sauce and simmering vegetables filled the air, a fragrant promise of the vegan *kare-kare* that awaited us. It was a comforting scent, grounding me in the present moment amidst the emotional intensity of self-reflection that had characterized this journey thus far. Despite the exhaustion, sleep evaded me, leaving me restless and alert.

The day's Vipassana meditation sessions were particularly challenging. The instructions now involved a systematic scanning of the body, noting every sensation that arose. The teacher had warned us that certain body parts might hold "sankharas," or stored energies of our past, which could manifest as intense or unpleasant sensations. He emphasized the importance of merely observing these sensations without reacting, resisting, or judging them.

I couldn't help but wonder where my own *sankharas* might be lurking. A sense of dread crept into my awareness as I contemplated scanning the area around my heart and shoulders, where I often felt the weight of anxiety and emotional pain. *Just this morning, the harsh clang of the gong and the unfamiliar surroundings had triggered a flood of emotions I thought I had long forgotten. Tears had streamed down my face, a silent torrent of grief and longing. It was a childhood memory, a wound I had buried deep within, resurfacing with unexpected force. In that moment of vulnerability, I remembered the Teacher's words: "It's okay to cry, but don't get swept away by the emotion. Just allow it to flow and observe." And so I had, surrendering to the tears, letting them wash over me like a cleansing rain.*

Just then, a muffled sob echoed from the girl's area, a stark reminder of the shared vulnerability that permeated this silent retreat.

As the sun dipped below the horizon, casting long shadows across the retreat grounds, I sought solace in the spartan comfort of my room. The chirping of crickets and the rustling of leaves in the night breeze filled the air as I drifted off to sleep, unaware of the turmoil that awaited me in the darkness.

The clock struck midnight, but sleep, when it finally came, was ripped apart in the dead of night. I awoke with a gasp, my heart thundering in my chest like a frantic drummer. An icy grip seized my chest, each breath a desperate gasp for air. My vision blurred, the darkness of the room closing in around me like a suffocating shroud. I had never known such fear, such utter despair.

This is it. I'm losing my mind. All those buried fears, all the pain I've been trying to ignore—it's all coming back to haunt me.

Gasping for air, I stumbled from my bed, desperate to escape the suffocating darkness of my room. The hallway seemed to stretch endlessly before me as I fumbled my way towards the manager's quarters, a strangled cry for help escaping my lips.

A stranger's face greeted me, but I could barely focus. "Please," I gasped, my voice barely audible, "I don't know... something's wrong!"

His response was a gentle touch, a lifeline amidst the chaos. "Sit," he urged, his voice low and steady. He placed his hand on my wrist, a physical anchor. "You are safe. Remember your breath."

Anapana. How could I have forgotten? Frantically, I focused on my nostrils, the coolness of inhaled air, the warmth leaving...battling the terror that threatened to consume me. It was like wrestling with a demon, the server's touch the only thing holding me on this side of sanity.

"I understand now," I said, catching my breath. "I think I've opened Pandora's Box. Today was the Vipassana day, and during the body scanning earlier, I scanned all parts of my body. The trapped energy must have been waiting for a release, and now this happened."

He listened quietly in the darkness. I couldn't quite make out his face, but I didn't think it was Marcus. I thought it was that tall guy from before, the one who helped me with the hot water. I think his name was Noah.

"This is not uncommon," Noah said, his voice a steady anchor in the storm. "The practice can bring up deep-seated emotions and anxieties. You faced something difficult tonight, but you also showed great courage in seeking help."

He offered a choice: his room, where I could be monitored, or my own bed. I chose to remain, too afraid to trust the solitude of my quarters. "Good choice," he said. "We'll talk to the Teacher in the morning. Now, try to rest."

I lay back on the narrow bed beside Noah's, my body still trembling with the aftershocks of fear. Sleep seemed like a distant dream. Each creak of the container house, each rustle of leaves outside, amplified the echoes of the night's terror in my mind.

The first rays of dawn filtered through the window, casting a soft glow on the room. It was a stark contrast to the suffocating darkness I had faced just hours before. The darkness of my room had mirrored the darkness within me, the shadows of my past threatening to engulf me. As I stepped outside, the cool morning air filled my lungs, a welcome relief after the night's breathlessness.

Rest was elusive. But I had fought a battle that night, and in a way, I had won.

Day 5:
Barely slept, head still buzzing...but I found myself face-to-face with the Teacher at 7:30 am. I recounted the night's terror, my voice still ragged with the echoes of panic.

"You've done well," he said, a warmth in his eyes that surprised me. "A great challenge met, and overcome."

Confusion warred with a flicker of pride. I needed guidance, not praise. "When it happens again..." I stammered, "...can I handle it alone? I don't want to disturb anyone."

He smiled, then demonstrated a simple shift in a meditation posture: hands turned open, palms facing upward. "This will help you anchor yourself in sensation," he explained. "Focus on the physical feeling of your hands. Now, imagine the tremor returning. Feel the vibrations in your palms, a ripple of energy passing through your body. Don't fight it, resist it, or judge it. Simply observe it with detached awareness, like a scientist studying a natural phenomenon."

"Sankharas are old impressions, buried deep within," the Teacher said with a gentle chuckle. "They rise like knots of energy, causing discomfort. But this is a release, a letting go. Like a gong's sound, the intensity will peak, then fade, leaving you lighter, freer."

His words offered a glimmer of understanding. It would be a long journey, but I was determined to face it head-on.

Back in my room, I hoped for a reprieve from group meditation. No such luck. The schedule, it seemed, was carved in stone, even for those battling internal storms.

The first hours blurred together - meditation, meals, more meditation. My body ached with exhaustion. The Teacher's words echoed in my head, "No exceptions. Don't give power to fear."

Grit and willpower were all that kept me going. Yet, even as my physical strength waned, I felt an odd surge of energy within - a crackling intensity, like my very essence was straining to break free. *Goku gathering his power,* I mused, my inner child seeking refuge in a familiar image. Perhaps this was what they meant by a 'spiritual body,' this ethereal source of strength.

Teacher Talk time rolled around again—a chance to seek clarification, guidance, or simply connect with another human being after so much isolation. The sign-up list, just a meter from me, caught my attention after lunch. A short list of names, some familiar like Alec and Ethan, others unknown: Kiran and another Alec? Only four signed up; I didn't this time. That left me and the middle-aged Filipino man out. Who were Kiran and the second Alec? The mystery lingered, as we hadn't had the chance to introduce ourselves properly. A curious guessing game for the next few days, bound together by this strange shared experience. We'd barely glanced at each other for days. Yet, I played by the rules. The enforced separation chafed, but change had to start within, I reminded myself.

Days 6 & 7:

These "Teacher-free" days became my proving ground. I'd learned to sit with my anxiety, to observe it without getting swept away by its currents. It was as if I were building a muscle, one that could withstand the onslaught of unpleasant sensations and emotions. The Teacher's words echoed in my ears, "You are stronger than you think."

I delved deeper into the practice of Vipassana, exploring the sensations in every part of my body. A dull ache throbbed in my knees, a testament to the hours spent in stillness. My breath, once shallow and erratic, now flowed in and out with a steady rhythm. But the area around my heart remained a source of unease, a territory I had touched upon but still feared to fully explore. The mere thought of scanning that region sent a familiar heaviness to my shoulders, as if I were carrying the weight of the world. *Enough*, a voice whispered within me. *I've shouldered enough.*

But despite my growing resistance, the routine of the retreat continued relentlessly.

As the seventh day dawned, I found myself seeking solace in the simple act of observing nature. *Perhaps that's why I'm drawn to these ants*, I thought as I sat in the grass, watching a colony of them marching purposefully across the earth. Their tiny bodies, each carrying a burden many times their size, mirrored the persistence of my own anxieties. *Relentless, unwavering, always seeking a way forward.* Yet, there was also a sense of interconnectedness in their tireless labor, a reminder that we are all part of a larger whole, each playing our role in the intricate dance of life.

Lost in these thoughts, I barely registered the gentle "pssst" that startled me back to the present. The long-haired man, who I assumed to be Kiran, pointed towards Marcus, who was calling from afar. I immediately stood up and approached him.

"The Teacher wants to talk to you," Marcus said, a hint of surprise in his voice.

He can do whatever he wants. He's the Teacher, after all. A wave of resentment washed over me, a familiar defiance against authority. *Why can't he just leave me alone?* Yet, a quieter voice reminded me that I had asked for his support. With a sigh, I resigned myself to the inevitable. *Perhaps he sees something in me that I'm too afraid to acknowledge.*

As I approached the Meditation Hall, a sense of anticipation mingled with apprehension. I paused outside, peeking through the screen window. The bearded man was still inside, engaged in a deep conversation with the Teacher. Outside, Marcus and the long-haired dude—Kiran, I now realized—stood in silent vigil. Both were holding a forward bending yoga pose, their bodies folded gracefully towards the earth. It wasn't the first time I'd noticed them practicing yoga; in the quietude of the retreat, their movements had become a familiar part of the landscape.

In the last few days of silent support, my impression of Marcus had shifted. The stern facade had softened, replaced by a quiet attentiveness. His interactions with the other students, though wordless, were filled with a gentle compassion. Goenka's words echoed in my mind: there's a different level of fulfillment in serving others. To think that this man, who bore such a resemblance to my father, had chosen this path of service... Was it possible that even my father, in his own way, was seeking solace and transformation? Was this his way of making amends, even in another lifetime? The thought, though absurd, brought a flicker of warmth to my heart. Maybe this was its way of guiding me towards healing.

Just then, the bearded man emerged from the Meditation Hall, a look of quiet contemplation on his face. Our eyes met briefly, but we both quickly averted our gaze, respecting the noble silence. Taking a deep breath, I pushed open the door and stepped inside, trying to mask my conflicting emotions with a practiced smile. The Teacher was waiting, a serene expression on his face.

"I didn't hear from you in the last few days," he said. "Just wanted to check on you."

"Oh, I'm fine, sir," I replied, my voice a bit tight. "Just managing things on my own."

He looked me in the eye, a hint of concern in his gaze. Suddenly, a pang of regret pierced my heart. *I had asked for his support, and here he was, fulfilling his promise, while I had shut him out.* The fear of vulnerability, the belief that I was unloved and alone, had driven me to erect walls around my heart. It was a pattern I had learned from my father, a facade I had perfected over the years.

"I apologize for my behavior," I said, my voice barely above a whisper. "I've been struggling, but I'm managing. Thank you for checking in."

A warm smile spread across the Teacher's face. It was a smile that held no judgment, only compassion - a stark contrast to the disapproving scowls I had received from my father. The Teacher's unexpected gesture of care, like a ray of sunlight piercing through the clouds, symbolized the possibility of healing and connection. "Remember, you're not alone in this journey," he said gently. "We're all here to support each other."

I nodded, a renewed sense of gratitude filling me. The Teacher's words had chipped away at the fortress around my heart, reminding me of the interconnectedness that was at the heart of Vipassana. With a bow, I left the hall, a newfound determination to embrace the challenges of the retreat coursing through me.

Day 8:

By the eighth day, a growing agitation gnawed at me. The retreat, once a sanctuary, now felt like a suffocating cage. The silence, once a balm, now pressed in on me, amplifying the restlessness that throbbed beneath the surface. I paced the grounds, my footsteps echoing the frantic beat of my heart. The other participants, once a source of silent camaraderie, now seemed like strangers trapped in their own private hells. There was Ethan, pacing relentlessly after meals, a haze of constant motion. Kiran, the long-haired dude, sprawled on the grass, seemingly entranced by a passing ant. Alec, nodding off post-lunch despite the risks to his digestion... And then there were the others, like the Filipino middle-aged guy and the bearded guy, who seemed to prefer the solitude of their rooms. *Were we all just running away from something? Seeking an escape from the noise and chaos of our lives? Or was there a deeper yearning, a shared hunger for something more?*

The cycle, relentlessly predictable: meditate, break, meditate again. Groundhog Day, with a dash of spiritual ambition thrown in. No outside world, no concept of time, just the intensity of sensation. Once, while washing my hands in the bathroom, I noticed a rope dangling from a wooden beam near the ceiling. The rough fibers brushed against my fingertips, a stark contrast to the smooth porcelain of the sink. It triggered a wave of unsettling thoughts. Suicidal ideations, alien and terrifying, crept into my awareness. *Was I losing control? Had my own mind become an enemy?*

My reflection in the mirror stared back at me, a stranger's eyes filled with fear and confusion. "What's happening to me?" I whispered, my voice echoing in the small, sterile space. "Am I losing my mind?"

A chilling thought crossed my mind: *Ego death.* I'd read about it in Vipassana literature, a complete dissolution of the sense of self, a terrifying yet potentially transformative experience. Was this what I was going through? The boundaries between myself and the world dissolving, the familiar anchor of my identity slipping away?

Panic clawed at my throat. I stumbled back from the mirror, my breath coming in ragged gasps. "They believed in me." I clenched my fists, digging my nails into my palms. "I can't let them down. All their sacrifices will be in vain." My voice cracked. "If I don't believe in myself, at least I gotta believe in the people who believed in me."

I bolted from the bathroom, a primal urge to escape the confines of the building propelling me forward. I ran until my lungs burned, until my legs ached, finally collapsing onto the gentle earth of the grassy hill I'd found earlier. It became my anchor, a place of solace where I could reconnect with the quiet hum of reality.

Day 9:

The same blur of motion seemed to continue. Until I made a few differences on that day. I saw three brown hens in the middle of the day, just after lunch. I didn't sign up for the Teacher's talk. *Just one more day,* I thought to myself, a flicker of anticipation stirring within me.

Just then, I remembered I had some cashews in my backpack and decided to feed the hens very discreetly. I unzipped my bag, the soft rustle of fabric breaking the silence. I carefully retrieved a handful of nuts, their salty aroma teasing my nostrils. With a gentle underhand toss, I scattered the cashews onto the ground. They landed with a satisfying *crunch*, instantly attracting the attention of the hens. Their beaks pecked at the earth, a chorus of eager clucks filling the air. The sun beat down on my back, a comforting warmth that eased the tension in my shoulders as I watched their playful scramble.

Suddenly, I felt a presence behind me. I turned to see Marcus, a ghost of a smile playing on his lips. He raised an eyebrow, then glanced at the scattering hens. A silent question hung in the air. *Was this allowed?* I held my breath, unsure of his reaction. But then, to my surprise, a chuckle escaped his lips, and he gave a subtle nod of approval. I couldn't help but grin back, the warmth of the shared moment spreading through me.

In that instant, something shifted. The stern manager, the echo of my father, faded away, replaced by a man who, like me, found joy in the simple act of feeding chickens. Perhaps, beneath the disciplined exterior, there was a shared humanity, a connection forged in the crucible of this retreat. As Marcus turned and walked away, I felt a pang of gratitude. In this place of silence and introspection, unexpected bonds were forming, a sense of belonging I had rarely experienced in the outside world.

Restlessness soon returned, though. The meditation felt stagnant, my mind rebelling against the endless hours of introspection. *I've learned what I needed to learn.* The thought of rejoining the world, of engaging with its vibrant chaos, filled me with a sense of excitement. *I'm ready,* I thought. *I'm ready to face whatever comes next.*

Driven by this newfound resolve, I spent the rest of the day exploring the grounds, watching the wildlife, and simply allowing myself to be present in the moment. I'd already counted more than ten kinds of butterflies and named all the trees around. I had toured every nook and cranny and hidden passage. *What else was missing?* I thought to myself. *The freedom to speak, to laugh, to simply be myself without the constraints of noble silence.* Even after all these days, my adventurer's spirit still pulled through.

The warm afternoon sun beckoned me towards a secluded clearing, where a lone mango tree stood sentinel. Its branches, heavy with ripening fruit, seemed to bow under the weight of their bounty, a stark contrast to the barrenness of the retreat's disciplined routine. The mango tree, in its solitary splendor, was a reminder that life could be simple, that abundance and sweetness could be found even in the most unexpected places.

I settled beneath its canopy, feeling the soft grass beneath me, the gentle breeze against my skin. The sounds of the retreat faded away, replaced by the symphony of nature. I watched a butterfly flutter past, its wings a kaleidoscope of color against the blue sky - a symbol of transformation and the delicate beauty of the present moment. I followed the lazy flight of a dragonfly, its iridescent body shimmering in the sunlight, a reminder of the fleeting nature of thoughts and emotions, always dancing and shifting in the light of awareness. I observed a colony of ants marching in perfect formation, each carrying a tiny burden. *Perhaps they too felt the weight of their duties, the relentless cycle of their existence.*

As the sun began its descent, casting long shadows across the clearing, a sense of peace settled over me, deeper and more profound than any I had experienced before. The retreat had been a challenge, but it had also been a gift. It had given me the space to quiet my mind, to confront my fears, and to reconnect with my inner self. I had learned that each of us has our own journey, that we don't have to hasten it. We have to be patient, and in due time, our time will come. Like for me, I had come here to better under-stand myself, all of the happenings in my life, and my place in it. And now, on this penultimate day, as the sun dipped below the horizon painting the sky in hues of orange and purple, a sense of anticipation mingled with the newfound peace. *Tomorrow, the silence would end.*

Day 10:

The final day dawned, a wave of excitement rippling through the retreat. The schedule shifted: after the first group meditation, the noble silence would end.

A decade of silence, then... boom! Talk! As if they could turn it back on at the tap. Ridiculous. True, I'd mumbled to myself on occasions, a lifeline to sanity. But now, even the muffled sounds of conversation filtering towards my room were overwhelming. *Decision made.* I sought a moment of solace in the washroom, then headed towards the grassy hill, hoping the quiet would soothe my frazzled nerves. There they were – my feathered companions, the three brown hens, pecking at the dirt near the grassy hill with single-minded focus.

While others flocked to their quarters, eager to break the silence, I chose solitude. The cafeteria seemed a safe bet. But to my dismay, Marcus and Kiran were already there, their voices shattering the tranquility I craved.

"Congratulations, Raymond," Marcus said, his voice surprisingly gentle. "I'm proud of you for making it through."

Kiran nodded in agreement. "How are you feeling?" he asked, his eyes filled with curiosity.

I simply nodded, a tightness in my chest preventing me from speaking. The sudden onslaught of noise was overwhelming. I covered my ears with my hands, a futile attempt to block out the chatter, and quickly filled my water bottle from the dispenser. I saw Mr. Spidey while doing my last round check of the cafeteria. Then, seeking refuge from the noise, I went out and eased myself down onto the sun-warmed grass, nestled between a weathered mango tree and a cluster of young trees. This open space, this was my sanctuary.

During the morning meditation, I recalled the teacher's reminder that although noble silence was lifted, we were still expected to maintain a meditative mindset.

Day 11: The Final Farewell

The next morning, we gathered in the Meditation Hall one last time. The pre-dawn air crackled with a nervous energy, a mix of anticipation and sadness. As we settled onto our cushions, the familiar routine felt both comforting and bittersweet. This would be our final meditation, our last opportunity to bask in the shared silence that had bound us together for the past ten days.

The gong resonated through the hall, its deep vibrations stirring something deep within me. I closed my eyes and focused on my breath, the familiar anchor that had guided me through the storms of the past week. The sensations in my body, once a source of anxiety and confusion, now felt like old friends, their impermanence a gentle reminder of the ever-changing nature of reality.

As the meditation drew to a close, a sense of profound gratitude washed over me. I had come to this retreat seeking solace from my anxieties, and I had found so much more. I had faced my deepest fears, shed tears for long-buried wounds, and glimpsed a profound sense of interconnectedness that transcended the boundaries of self.

The final Dhamma Talk, Goenka's wise words echoing through the hall, served as a gentle reminder of the journey ahead. The practice of Vipassana was not confined to these ten days; it was a lifelong commitment to self-awareness and compassion.

During this final gathering, one of the girls shared her experience. She had initially planned to leave on day six, overwhelmed by the intensity of the retreat. But something had shifted within her, a newfound strength that allowed her to stay. "What we have experienced here is something we will carry for the rest of our lives," she said, her voice filled with conviction. "It's not about escaping, it's about facing ourselves, about finding the strength to navigate the storms within."

Her words resonated deeply, mirroring my own journey of self-discovery and healing. *The retreat had given me the tools to navigate the storms within, and now it was time to put those tools into practice, even in the simple act of service.*

With practiced ease, we sorted ourselves into cleaning crews. My name went down under 'room quarters,' my final act of service to this place of transformation. The crunch of gravel underfoot, the rhythmic swish of my broom... each sound was a bittersweet farewell. Ten days ago, I'd arrived here a tangle of anxieties, terrified of the unknown. Now, a sense of calm certainty filled me.

My own inner mystery, it seemed, had yielded some of its secrets. The retreat had been a crucible, forging a stronger, more resilient version of myself. I had learned to sit with discomfort, to observe my thoughts and emotions without judgment, and to embrace the impermanence of all things. I knew I still had much to learn, many more layers to peel back, but for the first time in years, I felt a glimmer of hope. The path ahead was still uncertain, but I was ready to face it with newfound clarity and resilience. The lessons of Vipassana would be my compass, guiding me through the inevitable storms of life, reminding me to always return to the present moment, to breathe, and to simply be.

With a heavy heart, I said my goodbyes and stepped onto the van that would take me back to the city. As we drove away, I glanced back at the retreat center, nestled amidst the trees, a beacon of hope and transformation. The path ahead was still uncertain, but I was no longer afraid. I carried the lessons of Vipassana within me, a compass to guide me through the inevitable storms of life.

I am ready.

Chapter 22

Epiphanies in Brotherhood

Alec the Great
The cafeteria buzzed with voices, a cacophony of laughter, greetings, and animated conversations that echoed off the tin roof and mingled with the clinking of spoons against bowls. A lone figure, head bowed over his phone, remained oblivious to the chatter. Alec, the tall Aussie with the booming laugh and easy-going nature—he was the last one on my 'to-talk-to' list. I remembered him leaving a meditation session early, his broad back disappearing through the doorway like a ghost.

"Hey, mate," I slid into the seat across from him, "how's the stomach?"

He looked up, startled, then a grin spread across his tanned face. "Ah, it's good now. Bit of a rough patch back on Day 3, but Marcus sorted me out."

"I noticed you leaving a session early. Made me wonder...didn't they say we couldn't just bail in the middle?"

He chuckled, "Only for emergencies, like a bathroom crisis." A flash of self-deprecation crossed his face. "And yeah, maybe the food that day...I wasn't the only one feeling a bit off."

"Guess so. Now that you're back in form, tell me about your first Vipassana. Was it just as hard? Or is the intensity different from one group to the next?" I asked.

"Oh, that, well the crowd is a bit different, by average there's an equal number of males and females, about 30 each. And by energy and intensity, it's different. I can't pinpoint what it is, but all I can say is the experience is different. It was also hard," he said.

"So, easier this time 'round, yeah? Being a second-timer an' all?" I asked.

"Nah, mate," he said firmly. "This is still tough, just in its own way. Place, food, the whole lot... changes the game, y'know?"

"Fair enough. I always figured things get easier the next go."

"Depends on the bloke," he shrugged. Then, leaning in, I shifted gears. "Speaking of spirituality, I overheard you and Ethan earlier. Do you know about the Akashic Records? Think I might've stumbled into mine during meditation..."

"Yes, isn't that the library of knowledge? I've also met someone on the first retreat who could do that," he said.

"So why did you go there, what did you see? Did you set a specific intention beforehand?" he asked in quick succession, his eyes locked on mine.

Alec leaned forward, his piercing blue eyes locking onto mine with an intensity that made me squirm. It was as if he could see right through me, stripping away the carefully constructed layers I'd built over the years.

"Truthfully..." I began, a hint of hesitation in my voice. "I know Goenka frowns on this, but...well, my mind drifted. Tried a few things out while I was deep in the trance."

"Won't tell a soul," he said, a mischievous glint in his Aussie eyes. "So, what happened? Did this Akashic library cough up any answers?"

"I set a small intention...wanted to see a past life, then why we were all gathered here. And for a while...it wasn't Goenka's voice in my head anymore."

"Right. And what did you see?" His unwavering gaze held a mixture of curiosity and challenge.

"First, this monk figure, climbing a staircase towards a circle of white statues, like famous people from history. Above it all, a blinding sun...almost like looking down from above."

"Was the monk you?" The question hung in the air between us.

"Maybe... Hard to say. Then..." I trailed off, images flashing through my mind. "Rows of silent Buddha statues. It felt...oddly familiar."

He simply nodded, prompting me to continue.

"No real scenes, just flashes after that. The Taj Mahal, or something like it. Ancient Mayan ruins. And Egypt...not just the pyramids we know, but other structures."

"So what did you find about all of us here?" he asked

"We're here because we've already done this before. All of us here reconnected in order to remind each other, why we came in the first place" I said

"What do you mean?"

"It's hard to contextualize. But it feels like all of us here met somewhere before, like a déjà vu. That you became close to someone even though you met them for the first time, the sense of familiarity."

"Hmmm, it makes sense. The experience here is quite different than my first and it's also hard in a different way. The familiarity is also uncanny," Alec continued

"Heh, I actually don't know what I said makes sense."

"Hey, you have a gift," Alec continued

"Really? I thought it's just my imagination as the teacher pointed out." I sighed

"You could be like Mattias de Stefano who knows his past if you practice hard enough," he added

"I don't know man if I want to go that route. He is great no doubt, but I want to continue with my own adventure and love for writing."

"You write?"

"Yes, I'm in the middle of my writing so to speak. I believe our overall experience here will be an important chapter in my book," I replied shyly

"You don't seem sound so confident."

"Yeah, what if the world is not ready for it? What if people will judge me? So many what ifs," I said

"Fortune favors the brave," Alec quoted, his smile wry. "Remember old Terence?"

"Thanks," I said quietly. I took a sip of my tea, the warmth spreading through my chest. "Enough about me. What do you do when you're not seeking enlightenment?"

"Military," he said, his voice low and rough. "Left halfway through. Couldn't stomach the path...the violence they were grooming us for."

His words hung in the air, a testament to the courage it takes to walk away from a path that no longer serves you, even when it means facing uncertainty and forging a new direction. I felt a surge of respect for him, a kinship with his struggle to find his true calling.

"Australia's not the worst place for that," he continued, staring at his plate. "But it still adds up. Realizing you're just a pawn in someone else's bloody game...that'll sit heavy on your soul."

"Don't want that life. Ghost of it would haunt me," he said, finally meeting my gaze.

"Heard enough war stories...glad you took the other road," I managed, a tightness in my chest.

Alec's gaze drifted towards the window, his fingers tracing the worn edges of the wooden table. The silence stretched between us, thick with the unspoken weight of past battles.

"Here I am," he finally said, a wry smile playing on his lips. "Trying to figure out what the hell comes next."

"That first step's a big one, mate," I said sincerely.

It was...different, talking like this. Heart to heart, with a man I barely knew, but whose story resonated so deeply. Not the kind of conversation that happened every day. It struck me that if more men in the world allowed themselves to open their hearts like this, to share their vulnerabilities and connect on a deeper level, perhaps the world would be a better place.

Arjun the Judge

Day 10 dawned with a joyous buzz of voices filling the air. I held a borrowed copy of Goenka's discourses in my hand, planning to sip chamomile tea in my room while reading a few pages to clear my head. Afterward, I'd head to the grassy field with the book, hoping to ward off any lingering drowsiness.

As I stepped out of my room, the morning air, still cool and damp from the night's dew, carried the delicate fragrance of *ilang-ilang* (ylang-ylang) blossoms. I spotted a familiar figure standing near a row of vibrant hibiscus plants, their crimson petals a stark contrast to the muted greens of the surrounding foliage. It was Sir Arjun, the older Filipino gentleman who had shared his wisdom with us on the first day. His presence exuded a quiet strength, a sense of groundedness that I found both comforting and intimidating.

Despite our limited interactions, I felt a deep respect for him. He was a man who had walked the path of Vipassana many times before, a seasoned traveler on this inner journey. His dedication to the practice, evident in his early morning bell-ringing and his tales of long retreats, inspired a sense of awe within me. Yet, there was also a hint of trepidation. His quiet intensity reminded me of my father, a man whose approval I had always craved but rarely received.

He spotted me, a warm smile spreading across his face. "Good morning, Raymond," he greeted me.

"Good morning, Sir Arjun," I replied, bowing my head slightly in respect.

His eyes flickered towards the book in my hand. "What are you reading?" he inquired, his voice gentle.

"Goenka's discourses, sir," I explained. "Thought they might help if I doze off again."

"That's good," he said, nodding approvingly. "You can find it all on YouTube, anytime you need."

"Thank you, Sir Arjun," I said, grateful for his advice.

A comfortable silence settled between us, punctuated only by the chirping of birds and the rustling of leaves. Then, with a hint of concern in his eyes, he asked, "How are you, really? Did you ever find the root of that...incident...on the first day?"

That simple question triggered a rush of memories. He'd told me not to overthink on Day 1...was he implying it was all in my head? And yet, there was true concern in his eyes. The first person to ask. Something shifted inside me.

"You remember, huh?" I began hesitantly, then the words spilled out. "Trauma, sir. It happened when I was a child. Surfaced on Day 4, early morning meditation."

His eyes held mine, unwavering, like a silent demand to continue.

"Thought I'd put it behind me," I managed, my voice thick. "Self-work, trying to work through it mentally. Turns out..." I swallowed hard. "The body remembers what the mind tries to forget. That's where it was stuck, waiting to be released."

"Then the next one happened at midnight," I continued, my voice shaking. "That's when it hit. The breakdown...it felt like a physical blow. One minute, peaceful slumber...the next, drowning in pure terror. My heart pounded, a desperate drumbeat against my ribs. Each ragged gasp seemed stolen from thin air. Panic clawed its way up my throat, an invisible hand squeezing the life out of me. The techniques, all that discipline...gone, like dust in the wind. I stumbled out, driven only by the animal instinct for survival."

Sir Arjun listened intently, his expression a mask of compassion and understanding. His presence felt calming, a balm to my raw nerves. In his eyes, I saw not judgment, but a deep empathy that held me steady. After a moment of silence, he spoke, his voice calm and reassuring.

"I'm glad you overcame it," he said. "It sounds like you faced a formidable challenge."

A sense of relief engulfed me, knowing that he understood the depths of my experience. "It makes sense now," I replied, my voice steadier. "What the Teacher meant...about battles only we can fight. Turns out, that was mine. Still...glad I wasn't alone. Coming here, it felt right."

He remained silent for a moment, his gaze unwavering, an anchor in the storm of emotions swirling within me. Then, with a subtle shift in his posture, he relaxed slightly, leaning back against the wall. It was as if my vulnerability had opened a door between us, allowing for a deeper connection.

I asked him, "I overheard someone in the cafeteria say you were a judge. Is that true?"

He chuckled. "Sometimes I do find myself shouting at lawyers, yes."

"Wouldn't have guessed," I said, surprised by his candor. Curiosity piqued, I asked, "So, how is the retreat treating you? Must be a breeze compared to your thirty-day stints, huh?"

His answer surprised me. "Not at all. Struggle is part of it, I think. For everyone."

"Didn't expect that, honestly."

"It varies," he said, his voice calm. "Person to person. The challenges we face here are often reflections of our own internal battles."

A quiet understanding settled between us. *Perhaps that's why we were all drawn here, each of us carrying our own burdens, seeking solace and transformation in the depths of silence and introspection. Just like Sir Arjun, a judge in the outside world, seeking balance and equanimity within.*

"You're probably right," I mumbled, then added, "Not sure about another retreat myself. Gotta let this one sink in first."

"It'll come when the time's right," he said, a knowing smile gracing his lips.

With that, our conversation ended. I felt a sense of gratitude for his understanding and support, a silent acknowledgement passing between us. As I walked away, I pondered his words, recognizing the truth in them. The struggle was indeed part of the journey, and perhaps that was where the greatest growth occurred.

Ethan the Hiker

On the way back to my room, I finally caught sight of Ethan. He was standing near the container house, his phone held aloft, capturing the lush greenery that surrounded us.

"Hey Ethan!" I called out as he reached the top of the stairs leading up from the container houses.

He paused, ending a voice memo on his phone. "Raymond, man! What's happening?" His voice boomed with an enthusiasm that surprised me, a stark contrast to the hushed whispers of the past ten days.

"Been meaning to catch you again," I said, a smile tugging at my lips. "It's good to finally hear your voice after all these days of silence. I remember those shared meals, us trying to communicate with just our eyes and nods. It was quite the adventure, wasn't it?"

As we walked, I couldn't help but feel a sense of gratitude towards Ethan. His simple act of kindness on that first day, offering the breathing technique, had been a lifeline during my initial panic. Now, seeing him here, on the cusp of completing the retreat, filled me with a sense of shared accomplishment.

"Heh, 'do' is a strong word," he chuckled, his eyes sparkling with excitement. "Help out with a friend's business in Canada. Actually, I just got back from Japan, meeting up with friends here before heading back."

"Nice! Been to Japan myself," I said. "Great country."

"Tokyo was a blast," he agreed, his phone already back in his hand, capturing the sights and sounds of the retreat. "So, what about you? More travels after this? I think you mentioned you were on the road before?"

"Yeah, well...not sure where next. But London, Egypt, and Bali top the list."

"Woah, talk about spiritual destinations!" he said. "I've always wanted to explore those places too. Maybe we'll cross paths again on our journeys."

"Speaking of, I actually overheard you and Alec," I hesitated, unsure if I was overstepping. "I'm a total newbie to the whole spirituality thing." He looked down at the cobblestones as we walked, seemingly lost in thought.

"Hey, no pressure," I said. "Spirituality's a journey for everyone, different paces."

"I know, but..." He paused. "After that first day, man, I was worried. Saw your empty seat at meals, figured you'd bailed."

"Hah!" I barked out a laugh. "Brutal first few days. Just kept telling myself, gotta show up, gotta see this through."

The relief in his eyes was unmistakable. It seemed my presence, or rather, my perseverance, had offered him some solace as well. *Perhaps we were all mirrors for each other, reflecting both strengths and weaknesses, fears and hopes. In this strange and silent world, we had found a connection, a sense of belonging that transcended words.*

Silence hung between us as we reached the cafeteria. He seemed lost in his own thoughts, the retreat's effects clearly stirring something deep within him. His fingers tapped rhythmically against his phone, as if trying to capture the fleeting thoughts and emotions that swirled within.

"Well...thanks," he mumbled, finally breaking the silence. "Safe travels."

"You too."

I watched him walk away, a sense of curiosity and concern lingering. It was clear that the retreat had touched him in some way, but the nature of that touch remained a mystery. *Perhaps he, like many of us, was still processing the profound experience we had shared, the layers of our true selves slowly unraveling. Or perhaps, he was already planning his next adventure, eager to capture the world through his lens and share it with others.*

Kiran the Young Yogi

That first day, Kiran – the guy with the long hair and a jolt of energy that rivaled my own anxiety – had surprised me with a playful poke in the back. A bizarre greeting, but he was the kind of person who operated off his own compass. Right away, I felt a sense of kinship with him, a shared spark of mischief amidst the solemn atmosphere of the retreat.

"Do you do yoga?" he asked as we crossed paths at our rooms.

"Uhh, yeah," I stammered, "I watch YouTube videos, some poses here and there..." Not exactly mastery, but at least it was something.

He became my silent guardian angel on our daily hikes, a soft "psst" snapping me back to the present when I drifted too far into my thoughts – which, with Marcus leading the way, happened more often than I cared to admit. *Kiran, with his gentle spirit and keen observation, seemed to sense my inner struggles even without words. His presence was a comforting reminder that I wasn't alone in this journey.* Kiran, in his long brown malong with that big circle-of-life pattern in the center, moved with a surprising ease, as if barely connected to the ground. *The circle on his malong, a symbol of interconnectedness and the cyclical nature of existence, seemed to resonate with the very essence of Vipassana.* Each time he passed, I felt a prickle of awareness, like the air shifted around him. He had a way of noticing things unseen, an undeniable aura that set him apart. One time, I saw him watching intently at a patch of dirt off the ground. After he moved on, I curiously checked and saw a line of black ants diligently trying to build a nest. "You don't see that kind of observation every day," I mused, "He's truly in tune with his surroundings, such a rare ability for a man."

On Day 10, I found myself in the library. I saw him again.

"Think they care if you grab two?" He muttered to himself.

"Hey, what are those?" I asked. "One looked kind of orange..."

He shrugged, and said, "This 'Meditation for Men' deal by Goenka. Maybe it's got something useful..."

We were busy picking what books to borrow before heading back to our rooms. Back at my quarters, my brain was on hyperdrive. What to wear, what to pack... damn, I'd already forgotten the new schedule. Heard those light footsteps – had to be Kiran – and figured, why not just ask?

"Hey, Kiran," I called out. "Do you remember if that crazy early wake-up call tomorrow is 4 AM sharp? And what's after that again?"

"Yeah, 4 AM at the meditation hall, and all that jazz, then Goenka talks until 7:30-ish," he said.

"Right, got it." I gave my thanks.

"By the way, ever tried talking to Alec?" He meant the bearded Alec.

"Nah, why?"

"Haha, okay, I'll give it a shot," I said, intrigued by Kiran's cryptic comment.

"Good to hear," Kiran said, then caught my eye, a playful glint in his own. "You know I heard you talking to the teacher about feeling energy in meditation?"

"Yeah, I get all hot and tingly. What about you?"

"Energy all over, for me," he said. I grinned. "Mr. Energy, huh?"

"Hey, I'm serious." He raised an eyebrow, a mix of amusement and challenge in his expression.

A smile tugged at my lips. "Just kidding," I said. "Seriously though, of all the guys here, you seem the most into spirituality stuff. How'd you end up on this retreat?"

"Ah, my yoga teacher," he said, a nostalgic smile gracing his lips. "Back home in Pampanga, he was the one who introduced me to meditation after his own Vipassana experience. Now he teaches yoga."

A comfortable silence settled between us as we walked, the crunch of gravel underfoot the only sound breaking the stillness. We shared a knowing glance, acknowledging the unspoken connection forged in the crucible of the retreat.

"Hey, you know that first day? With the anxiety and everything...you could feel that, huh?" I finally asked, breaking the silence.

Kiran's smile faded, replaced by a look of empathy. "Yeah, definitely," he said, his voice softening. "We were seatmates in the hall, so I got a strong sense of it. That's actually why I moved back, needed to focus on my own meditation."

"No worries," I reassured him. "I was battling some stuff too, so yeah, wasn't easy."

Later, Kiran and I were taking pictures outside the center. He undid his braids, joking, "Time to channel my feminine side in front of the Meditation Hall." I commented on the importance of balancing yin and yang, and Kiran's face lit up with a genuine smile. We both did a little yogi bow, and I snapped a few shots. Marcus and the other guys joined us, and soon we were all posing, a group of strangers turned brothers, united by a shared experience of introspection and growth.

Finally, it was time to leave. Kiran gathered his belongings, headed for his car, and was off back to Pampanga. *I hope to see you again, my friend,* I thought to myself, a wave of warmth washing over me as I realized the depth of connection I had formed with this enigmatic young yogi in just ten days of silence. Meeting such a diverse group of people on this retreat was a revelation in itself. It truly showed me how complex and fascinating we all are, each with our own unique stories and paths to walk.

But it was Kiran who left the most lasting impression, his gentle presence and unwavering support a beacon of light during my darkest moments. Our connection transcended words, a silent understanding forged in the crucible of shared experience. Whether a guardian angel or a kindred spirit, I knew our encounter was no mere coincidence. It was a serendipitous meeting that would forever shape my understanding of myself and the world around me.

Alec the Second

Alec, the bearded guy I'd helped find his way on the first day, was a young man with the same youthful energy as Kiran. He was quiet, with an intensity that often manifested as solitude. Alec carried himself with a maturity that hinted at hidden depths. Our interactions were minimal; he always seemed to be lost in his own world, his gaze often fixed on some distant point.

Yet, fate intertwined our paths in unexpected ways. Kiran, Alec, and I were consistently the first called to share our meditation experiences. While mine were filled with heat and tingling, and Kiran spoke of energy surges, Alec remained silent, a blank slate amidst our eager sharing. He even declined joining the group photo at the end, choosing to remain apart.

His aloofness intrigued me. It mirrored my own past self – the one who craved isolation, who feared vulnerability. *Perhaps, I wondered, being grouped with us, hearing about our experiences, had stirred something within him. After all, this was a journey of self-discovery, and not everyone progressed at the same pace.* Perhaps Alec simply needed time, slowly unraveling the layers of his own inner mystery. Or perhaps, he had already found what he was seeking, the silence a testament to a profound inner peace that needed no words. *Alec's silence was both intriguing and frustrating. It reminded me of my own past tendency to retreat into myself, to build walls around my heart. Did he carry the same burdens, the same fears of vulnerability? Or was his silence a sign of a peace I had yet to attain?*

Later that day, curiosity got the better of me, and I approached Alec. He was carrying cleaning supplies towards the wash area. "Hey Alec," I began, "need a hand with that?"

He looked up, a hint of surprise in his eyes, then shook his head. "No, I'm good," he muttered, his voice barely above a whisper. He continued on his way, leaving me to ponder his reserved demeanor.

As Alec walked away, the cleaning supplies clutched tightly in his hands, I couldn't help but see them as a metaphor for his own inner cleansing, a silent scrubbing away of the past to make space for something new. Was he, like the rest of us, fighting his own battles, finding the strength to navigate the storms within?

The gong's harsh clang shattered the stillness, signaling lunchtime. As faces flooded back into the cafeteria, it wasn't just hunger driving the smiles and eager chatter. A newfound warmth radiated from the men, a shared sense of accomplishment after days of silent introspection. In the last ten days, while little had changed outwardly, we had each undergone our own trials, fought our own battles, and emerged transformed. It was a silent victory, etched on our faces, testament to facing inner demons. *Perhaps, even Alec, in his quiet way, had found a measure of peace within the storm.*

Chapter 23

Like Father, Like Son

I was becoming my father. The very person I'd sworn I'd never be like.

Growing up, my mother's warning echoed constantly: "Don't be like your father when you grow up." I absorbed her words, but resisting his influence felt unnatural, like denying a part of myself.

During the Vipassana retreat, I'd glimpsed something in my own mind that looked terrifyingly familiar - the same patterns, the same struggles he'd faced. The vision I described in Chapter 21 wasn't just about my own psyche. It was about understanding his.

"The very thing you detest the most is often the very thing you end up becoming."

Even as a kid, I'd watch him from my spot at the dining table. He'd be on the red linen sofa with its intricate floral design, fingers intertwined, staring at the glass table or gazing at the walls as if seeking solace in their silent embrace. The square clock with the eagle design hung just above where he sat. A vase of flowers on the center table. Everything in its place, but him somewhere else entirely.

"What is he doing this time?" I'd silently wonder as I chewed my meal, a young observer trying to understand something I had no framework for yet. I wanted to bridge the gap between us, to unravel the mysteries of his mind. But I couldn't.

Exploring the Masculine Psyche

In my exploration of the silent epidemic affecting men, I turned to literature that echoed my own experiences. The works of James Hollis and Robert Moore and Douglas Gillette provided valuable insights into the complexities of masculine psychology and the father-son dynamic.

In *Under Saturn's Shadow: The Wounding and Healing of Men*, James Hollis explores the concept of "father hunger," a deep yearning in men for guidance, affirmation, and a healthy masculine role model. This concept struck a chord within me as I grappled with the ambivalent legacy of my father. Hollis's insights helped me understand that my father's struggles were not unique but rather part of a larger pattern of wounded masculinity passed down through generations.

Hollis's exploration of the mother complex also shed light on the intricate dynamics between mothers and sons. He emphasizes that a mother's influence, whether positive or negative, can profoundly shape a man's relationship with himself, others, and the feminine principle. In my own life, I recognized the complex interplay between my mother's protective instincts and my father's emotional distance, both of which contributed to my own anxieties and insecurities.

The absence of positive male role models and the lack of rituals that facilitate the transition from boyhood to manhood, as highlighted by Hollis, have left many men feeling lost and adrift. This lack of guidance and initiation can lead to a distorted sense of masculinity, where men may overcompensate by adopting aggressive or dominant behaviors, or conversely, withdraw into isolation and emotional suppression. In my own life, I recognized the impact of this absence, as I struggled to define my own masculinity and find my place in the world.

This realization led me to further explore the archetypes that shape men's lives, seeking a deeper understanding of the forces that had shaped both my father and myself.

King, Warrior, Magician, Lover

The next book I've read is *King, Warrior, Magician, Lover* by Robert Moore and Douglas Gillette. It wasn't just another book; it was a journey into the depths of masculine psychology, a roadmap for understanding the archetypes that shape men's lives. As I delved into each archetype, I realized that these are not rigid categories, but rather fluid energies that can coexist and even complement each other within a single individual. The goal is not to identify with just one, but to cultivate a healthy balance of all four.

The King: The King archetype, in its fullness, embodies order, responsibility, and generativity. He is the one who creates a safe and stable environment, who provides for his people, and who ensures the continuation of life and culture. The King's energy is one of benevolent leadership, of holding a vision for the future, and of inspiring others to work towards a common good. In his shadow aspect, however, the King can become a tyrant, abusing his power, becoming rigid and controlling, or abdicating his responsibilities altogether.

My grandfather, despite his humble beginnings as a seafarer, embodied the regal qualities of the King, though he also possessed a warrior's determination and a magician's wisdom. He led our family with quiet dignity, offering wisdom and guidance drawn from a life lived fully. His decisions, always made with the collective well-being in mind, instilled in me a deep respect for authority and a desire to lead with integrity. However, his strict disciplinary measures, like the sharp slap I received for making my cousin cry, also hinted at the shadow side of the King—a potential for rigidity and control.

The Warrior: The Warrior archetype represents courage,

discipline, and the ability to take action. He is the protector, the defender, the one who stands up for what is right and fights for justice. The Warrior's energy is focused, determined, and unwavering in the face of adversity. In his shadow form, the Warrior can become a sadist, using violence and aggression to dominate others, or a masochist, turning his destructive tendencies inward.

My father, in his youth, embodied the Warrior spirit above all else, yet his love for his family (a Lover quality) and his moments of quiet reflection (a Magician trait) also shaped his actions. Tales of his athletic prowess on the basketball court and his unwavering determination in overcoming challenges painted a picture of a man who faced life head-on. His example instilled in me a sense of courage and resilience, a belief that I could overcome any obstacle if I set my mind to it. However, his struggles with addiction and the influence of negative peer pressure also revealed the shadow side of the Warrior—the destructive potential of unchecked aggression and the vulnerability to self-sabotage. This imbalance in the Warrior archetype, as described by Moore and Gillette, can manifest as a toxic masculinity that prioritizes dominance and control over empathy and vulnerability. It can lead to a suppression of emotions, a fear of vulnerability, and a reliance on aggression as a means of asserting power. In my father's case, the pressures of societal expectations and the lack of healthy emotional outlets contributed to his struggles with addiction and ultimately, his untimely demise.

The Magician: The Magician archetype embodies transformation, knowledge, and the power of the unseen. He is the shaman, the healer, the one who bridges the gap between the physical and spiritual realms. The Magician's energy is one of mystery, intuition, and the ability to see beyond the surface of things. In his shadow aspect, the Magician can become a manipulator, using his knowledge and power for selfish gain, or a detached observer, losing touch with the emotional needs of himself and others. He can also succumb to self-doubt, questioning his own abilities and wisdom.

The Magician archetype resonated deeply with me, perhaps more than any other. Yet, I recognized the King's leadership within me, the Warrior's resilience, and the Lover's passion, all vying for expression. The mystical visions I experienced during meditation, the sense of interconnectedness, and the insights into my father's pain all hinted at the transformative power that lies beyond the ordinary. My own journey of self-discovery, of unraveling the mysteries of my mind and my family history, felt like a quest for hidden knowledge, a path towards personal alchemy. Yet, I also recognized the shadow of the Magician within me—the tendency to doubt my own intuition and to rely on external validation. The retreat has taught me to trust my inner knowing and to embrace the power of transformation that lies within.

The Lover: The Lover archetype, the final aspect, embodies masculinity's essence of passion, connection, and the joy of being alive. He is the romantic, the artist, the one who finds beauty and meaning in the world around him. The Lover's energy is one of empathy, vulnerability, and the ability to form deep and mean-ingful relationships with others. In his shadow form, the Lover can become addicted to pleasure, seeking external validation and losing touch with his own inner worth, or become impotent, with-drawing from emotional connection and intimacy.

I, too, resonate with the Lover archetype, though perhaps not to its fullest extent before. Yet, the King's desire for order, the Warrior's determination, and the Magician's intuition all reside within me, waiting to be integrated into a harmonious whole. I've always been passionate and expressive, drawn to the beauty of the natural world and the emotional depths of human connection. As a child, I would spend hours playing in the fields with my cousins, flying kites and chasing each other under the vast expanse of the sky. I felt a deep connection to the earth, the wind, and the sun, a sense of belonging that transcended words. I even had an affinity for the chickens we raised, often spending time in their coop, imagining it as my own little house.

Later in life, my passion found an outlet in creative pursuits. I remember the exhilaration of shooting a music video for a college project, a hilarious endeavor filled with laughter, camaraderie, and a shared sense of purpose. It was a reminder that joy and connection could be found in the most unexpected places. The Lover archetype, while often associated with romantic love, extends far beyond it. It encompasses the deep affection and connection we share with our animal companions, our friends, and even our own passions and creative pursuits.

The Lover archetype reminds me that true strength lies not in denying our emotions, but in embracing them fully, allowing ourselves to be vulnerable, and connecting with the world and others from a place of love and authenticity. The retreat has taught me the importance of putting myself out there, of risking intimacy and connection, even in the face of potential rejection or hurt. It's a lesson I'll carry with me as I continue my journey, seeking deeper connections with both myself and the world around me.

However, the Lover archetype, like the others, can be distorted by societal pressures and expectations. In a culture that often equates masculinity with emotional stoicism and detachment, the Lover's vulnerability can be seen as a weakness. This can lead men to suppress their emotions, avoid intimacy, and seek validation through superficial connections or addictive behaviors. In my own life, I've struggled with the shadow side of the Lover, seeking external validation and numbing my pain through escapism.

The retreat, with its emphasis on self-reflection and emotional awareness, has helped me to recognize and heal these patterns. It has shown me that true strength lies not in denying our emotions, but in embracing them fully, allowing ourselves to be vulnerable, and connecting with the world and others from a place of love and authenticity. It's a lesson I'll carry with me as I continue my journey, seeking deeper connections with both myself and the world around me.

It's important to acknowledge that the journey towards a healthy and integrated masculinity is ongoing. There will be setbacks, challenges, and moments of doubt. But by embracing the full spectrum of our emotions, strengths, and vulnerabilities, we can break free from the limitations of toxic masculinity and create a new paradigm for what it means to be a man.

Revisiting His Past

In my quest to move forward, I delved into the secrets of my past, seeking to unravel the enigma that shrouded my father's history. My investigative journey led me to the roots of my paternal lineage, tracing back to Bacolod City, an island situated just across the waters from my upbringing in Iloilo City.

My grandfather, a seafarer like my father, ventured from Bacolod to Iloilo in pursuit of work. It was in Iloilo City that he crossed paths with my grandmother, the matriarch of our family. Together, they raised six children, with my father claiming the position of the third sibling among four brothers and two sisters. Their residence, conveniently adjacent to our concrete house, presented a peculiar contrast – our modern abode juxtaposed with their unique wooden home, resembling a treehouse from my childhood fantasies.

The wooden structure was a marvel to behold, featuring a slanting door that needed to be pulled down for the night, and floors crafted from an assortment of wooden pieces, each size contributing to the overall tapestry of memories. I often found myself intrigued by the gaps between the wooden floorboards, sparking my curiosity about the mysterious realm beneath.

Reflecting the family's maritime legacy, my grandfather's occupation as a seaman mirrored my father's eventual profession. The allure of a high-paying job in those times drove both men to navigate the vast seas. As a child, I was fortunate to experience the presence of both sets of grandparents. Their influence, however, came with its share of challenges.

My grandfather, strict and disciplinary, didn't hesitate to administer a stern punishment when I inadvertently made my younger cousin cry. The memory of a sharp slap on my diapered behind lingers, a reminder of his uncompromising approach. Yet, on the opposite end of the spectrum, amidst times of illness, he displayed a tender side. His remedy for a cold involved crafting a delicious calamansi juice, a gesture that remains etched in the fabric of my early memories.

Later in life, my grandfather succumbed to colon cancer. At the time, I was too young to fully grasp the weight of his passing. However, he left behind an important memento: my name, Raymond. He bestowed it upon me in honor of his favorite young captain, a man he admired for his wisdom beyond his years. While I once harbored resentment towards this name, I now realize its honor and legacy.

Just as my grandfather imparted his wisdom to my father, so too did my father pass on his knowledge to me. Despite sharing the same elementary and high schools, my father's journey diverged from the successes of his youth. Although he graduated with honors, excelled on the varsity team, and captured the attention of many admirers, he succumbed to life's vices, experimenting with drugs and alcohol during his fraternity years.

Final Closure

Reflecting on my journey, I recognize that experiences, no matter how challenging, serve as catalysts for growth. Lacking a healthy father figure growing up, I turned to the protagonists of video games for guidance and inspiration. Their journeys of overcoming obstacles and achieving greatness resonated with my own yearning for purpose and direction.

My rites of passage into adulthood unfolded organically after college when the urge to explore beyond my hometown became irresistible. Determined to embrace life beyond familiar boundaries, I set forth on a journey to Metro Manila, relying solely on my instincts. Stepping into a world vastly different from my upbringing was a daunting transition. Tito N, my father's younger brother, provided me with temporary shelter, but beyond that, I had to navigate the complexities of life on my own. As a "provinciano," adapting to the fast-paced urban lifestyle posed its own set of challenges. Yet, with each obstacle encountered, I gained invaluable insights and forged my path in the world.

My journey continued as I embarked on travels, initially with the support of my sister, who encouraged me to step outside my comfort zone. I found myself in unfamiliar territories, grappling with language barriers and getting lost countless times. Each setback became a lesson, guiding me back on course and shaping my understanding of resilience. Eventually, my travels led me to Japan, where the cultural immersion and encounters with new perspectives further broadened my horizons and deepened my self-awareness.

Reflecting on my father's life, I couldn't help but draw parallels between his experiences and my own. His photographs from his travels across Europe sparked a desire within me to explore those same destinations someday. While I couldn't attribute all my qualities to him, I recognized the influence of video games and anime during my formative years, shaping my perception of masculinity and heroism.

In the wake of my father's passing, I sought solace in video games, immersing myself in virtual worlds as a form of escapism. Yet, his untimely death left unanswered questions lingering. I couldn't ignore the societal pressures that contributed to his struggles, nor could I dismiss the importance of addressing unresolved trauma within our lineage. His funeral brought to light the superficiality of societal connections, prompting me to question the authenticity of relationships built on fleeting pleasures. Amidst the uncertainty, I resolved to break free from societal expectations and chart my path with authenticity and purpose.

The retreat served as a mirror, reflecting both the strengths and weaknesses I inherited from my father and grandfather. I recognized the King in my grandfather's quiet dignity and leadership, the Warrior in my father's resilience and determination, and the Magician in my own thirst for knowledge and transformation. Yet, I realized the importance of embracing the Lover archetype, representing the positive aspects of the mature masculine, to achieve a balanced and integrated sense of self.

A true man, I now understand, is not defined by societal expectations or external achievements. He is a man who:

- Embraces challenges as opportunities for growth.
- Believes in his potential for greatness and confronts obstacles with unwavering ambition.
- Carries the weight of his loved ones' troubles with strength and compassion.
- Shapes his world according to his vision, inviting his family to share in its evolution.
- Safeguards his realm from harm, continuously striving for self-improvement.
- Enriches the lives of those around him, standing against wrongdoing and confronting danger to secure valuable resources.
- Embraces vulnerability and seeks help when needed.

As I continue on this journey of self-discovery, I carry my father's legacy within me, not as a burden, but as a guiding light. The retreat has shown me that true strength lies not in denying our emotions or conforming to societal expectations, but in embracing our vulnerabilities, connecting with our inner truth, and living a life of purpose and authenticity. It is through this integration of the King, Warrior, Magician, and Lover within myself that I can truly honor my father's memory and fulfill the mission that I cannot fail. And as I do, I see him – not the troubled figure of my childhood, but the young man with a bright smile in his graduation photo, full of potential and the promise of a life yet to be lived.

Chapter 24

Rewriting my Thirties

Why leave a comfortable career to chase an undefined path? It's the question I kept asking myself. Promotions and big salaries left me empty, but it was the sudden chill from former colleagues upon my resignation that crystallized the truth: the corporate world's inauthenticity wasn't for me. That, combined with years of stifled creativity and the echoing dread of Monday mornings, propelled me towards a different life.

This journey of rewriting my thirties is guided by **five principles**:

1. Reclaiming My Destiny: Navigating the Balance Between Ambition and Authenticity

From a young age, I was driven to achieve. I excelled in academics, won awards in competitions, and graduated with honors. The corporate world, with its promise of success and stability, seemed like the logical next step. However, after years of climbing the corporate ladder, a nagging question emerged: Is this truly what I want?

I had achieved the external markers of success – a stable job, a decent salary, and recognition from my peers. Yet, a growing sense of emptiness gnawed at me. There was a disconnect between my external achievements and my internal desires. A feeling nagged at me that I was meant for something bigger, something more than just being a cog in a machine.

Traveling opened my eyes to the fleeting nature of life and ignited a yearning for work that aligned with my values of creativity, freedom, and making a meaningful impact. I began to question the societal norms and expectations that had guided my choices thus far. Was external validation truly the key to happiness? Or was there a way to balance the practicality of earning a living with a deeper sense of purpose?

I realized that I had unknowingly subscribed to a form of *empire consciousness*, a mindset that values power, control, and external validation above all else. This mindset was reinforced by the corporate culture, which emphasized competition, hierarchy, and profit maximization. But I also recognized that not all work within established structures is inherently soul-crushing. Many find meaning and fulfillment in their careers, contributing to a greater good or expressing their creativity within existing roles.

This realization marked the beginning of my journey to reclaim my destiny. It wasn't about rejecting work altogether, but about redefining my relationship with it. I yearned for a career path that was an extension of my values and passions, a path that reflected my authentic self. It was time to redefine success on my own terms and forge a career that resonated with my soul

2. **Embracing Vulnerability:** Unveiling Authenticity and
   Cultivating Deeper Connections

In the office, I was a carefully curated version of myself. Smiles were plastered on, opinions were muted, and my true self was carefully tucked away, like a cherished memento hidden in a dusty attic. This wasn't unique to the office. In social settings, I'd often find myself echoing the sentiments of others, afraid to voice unpopular opinions or reveal my quirks. The fear of judgment was a constant companion, whispering doubts in my ear and urging me to conform.

But leaving that world cracked open a door I hadn't realized was closed. It wasn't an immediate flood of unfiltered emotions and revelations. Instead, it was a gradual reawakening of my true self, a process Brené Brown so aptly describes as "letting go of who we think we're supposed to be and embracing who we are." I began to question the masks I'd worn for so long. Why did I feel the need to dim my light to fit in?

Even as a child, I'd embraced my passions wholeheartedly. Whether it was my love for certain books, movies, or hobbies, I never shied away from expressing my enthusiasm. Some mistook this passion for fandom, but it was simply my way of being authentic and true to myself. I started to wonder if I could bring that same level of authenticity into my adult life.

It wasn't about abandoning all social graces or becoming a bulldozer of unfiltered thoughts. It was about finding a balance. In professional settings, I learned to maintain boundaries while still expressing my unique perspective. In social circles, I practiced sharing my opinions, even if they differed from the majority.

This journey of embracing vulnerability hasn't been without its challenges. There have been moments of self-doubt, of wondering if I'd gone too far or revealed too much. But with each step, I've gained a deeper understanding of myself and forged more meaningful connections with others.

I've learned that vulnerability doesn't mean oversharing or being unprofessional. It means showing up as my true self, with my unique passions, quirks, and perspectives. It means being honest about my strengths and weaknesses, and not being afraid to express my emotions in a healthy way. It's an ongoing process of self-discovery, of shedding layers of inauthenticity to reveal the person I was always meant to be.

3. **Adventure:** a Catalyst for Self-Discovery and Transformation

The allure of materialism, a relentless contest of who has the biggest house or the fastest car, had always left me feeling empty. I'd witnessed firsthand the deep-seated unhappiness that often lurked beneath the surface of those who over-identified with possessions. In contrast, my travels opened my eyes to a world of experiences that money couldn't buy, experiences that enriched my life in ways that material possessions never could.

The towering cliffs of El Nido were a metaphor for the challenges I faced in leaving my comfort zone. As I stood on the edge, heart pounding, I knew that if I didn't take the leap, I would never know what lay beyond my fears. The exhilaration of jumping, the feeling of the wind rushing past me, and the breathtaking view from the top of Taraw Cliff were a visceral reminder that sometimes, the most rewarding experiences come from embracing the unknown.

I realized there was so much more to life than the lukewarm coffee and endless spreadsheets that had defined my corporate existence. Travel offered a stark contrast, a vibrant tapestry of experiences that ignited my curiosity and expanded my horizons. As I navigated the bustling streets of Tokyo, lost and overwhelmed, I felt a surge of panic. But instead of retreating to the safety of my hotel room, I decided to embrace the discomfort. I wandered aimlessly, striking up conversations with locals, trying new foods, and simply observing the rhythm of this unfamiliar city. It was in those moments of vulnerability and uncertainty that I felt most alive, most connected to the world around me.

But adventure isn't just about hopping on a plane. It's a mindset, a way of approaching life with curiosity and openness. It's about seeking out new experiences, even in the mundane, and embracing the unexpected with open arms. Whether it's exploring a new neighborhood in my own city, trying a new hobby, or simply taking a different route to work, I've learned that adventure can be found in the everyday if I'm willing to look for it.

Through these journeys, both near and far, I learned to appreciate the simple pleasures: the mischievous antics of monkeys in a Balinese temple, their playful energy a reminder to embrace the lighter side of life; the laughter shared with new friends, the feeling of the sun on my face as I wandered through ancient ruins. I discovered the joy of being fully present, of savoring each moment, and of finding fulfillment beyond the pursuit of material wealth.

Adventure has become more than just a pastime; it's a way of life. It has taught me resilience, resourcefulness, and the importance of staying open to new possibilities. It has challenged me to step outside my comfort zone, confront my fears, and embrace the unknown. And in doing so, it has transformed me into a more open-minded, compassionate, and adventurous individual. It has shown me that true wealth lies not in material possessions alone, but in the richness of our experiences, the depth of our connections, and the pursuit of a life that is aligned with our true purpose.

4. **Forging an Independent Path:** Embracing Individuality While Recognizing the Power of Community

Independence has always been a core part of my identity. From a young age, I was raised to be self-reliant, a skill that seamlessly transitioned into my corporate life. Every project, every initiative, bore the mark of my independent spirit. I thrived on taking ownership, leading from the front, and crafting solutions on my own.

But over time, I discovered that unbridled independence can

be a double-edged sword. While it fueled my drive and determination, it also left me feeling isolated at times. The weight of every decision rested solely on my shoulders, and the lack of a sounding board or a supportive hand could be overwhelming.

My travels became a turning point. As I ventured into unfamiliar territories, I encountered diverse communities that challenged my assumptions about independence. I met fellow solo travelers who, like me, craved autonomy yet found solace and strength in connecting with others who shared their values and passions. It was through these encounters that I discovered the power of community, a realization that shifted my perspective on what it meant to be truly independent.

I learned that true independence isn't about isolation or self-sufficiency. It's about having the freedom to make choices that align with my values and passions, regardless of societal expectations. It's about trusting my own instincts and decisions, even when they go against the grain. But it's also about recognizing that we don't have to walk this path alone.

Having a supportive network of friends, mentors, and like-minded individuals can amplify our independence. They provide a safe space for us to share our struggles, celebrate our victories, and learn from each other's experiences. They challenge us to grow, offer different perspectives, and remind us that we are not alone on this journey.

Over time, I found it fascinating to balance both worlds. I learned to hone in and focus on the things I wanted to do in life, cultivating a deeper level of awareness about my environment. But I also learned to lean on my community when I needed support, guidance, or simply a listening ear.

Being independent is one thing, but having friends and people going with you along the way can be even more fun. It's a reminder that we are social creatures, wired for connection and belonging. And it's in that connection that we often find the strength and courage to forge our own unique paths.

If there's one piece of advice I can offer to those seeking independence, it's this: find your people. They exist, and they're out there. Seek out communities, both online and offline, where you can connect with individuals who share your passions, values, and aspirations. Don't be afraid to ask for help, offer support, and learn from each other's journeys. Remember, true independence is not about going it alone, but about building a strong foundation of support that allows us to thrive as our authentic selves.

5. **Trusting Intuition:** Navigating Life with a Balanced Approach

As a child, I navigated the world with an almost uncanny intuition. I remember the time my cousin gasped in amazement when I accurately predicted the ending of a movie we were watching. It was like a game to me, sensing the subtle currents of energy that hinted at what was to come. Even my dreams were often prophetic, revealing glimpses of future events that would later unfold.

But as I grew older, the demands of the "real world" began to chip away at this innate ability. The corporate world, with its emphasis on logic, data, and linear thinking, subtly silenced my inner voice. I learned to suppress my gut feelings, to prioritize spreadsheets over serendipity, and to rely on external validation rather than my own internal compass.

Yet, even as I conformed to the expectations of my career, a flicker of my intuition remained. It whispered to me in quiet moments, urging me to question the status quo and seek a path that resonated with my soul. But I'd grown adept at ignoring those whispers, convincing myself that logic and reason were the only reliable guides.

Then, a chance encounter with a colleague who was deeply immersed in spirituality and meditation rekindled the flame. She introduced me to practices that allowed me to reconnect with my inner wisdom, to hear the whispers more clearly, and to trust their guidance. Meditation became my sanctuary, a space where I could silence the noise of the world and tune into the subtle signals of my intuition.

It was during my travels, particularly a transformative trip to Japan, where I truly learned to integrate intuition and logic. In this country steeped in tradition and spirituality, I found myself navigating a delicate dance between the two. There were moments when I meticulously planned every detail of my itinerary, only to have a spontaneous encounter or hidden gem completely change the course of my day. I learned that while logic provided a framework, intuition added the magic, the serendipity that made each experience unique and unforgettable.

But there were also times when I overindulged in the intuitive realm, getting lost in my imagination and losing sight of practical considerations. I learned that too much of a good thing can be detrimental, that a healthy dose of logic was necessary to ground me and make informed decisions.

My travels became my testing ground, a place where I could experiment with different approaches to decision-making, to find the sweet spot where intuition and logic worked in harmony. It was a journey of self-discovery, of learning to trust my inner compass while also acknowledging the importance of gathering information and considering different perspectives.

Through this process, I've come to realize that intuition is not a replacement for logic, but a powerful complement to it. It's the bridge between our conscious and subconscious minds, a channel through which we can access deeper wisdom and guidance. By learning to listen to our intuition, we open ourselves up to a world of possibilities, a world where magic and meaning can be found in the most unexpected places.

Chapter 25

The Greatest Intersection

As I stand at this crossroads, reflecting on the journey that led me here, I can't help but marvel at how far I've come. The person I was at the beginning of this story – the anxious young man navigating his first job in Manila, seeking solace in video games and struggling to find his place in the world – feels like a distant memory, a shadow of the man I am today.

This journey has been a winding road, filled with unexpected detours and breathtaking vistas. It's a tapestry woven with threads of joy and sorrow, triumphs and setbacks, love and loss. I've encountered a cast of characters who have shaped my life in profound ways, each one leaving an indelible mark on my heart and soul.

My mother and sister, the two pillars of feminine strength in my life, have taught me the unwavering power of unconditional love and the importance of *embracing vulnerability*. Their unwavering support and encouragement have been my bedrock, empowering me to shed the masks I once wore and embrace my authentic self. This was especially true after my father's passing, when our bond deepened, woven together by shared grief and a fierce determination to support one another. It was in those moments of raw vulnerability that I felt most seen, most loved, and most supported.

My father's absence, a wound that once felt raw and gaping, has been a catalyst for my personal growth. It has taught me the importance of cherishing the time we have with our loved ones, the power of forgiveness, and the importance of seeking out healthy masculine role models. Through this healing process, I have come to understand that the pain I felt wasn't his fault, but my own trauma resurfacing, seeking resolution. The "Mission I cannot fail" – the mission to embody a healthy and integrated masculinity – took on a new dimension. It became not just about honoring my father's memory, but also about breaking free from the cycles of pain and dysfunction that had been passed down through generations. It became about healing myself and creating a new legacy for future generations of men.

Reclaiming my destiny began as a whisper amidst the cacophony of corporate life. The suffocating routine, lack of autonomy, and misalignment with my values pushed me to a breaking point. The alarm blared one morning, and a wave of nausea enveloped me. I couldn't face another day of spreadsheets, meetings, and the suffocating routine. With a sudden surge of determination, I flung the covers back and sat up, a silent vow echoing in my mind: "This ends today." The decision to resign was a leap of faith, a declaration of independence from the expectations that had been placed upon me.

Even during my college to early corporate years, I sought solace and a sense of agency in virtual worlds like Pokemon. These digital adventures, where I could be the protagonist and shape my own destiny, sparked a desire for exploration and discovery that would eventually lead me to embrace the transformative power of travel. It was through online gaming forums that I met Jacob, Elio, and Flyffers, some of whom would become dear friends in real life. Their lightheartedness and camaraderie reminded me not to take life too seriously, and their friendship offered a much-needed respite from the pressures of the real world.

My experience directing a college play further solidified my understanding of the power of collaboration and creative expression. The positive feedback and recognition from my college classmates fueled my desire to create and share my work with a wider audience. It was through these shared experiences, both virtual and real, that I began to forge my own path, one that would eventually lead me away from the corporate world and towards a life of adventure, creativity, and self-discovery.

Uncertainty and self-doubt swirled after my resignation, but it was also a time of liberation and exploration. I began to question everything I had been taught about success and happiness, and to seek out alternative paths that aligned with my true values and passions. This exploration led me to embrace adventure and travel, to seek out the guidance of my Tita N and cousin Jil, who became my second family as I navigated the intricate city of Manila and introduced me to the world of self-help and spirituality.

One of the most pivotal figures during this time was Ms. Kris, an aspiring life coach. Her tough love approach pushed me out of my comfort zone and challenged me to confront my deepest fears and insecurities. Through her guidance, I discovered the transformative power of meditation and self-reflection, tools that have become essential in my journey of self-discovery and personal growth.

A chance encounter with an officemate, Pat, opened my eyes to the world of psychics and esoteric knowledge. Her own spiritual journey, including a past-life regression that revealed her as a priestess from Atlantis, sparked my curiosity and encouraged me to explore alternative paths to healing and self-discovery. Our conversations about energy, meditation, and the interconnectedness of all things deepened my understanding of the world and my place in it. It was through Pat's encouragement that I sought out a psychic reading, a pivotal moment that would later shape my understanding of my life's purpose and direction.

From the vibrant streets of Singapore, where my sister and I navigated our differences with newfound appreciation, to the serene temples, each experience was a stepping stone on my path to wholeness.

In Ilocos Norte, I found freedom in solitude, defying the insistence of others to have a travel companion. This solo adventure helped me overcome my anxiety and unlock a newfound confidence. I learned to *trust my intuition* as I navigated unfamiliar terrain, embracing the unexpected twists and turns of the journey.

Scaling the Taraw Cliff in El Nido with Tony taught me to confront my fears and seize opportunities. His spontaneous spirit reminded me that life is meant to be lived fully, and the greatest adventures are often unplanned. We shared laughter, adrenaline, and a deep appreciation for the natural beauty of the Philippines.

In Japan, two individuals crossed my path, forever leaving their mark on my soul. Kaito, a salaryman with dreams of returning to Africa, showed me the power of following one's heart, no matter how unconventional the path. His unwavering determination resonated deeply, reminding me that true happiness lies in pursuing our passions.

Astrid, a fellow adventurer in the snowy slopes of Niseko, embodied resilience and determination. As we navigated the icy terrain together, her unwavering support and encouragement taught me the power of perseverance in the face of challenges. Her infectious spirit reminded me that I was capable of achieving far more than I had ever imagined.

It was in Japan that I truly connected with the natural world. The meticulous care with which the Japanese tended to their gardens, the reverence they showed for ancient trees, and the pristine cleanliness of their cities all spoke to a deep respect for nature. Hiking through bamboo forests, witnessing the delicate beauty of cherry blossoms, and experiencing the tranquility of traditional tea ceremonies, I felt a sense of peace and harmony that I had never known before. This deep connection to nature further solidified my rejection of the empty pursuit of material wealth and fueled my desire to create a meaningful legacy.

Taiwan, with its serene temples and colorful villages, offered a different kind of adventure. A chance meeting with Kaya, a Japanese girl with a gentle spirit, taught me to open my heart to unexpected connections. Her kindness was a reminder that genuine connection exists in the real world, not just in fiction.

A music festival under a starlit sky marked another pivotal moment. On my birthday, a shooting star streaked across the heavens, symbolizing new beginnings. It was a moment of pure magic, a fleeting friendship forged under the celestial canopy, reminding me of the beauty and interconnectedness of all things.

Through my travels, I learned to embrace the unexpected and find beauty in unplanned detours. In the Rainbow Village, the colorful houses burst with artistic energy, showcasing the power of creativity to transform even the most mundane spaces. In the Buddha Museum's stillness, I found solace, a refuge for meditation and reflection.

Returning home from my adventures, I felt a renewed sense of purpose and a yearning to share my experiences and insights with others. This led me to embrace my passion for writing and content creation, a path that allows me to *forge my own path*, express my creativity, connect with a global community, and leave a lasting impact on the world.

This very book you hold in your hands is a testament to that passion. It is a culmination of years of self-reflection, travel, and spiritual exploration. It is a testament to the transformative power of *embracing vulnerability, seeking adventure, trusting intuition, and forging one's own path*. It is a message of hope, resilience, and the unwavering belief in the human spirit.

The online communities I had built through gaming and travel became a source of inspiration and support, reminding me that I wasn't alone in my journey of self-discovery.

Trusting the flow became essential as I entered my thirties. The global upheaval of the COVID-19 pandemic in 2020, coinciding with my 30th birthday, forced me to turn inward and confront the anxieties simmering beneath the surface. It was a time of introspection and questioning, a time to re-evaluate my priorities and seek new sources of meaning. Guided by my intuition, I embarked on a journey of deeper self-exploration, delving into spiritual practices and self-reflection, refining my intuition along the way.

Ayahuasca ceremonies, under the guidance of experienced shamans, opened my eyes to the unseen realms of consciousness and helped me access a deeper level of inner wisdom. They provided a glimpse into the interconnectedness of all things and the infinite possibilities that exist beyond our limited perception. It was a profound reminder that we are all spiritual beings having a human experience, and that our true nature is one of love, compassion, and interconnectedness. While my spiritual journey is deeply personal, I believe that everyone has the potential to find their own truth and meaning in life, whatever their beliefs or worldview may be.

These experiences, along with the Vipassana retreat, emphasized the importance of honoring the present moment. Whether through the sacred rituals of Ayahuasca or the disciplined practice of Vipassana, I was constantly reminded to come back to my breath and anchor myself in the now. This mindfulness practice has become a cornerstone of my daily life, a way to find peace and clarity amidst the chaos of the world. It has taught me to appreciate the simple joys of life, to be fully present in my interactions with others, and to cultivate a deep sense of gratitude for each moment.

The year 2023 arrived, a harbinger of unexpected challenges

and profound loss. The passing of our beloved family dog, my aunt, and the end of a significant chapter in my career, was a time of immense grief and sorrow. While devastated by these losses, I also recognized that grief can be a powerful motivator and catalyst for change. It forced me to confront my own mortality, to re-evaluate my priorities, and to seek deeper meaning in life. The pain of loss illuminated a new path, one that led me towards healing, growth, and a deeper understanding of myself.

This led me to the Vipassana retreat, a ten-day silent meditation course nestled in the heart of nature. It was a refuge for healing, offering me the space and time to process my grief, confront my demons, and cultivate a deeper sense of self-awareness. The days were long and arduous, filled with hours of sitting in meditation, observing the sensations of my body and the fluctuations of my mind. But through this rigorous practice, I began to unravel the layers of conditioning that had shaped my beliefs and behaviors.

The retreat was not just about meditation; it was also about community, even in the absence of words. The shared experience of silence and introspection created a profound sense of connection with the other participants. Though we couldn't speak, we could see each other's struggles and triumphs in our eyes, and we could feel the collective energy of compassion and support that filled the meditation hall.

It was through this silent communion with others that I began to heal the wounds of my past, particularly those related to my relationship with my father and the absence of a healthy masculine influence in my upbringing. The vulnerability and authenticity I witnessed in the other meditators inspired me to embrace my own vulnerability and to forge deeper connections with others.

The Vipassana retreat was a turning point in my journey of self-discovery. It taught me the importance of mindfulness, compassion, and equanimity. It helped me to develop a deeper understanding of myself, my emotions, and my place in the world.

And it showed me the power of silence, stillness, and self-observation to create lasting transformation.

The lessons I learned through travel, spiritual practice, and the challenges of loss have all reinforced the importance of trusting the flow of life. It's a lesson I continue to learn and re-learn, as I navigate the ever-changing landscape of my own existence. I've come to realize that life is not about controlling every outcome, but about embracing the journey with all its twists and turns. It's about surrendering to the unknown, trusting my intuition, and having faith that everything unfolds exactly as it should.

That's where I am today, writing the final chapter of my story. Sharing my experiences, I believe, is an act of service, a way to connect with others who may be on their own journeys of self-discovery. I believe that stories have the power to inspire, heal, and transform. They are the threads that connect us, weaving together the tapestry of human experience.

As I reflect on my journey, I am reminded of the words of Napoleon Bonaparte: "Let him sleep. When he wakes, he will move mountains." This quote resonates with me deeply, as it speaks to the transformative power of introspection and self-discovery. It is through delving into the depths of our own being, facing our shadows, and embracing our light that we can truly awaken to our full potential.

I am no longer afraid to tell my truth when someone tramples on my boundaries. I say what needs to be said for proper communication. I have also started seeking out communities where I feel I belong, both online and in my local area. I see it as a learning opportunity to learn from different kinds of people, not just limited to travel.

The path to self-discovery is not a straight line. It is a winding road filled with unexpected twists and turns. There will be moments of joy and sorrow, triumphs and setbacks. But through it all, we have the power to choose our own adventure. We can choose to embrace the unknown, to trust our intuition, and to create a life that is authentically our own. For me, writing this book has been like a rebirth, a new beginning. It felt as if everything I learned in school needed to be unlearned, as I embarked on a new quest with a blank slate. It's as if I've reached a point in my life where I need to start fresh again.

And while my story may be unique, the lessons I've learned along the way are universal. The tools I've discovered through spiritual practices, like meditation and yoga, and even daily exercise, have become a foundation for connecting with the present moment and cultivating a calmer, more centered mind. I encourage you, dear reader, to embark on your own journey of self-discovery, whatever that may mean for you. Step outside your comfort zone, challenge your assumptions, and embrace the uncertainty that comes with exploring the unknown. Whether it's traveling to a new place, trying a new hobby, or simply spending time in quiet reflection, allow yourself to be open to the possibilities that life has to offer.

As an explorer of life, I will continue to journey forward, driven by an insatiable curiosity and a deep desire to connect with others. I will continue to share my hopes, dreams, and inspirations with people from all walks of life, in the hopes that they, too, will find their own unique path to fulfillment.

This book is my legacy, a testament to the transformative power of vulnerability, adventure, intuition, and the unwavering belief in the human spirit. It is my hope that this book will inspire you to create your own legacy, one that is authentic, meaningful, and uniquely yours. After all, it is not up to me to say what your life will look like—that permission belongs solely to you.

So go forth, dear reader, and embrace the adventure that awaits you. Trust your intuition, follow your heart, and never stop exploring the vast landscape of your own being. The journey may be challenging, but the rewards are immeasurable. May your path be filled with joy, love, and the unwavering belief that you are capable of creating a life that is beyond your wildest dreams.

This is my **awakening,** my **greatest intersection,** and my **trance formation.**

Acknowledgments

First and foremost, I would like to thank my mother and sister for their unwavering support. To my mother, the best mother in the world, for her loyalty, unconditional love, and unwavering care through life's challenges. To my sister, with whom I share a sometimes tumultuous, yet ultimately loving, bond. Thank you for pushing me outside my comfort zone and onto this grand adventure.

To my father, whom I miss dearly. Writing this book has been a journey of grappling with your absence. Growing up without you wasn't easy, but it fueled my desire to share my story, to offer solace to others who have experienced loss. I cherish our memories together, and I hope, wherever you are, you are proud of my journey and the legacy I hope to leave behind.

To Tito N and Tita N, my second parents in Metro Manila, thank you for your guidance and unwavering support as I found my path. I am deeply grateful for your presence and the love you've shown me.

To my cousin Jil, thank you for being my confidante and a second sister in Manila. Your listening ear and companionship were invaluable. And to Micah, thank you for suggesting the publisher for this book.

To Angeli, thank you for the four years of friendship during our high school days. We shared a love for Harry Potter, navigating the trials and tribulations of adolescence together. Our bond, forged over magic and shared experiences, is something I'll always treasure. I know you are in good hands now, and I wish you all the best.

To Ms. Kris, thank you for teaching me the invaluable tool of meditation. It has been a constant companion for 14 years, helping me cultivate peace and mindfulness. I'm grateful for our shared adventures and the wisdom you've imparted in metaphysics and finance.

To Pat, thank you for introducing me to the world of psychics. Your presence affirmed that there are others who seek deeper knowledge and understanding of the world's mysteries. I cherish our conversations and the shared moments of quiet contemplation.

To my officemates, thank you for helping me navigate the corporate world. While this path wasn't my calling, I'm grateful for the insights you provided on what needs to change and evolve within corporations.

To Jacob, Elio, and my friends in the Flyffers community, thank you for shaping my early online interactions. Your virtual camaraderie and genuine conversations during the rise of the internet showed me the power of connection and the potential for true friendships to blossom online.

To Tony, thank you for pushing me beyond my comfort zone during our travels. I never imagined I'd be climbing cliffs, diving in oceans, and exploring canyons. Your encouragement helped me realize my own potential for adventure.

To Kaito, our brief encounter in Osaka sparked a realization of my true calling. Thank you for sharing your dreams, which ignited my own epiphanies. I wish you success in Africa or wherever your journey takes you.

To Kaya, thank you for the serendipitous encounter in Taiwan. Our connection highlighted the magic of chance encounters and opened my eyes to new possibilities.

To Astrid, thank you for the fun-filled adventures in Niseko, Japan. Your help with snowboarding, building snowmen, and navigating snowy mishaps taught me the importance of human connection and support.

To Raychel, thank you for eleven years of unconditional love. You've left an enduring mark on my heart, always there as a loyal companion.

To my brothers in arms from the retreat, thank you for your authenticity and vulnerability during our shared experience. The silent struggles we overcame together will forever remain in my heart.

To my classmates, teachers, friends, and acquaintances, thank you for all the lessons you've taught me. I am grateful for the diverse encounters that have shaped my understanding of myself and the world.

To Joan, thank you for your invaluable assistance in bringing this book to fruition.

To Nin, thank you for your dedication and hard work in creating the stunning book cover design.

The journey doesn't end here. If you've found this book meaningful, please turn to the next page to see how you can share your thoughts and help others discover this story.

Review Request

Your words have power. They can illuminate the path for others. If "Trance Formation" has resonated with you in any way, please share your voice through a review on Amazon and Goodreads.

Your honest feedback, whether it be praise, critique, or simply a reflection of your experience, is invaluable. It helps me grow as an author and guides fellow seekers toward this story of transformation and hope.

Your review could be the spark that ignites another's journey. Let your voice be heard, and together, let's create a ripple of positive change in the world.

Review Links:
Amazon (US) Amazon (UK) Amazon (CA) Goodreads

If your country isn't listed above, please leave a review on the Amazon site where you purchased the book.

With heartfelt gratitude,

TheReal Rayster